Note to the reader

We want express our sincere hope that this book will enrich your spiritual journey. In these turbulent times, developing a personal connection with Christ is more important than ever.

We also want to let you know that we've designed this book to make it easier for you to find references within each paragraph. The two-column layout was specifically chosen to make the book more compact and easier to read.

We genuinely appreciate your decision to acquire this book and we hope that it exceeds your expectations. Thank you so much for choosing us!

Design by SaintilWay Productions

You are free to

Distribute, remix, adapt, and build upon the material in any medium or format for non-commercial purposes so long as attribution is given to the creator. If you remix, adapt, or build upon the material, you must license the modified material under identical terms.

We are providing this book with an incredibly low royalty fee, almost close to zero dollars. The pricing covers expenses for printing, shipping, and marketing. We would greatly appreciate any feedback on how we can enhance this offering.

Table of Contents

The Great Controversy

Chapter 1—The Fall of Satan

Chapter 2—The Creation

Chapter 3—The Temptation and Fall

Chapter 4—The Plan of Salvation

Chapter 5—Cain and Abel

Chapter 6—Seth and Enoch

Chapter 7—The Flood

Chapter 8—Disguised Infidelity

Chapter 9—The Tower of Babel

Chapter 10—Abraham

Chapter 11—Isaac

Chapter 12—Jacob and Esau

Chapter 13—Jacob and the Angel

Chapter 14—Joseph and his Brethren

Chapter 15—Moses

Chapter 16—The Plagues on Egypt

Chapter 17—The Passover

Chapter 18—Israel Leaves Egypt

Chapter 19—Their Journeyings

Chapter 20—The Law of God

Chapter 21—The Sanctuary

Chapter 22—Strange Fire

Chapter 23—The Quails

Chapter 24—Miriam

Chapter 25—Caleb and Joshua

Chapter 26—Korah, Dathan, and Abiram

Chapter 27—Aaron's Rod

Chapter 28—The Sin of Moses

Chapter 29—Fiery Serpents

Chapter 30—Balaam

Chapter 31—Death of Moses

Chapter 32—Joshua

Chapter 33—Samuel and Saul

Chapter 34—David

Chapter 35—Solomon

Chapter 36—The Ark of God

The Great Controversy

Chapter 1
The Fall of Satan

Satan in Heaven, before his rebellion, was a high and exalted angel, next in honor to God's dear Son. His countenance, like those of the other angels, was mild and expressive of happiness. His forehead was high and broad, showing a powerful intellect. His form was perfect; his bearing noble and majestic. A special light beamed in his countenance, and shone around him brighter and more beautiful than around the other angels; yet Jesus, God's dear Son, had the pre-eminence over all the angelic host. He was one with the Father before the angels were created. Satan was envious of Christ, and gradually assumed command which devolved on Christ alone. (1SP 17.1)

The great Creator assembled the heavenly host, that he might in the presence of all the angels confer special honor upon his Son. The Son was seated on the throne with the Father, and the heavenly throng of holy angels was gathered around them. The Father then made known that it was ordained by himself that Christ, his Son, should be equal with himself; so that wherever was the presence of his Son, it was as his own presence. The word of the Son was to be obeyed as readily as the word of the Father. His Son he had invested with authority to command the heavenly host. Especially was his Son to work in union with himself in the anticipated creation of the earth and every living thing that should exist upon the earth. His Son would carry out his will and his purposes, but would do nothing of himself alone. The Father's will would be fulfilled in him. (1SP 17.2)

Satan was envious and jealous of Jesus Christ. Yet when all the angels bowed to Jesus to acknowledge his supremacy and high authority and rightful rule, Satan bowed with them; but his heart was filled with envy and hatred. Christ had been taken into the special counsel of God in regard to his plans, while Satan was unacquainted with them. He did not understand, neither was he permitted to know, the purposes of God. But Christ was acknowledged sovereign of Heaven, his power and authority to be the same as that of God himself. Satan thought that he was himself a favorite in Heaven among the angels. He had been highly exalted; but this did not call forth from him gratitude and praise to his Creator. He aspired to the height of God himself. He gloried in his loftiness. He knew that he was honored by the angels. He had a special mission to execute. He had been near the great Creator, and the ceaseless beams of glorious light enshrouding the eternal God, had shone especially upon him. Satan thought how angels had obeyed his command with pleasurable alacrity. Were not his garments light and beautiful? Why should Christ thus be honored before himself? (1SP 18.1)

He left the immediate presence of the Father, dissatisfied, and filled with envy against Jesus Christ. Concealing his real purposes, he assembled the angelic host. He introduced his subject, which was himself. As one aggrieved, he related the preference God had given Jesus to the neglect of himself. He told them that henceforth all the sweet liberty the angels had enjoyed was at an end. For had not a ruler been appointed over them, to whom they from henceforth must yield servile honor? He stated to them that he had called them together to assure them that he no longer would submit to this invasion of his rights and theirs; that never would he again bow down to Christ; that he would take the honor upon himself which should have been conferred upon him, and would be the commander of all who would submit to follow him and obey his voice. There was contention among the angels. Satan and his sympathizers were striving to reform the government of God. They were discontented and unhappy because they could not look into his unsearchable wisdom and ascertain his purposes in exalting his Son Jesus, and endowing him with such unlimited power and command. They rebelled against the authority of the Son. (1SP 18.2)

Chapter 1 - The Fall of Satan (1SP 22.1)

Angels that were loyal and true sought to reconcile this mighty, rebellious angel to the will of his Creator. They justified the act of God in conferring honor upon Jesus Christ, and with forcible reasoning sought to convince Satan that no less honor was his now than before the Father had proclaimed the honor which he had conferred upon his Son. They clearly set forth that Jesus was the Son of God, existing with him before the angels were created; and that he had ever stood at the right hand of God, and his mild, loving authority had not heretofore been questioned; and that he had given no commands but what it was joy for the heavenly host to execute. They urged that Christ's receiving special honor from the Father, in the presence of the angels, did not detract from the honor that he had heretofore received. The angels wept. They anxiously sought to move Satan to renounce his wicked design and yield submission to their Creator; for all had heretofore been peace and harmony, and what could occasion this dissenting, rebellious voice? (1SP 19.1)

Satan refused to listen. And then he turned from the loyal and true angels, denouncing them as slaves. These angels, true to God, stood in amazement as they saw that Satan was successful in his effort to excite rebellion. He promised them a new and better government than they then had, in which all would be freedom. Great numbers signified their purpose to accept Satan as their leader and chief commander. As he saw his advances were met with success, he flattered himself that he should yet have all the angels on his side, and that he would be equal with God himself, and his voice of authority would be heard in commanding the entire host of Heaven. Again the loyal angels warned Satan, and assured him what must be the consequence if he persisted; that He who could create the angels, could by his power overturn all their authority, and in some signal manner punish their audacity and terrible rebellion. To think that an angel should resist the law of God which was as sacred as himself! They warned the rebellious to close their ears to Satan's deceptive reasonings, and advised Satan, and all who had been affected by him, to go to God and confess their wrong for even admitting a thought of questioning his authority. (1SP 20.1)

Many of Satan's sympathizers were inclined to heed the counsel of the loyal angels, and repent of their dissatisfaction, and be again received to the confidence of the Father and his dear Son. The mighty revolter then declared that he was acquainted with God's law, and if he should submit to servile obedience, his honor would be taken from him. No more would he be intrusted with his exalted mission. He told them that himself and they also had now gone too far to go back, and he would brave the consequences; for to bow in servile worship to the Son of God he never would; that God would not forgive, and now they must assert their liberty and gain by force the position and authority which was not willingly accorded to them. (1SP 20.2)

The loyal angels hasten speedily to the Son of God, and acquaint him with what is taking place among the angels. They find the Father in conference with his beloved Son, to determine the means by which, for the best good of the loyal angels, the assumed authority of Satan could be forever put down. The great God could at once have hurled this arch deceiver from Heaven; but this was not his purpose. He would give the rebellious an equal chance to measure strength and might with his own Son and his loyal angels. In this battle every angel would choose his own side, and be manifested to all. It would not have been safe to suffer any who united with Satan in his rebellion to continue to occupy Heaven. They had learned the lesson of genuine rebellion against the unchangeable law of God; and this is incurable. If God had exercised his power to punish this chief rebel, disaffected angels would not have been manifested; hence God took another course; for he would manifest distinctly to all the heavenly host his justice and his judgment. (1SP 21.1)

It was the highest crime to rebel against the government of God. All Heaven seemed in commotion. The angels were marshaled in companies, each division with a higher commanding angel at their head. Satan was warring against the law of God, because ambitious to exalt himself, and unwilling to submit to the authority of Gods' Son, Heaven's great commander. (1SP 22.1)

All the heavenly host were summoned to appear before the Father, to have each case determined. Satan unblushingly made known his dissatisfaction that Christ should be preferred before him. He stood up proudly and urged that he should be equal with God, and should be taken into conference with the Father and

Chapter 1 - The Fall of Satan (1SP 22.2)

understand his purposes. God informed Satan that to his Son alone he would reveal his secret purposes, and he required all the family in Heaven, even Satan, to yield him implicit, unquestioned obedience; but that he (Satan) had proved himself unworthy a place in Heaven. Then Satan exultingly pointed to his sympathizers, comprising nearly one half of all the angels, and exclaimed, These are with me! Will you expel these also, and make such a void in Heaven? He then declared that he was prepared to resist the authority of Christ, and to defend his place in Heaven by force of might, strength against strength. (1SP 22.2)

Good angels wept to hear the words of Satan, and his exulting boasts. God declared that the rebellious should remain in Heaven no longer. Their high and happy state had been held upon condition of obedience to the law which God had given to govern the high order of intelligences. But no provision had been made to save those who should venture to transgress his law. Satan grew bold in his rebellion, and expressed his contempt of the Creator's law. This Satan could not bear. He claimed that angels needed no law; but should be left free to follow their own will, which would ever guide them right; that law was a restriction of their liberty, and that to abolish law was one great object of his standing as he did. The condition of the angels he thought needed improvement. Not so the mind of God, who had made laws and exalted them equal to himself. The happiness of the angelic host consisted in their perfect obedience to law. Each had his special work assigned him; and until Satan rebelled, there had been perfect order and harmonious action in Heaven. Then there was war in Heaven. The Son of God, the Prince of Heaven, and his loyal angels, engaged in conflict with the arch rebel and those who united with him. The Son of God and true, loyal angels prevailed; and Satan and his sympathizers were expelled from Heaven. All the heavenly host acknowledged and adored the God of justice. Not a taint of rebellion was left in Heaven. All was again peaceful and harmonious as before. (1SP 22.3)

Angels in Heaven mourned the fate of those who had been their companions in happiness and bliss. Their loss was felt in Heaven. The Father consulted Jesus in regard to at once carrying out their purpose to make man to inhabit the earth. He would place man upon probation to test his loyalty, before he could be rendered eternally secure. If he endured the test wherewith God saw fit to prove him, he should eventually be equal with the angels. He was to have the favor of God, and he was to converse with angels, and they with him. He did not see fit to place them beyond the power of disobedience. (1SP 23.1)

*****

Chapter 2
The Creation

The Father and the Son engaged in the mighty, wondrous work they had contemplated, of creating the world. The earth came forth from the hand of the Creator exceedingly beautiful. There were mountains, and hills, and plains; and interspersed among them were rivers and bodies of water. The earth was not one extensive plain, but the monotony of the scenery was broken by hills and mountains, not high and ragged as they now are, but regular and beautiful in shape. The bare, high rocks were never seen upon them, but lay beneath the surface, answering as bones to the earth. The waters were regularly dispersed. The hills, mountains, and very beautiful plains, were adorned with plants and flowers, and tall, majestic trees of every description, which were many times larger, and much more beautiful, than trees now are. The air was pure and healthful, and the earth seemed like a noble palace. Angels beheld and rejoiced at the wonderful and beautiful works of God. (1SP 24.1)

After the earth was created, and the beasts upon it, the Father and Son carried out their purpose, which was designed before the fall of Satan, to make man in their own image. They had wrought together in the creation of the earth and every living thing upon it. And now God says to his Son, "Let us make man in our image." As Adam came forth from the hand of his Creator, he was of noble height, and of beautiful symmetry. He was more than twice as tall as men now living upon the earth, and was well proportioned. His features were perfect and beautiful. His complexion was neither white, nor sallow, but ruddy, glowing with the rich tint of health. Eve was not quite as tall as Adam. Her head reached a little above his shoulders. She, too, was noble-perfect in symmetry, and very beautiful. (1SP 24.2)

This sinless pair wore no artificial garments. They were clothed with a covering of light and glory, such as the angels wear. While they lived in obedience to God, this circle of light enshrouded them. Although everything God had made was in the perfection of beauty, and there seemed nothing wanting upon the earth which God had created to make Adam and Eve happy, yet he manifested his great love to them by planting a garden especially for them. A portion of their time was to be occupied in the happy employment of dressing the garden, and a portion in receiving the visits of angels, listening to their instruction, and in happy meditation. Their labor was not wearisome, but pleasant and invigorating. This beautiful garden was to be their home, their special residence. (1SP 25.1)

In this garden the Lord placed trees of every variety for usefulness and beauty. There were trees laden with luxuriant fruit, of rich fragrance, beautiful to the eye, and pleasant to the taste, designed of God to be food for the holy pair. There were the lovely vines which grew upright, laden with their burden of fruit, unlike anything man has seen since the fall. The fruit was very large, and of different colors; some nearly black, some purple, red, pink and light green. This beautiful and luxuriant growth of fruit upon the branches of the vine was called grapes. They did not trail upon the ground, although not supported by trellises, but the weight of the fruit bowed them down. It was the happy labor of Adam and Eve to form beautiful bowers from the branches of the vine, and train them, forming dwellings of nature's beautiful, living trees and foliage, laden with fragrant fruit. (1SP 25.2)

The earth was clothed with beautiful verdure, while myriads of fragrant flowers of every variety and hue sprang up in rich profusion around them. Everything was tastefully and gloriously arranged. In the midst of the garden stood the tree of life, the glory of which surpassed all other trees. Its fruit looked like apples of gold and silver, and was to perpetuate immortality. The leaves contained healing properties. (1SP 26.1)

Chapter 2 - The Creation (1SP 26.2)

Very happy were the holy pair in Eden. Unlimited control was given them over every living thing. The lion and the lamb sported together peacefully and harmlessly around them, or slumbered at their feet. Birds of every variety of color and plumage flitted among the trees and flowers, and about Adam and Eve, while their mellow-toned music echoed among the trees in sweet accord to the praises of their Creator. (1SP 26.2)

Adam and Eve were charmed with the beauties of their Eden home. They were delighted with the little songsters around them, wearing their bright yet graceful plumage, and warbling forth their happy, cheerful music. The holy pair united with them and raised their voices in harmonious songs of love, praise and adoration, to the Father and his dear Son, for the tokens of love which surrounded them. They recognized the order and harmony of creation, which spoke of wisdom and knowledge that were infinite. Some new beauty and additional glory of their Eden home they were continually discovering, which filled their hearts with deeper love, and brought from their lips expressions of gratitude and reverence to their Creator. (1SP 26.3)

*****

Chapter 3
The Temptation and Fall

In the midst of the garden, near the tree of life, stood the tree of knowledge of good and evil. This tree was especially designed of God to be the pledge of their obedience, faith and love to him. Of this tree the Lord commanded our first parents not to eat, neither to touch it, lest they die. He told them that they might freely eat of all the trees in the garden except one; but if they ate of that tree they should surely die. (1SP 27.1)

When Adam and Eve were placed in the beautiful garden, they had everything for their happiness which they could desire. But he chose, in his all-wise arrangements, to test their loyalty before they could be rendered eternally secure. They were to have his favor, and he was to converse with them, and they with him. Yet he did not place evil out of their reach. Satan was permitted to tempt them. If they endured the trial, they were to be in perpetual favor with God and the heavenly angels. (1SP 27.2)

Satan stood in amazement at his new condition. His happiness was gone. He looked upon the angels who, with him, were once so happy, but who had been expelled from Heaven with him. Before their fall, not a shade of discontent had marred their perfect bliss. Now all seemed changed. Countenances which had reflected the image of their Maker were gloomy and despairing. Strife, discord, and bitter recrimination, were among them. Previous to their rebellion these things had been unknown in Heaven. Satan now beholds the terrible results of his rebellion. He shuddered, and feared to face the future, and to contemplate the end of these things. (1SP 28.1)

The hour for joyful, happy songs of praise to God and his dear Son had come. Satan had led the heavenly choir. He had raised the first note, then all the angelic host united with him, and glorious strains of music had resounded through Heaven in honor of God and his dear Son. But now, instead of strains of sweetest music, discord and angry words fall upon the ear of the great rebel leader. Where was he? Was it not all a horrible dream? Was he shut out of Heaven? Were the gates of Heaven never more to open and admit him? The hour of worship draws nigh, when bright and holy angels bow before the Father. No more will he unite in heavenly song. No more will he bow in reverence and holy awe before the presence of the eternal God. Could he be again as he was when he was pure, true and loyal, gladly would he yield up the claims of his authority. But he was lost! beyond redemption, for his presumptuous rebellion! And this was not all; he had led others to rebellion and to the same lost condition with himself–angels, who had never thought to question the will of Heaven, or refuse obedience to the law of God till he had put it into their minds, presenting before them that they might enjoy a greater good, a higher and more glorious liberty. This had been the sophistry whereby he had deceived them. A responsibility now rests upon him from which he would fain be released. (1SP 28.2)

These spirits had become turbulent with disappointed hopes. Instead of greater good, they were experiencing the sad results of disobedience and disregard of law. Never more would these unhappy beings be swayed by the mild rule of Jesus Christ. Never more would their spirits be stirred by the deep, earnest love, peace, and joy, which his presence had ever inspired in them, to be returned to him in cheerful obedience and reverential honor. (1SP 29.1)

Satan trembled as he viewed his work. He was alone in meditation upon the past, the present, and his future plans. His mighty frame shook as with a tempest. An angel from Heaven was passing. He called him, and entreated an interview with Christ. This was granted him. He then related to the Son of God that he repented of his rebellion, and wished again the favor of God. He was willing to take the place God had previously assigned him, and be under his wise command. Christ wept at Satan's woe, but told

Chapter 3 - The Temptation and Fall (1SP 29.2)

him, as the mind of God, that he could never be received into Heaven. Heaven must not be placed in jeopardy. All Heaven would be marred should he be received back; for sin and rebellion originated with him. The seeds of rebellion were still within him. He had, in his rebellion, no occasion for his course, and he had not only hopelessly ruined himself, but the host of angels also, who would then have been happy in Heaven had he remained steadfast. The law of God could condemn, but could not pardon. (1SP 29.2)

He repented not of his rebellion because he saw the goodness of God which he had abused. It was not possible that his love for God had so increased since his fall that it would lead to cheerful submission and happy obedience to his law which had been despised. The wretchedness he realized in losing the sweet light of Heaven, and the sense of guilt which forced itself upon him, and the disappointment he experienced himself in not finding his expectations realized, were the cause of his grief. To be commander out of Heaven, was vastly different from being thus honored in Heaven. The loss he had sustained of all the privileges of Heaven seemed too much to be borne. He wished to regain these. (1SP 30.1)

This great change of position had not increased his love for God, nor for his wise and just law. When Satan became fully convinced that there was no possibility of his being re-instated in the favor of God, he manifested his malice with increased hatred and fiery vehemence. (1SP 30.2)

God knew that such determined rebellion would not remain inactive. Satan would invent means to annoy the heavenly angels, and show contempt for his authority. As he could not gain admission within the gates of Heaven, he would wait just at the entrance, to taunt the angels and seek contention with them as they went in and out. He would seek to destroy the happiness of Adam and Eve. He would endeavor to incite them to rebellion, knowing that this would cause grief in Heaven. (1SP 30.3)

His followers were seeking him; and he aroused himself and, assuming a look of defiance, informed them of his plans to wrest from God the noble Adam and his companion Eve. If he could, in any way, beguile them to disobedience, God would make some provision whereby they might be pardoned, and then himself and all the fallen angels would be in a fair way to share with them of God's mercy. If this should fail, they could unite with Adam and Eve; for when once they should transgress the law of God, they would be subjects of God's wrath, like themselves. Their transgression would place them also, in a state of rebellion; and they could unite with Adam and Eve, take possession of Eden, and hold it as their home. And if they could gain access to the tree of life in the midst of the garden, their strength would, they thought, be equal to that of the holy angels, and even God himself could not expel them. (1SP 30.4)

Satan held a consultation with his evil angels. They did not all readily unite to engage in this hazardous and terrible work. He told them that he would not intrust any one of them to accomplish this work; for he thought that he alone had wisdom sufficient to carry forward so important an enterprise. He wished them to consider the matter while he should leave them and seek retirement, to mature his plans. He sought to impress upon them that this was their last and only hope. If they failed here, all prospect of regaining and controlling Heaven, or any part of God's creation, was hopeless. (1SP 31.1)

Satan went alone to mature plans that would most surely secure the fall of Adam and Eve. He had fears that his purposes might be defeated. And again, even if he should be successful in leading Adam and Eve to disobey the commandment of God, and thus become transgressors of his law, and no good come to himself, his own case would not be improved; his guilt would only be increased. (1SP 31.2)

He shuddered at the thought of plunging the holy, happy pair into the misery and remorse he was himself enduring. He seemed in a state of indecision; at one time firm and determined, then hesitating and wavering. His angels were seeking him, their leader, to acquaint him with their decision. They will unite with Satan in his plans, and with him bear the responsibility, and share the consequences. (1SP 32.1)

Satan cast off his feelings of despair and weakness, and, as their leader, fortified himself to brave out the matter, and do all in his power to defy the authority of God and his Son. He acquainted them with his plans. If he should come boldly upon Adam and Eve and make complaints of God's own Son, they would not listen to him for a moment, but would be

Chapter 3 - The Temptation and Fall (1SP 34.3)

prepared for such an attack. Should he seek to intimidate them because of his power, so recently an angel in high authority, he could accomplish nothing. He decided that cunning and deceit would do what might, or force, could not. (1SP 32.2)

God assembled the angelic host to take measures to avert the threatened evil. It was decided in Heaven's council for angels to visit Eden and warn Adam that he was in danger from the foe. Two angels sped on their way to visit our first parents. The holy pair received them with joyful innocence, expressing their grateful thanks to their Creator for thus surrounding them with such a profusion of his bounty. Everything lovely and attractive was theirs to enjoy, and everything seemed wisely adapted to their wants; and that which they prized above all other blessings, was the society of the Son of God and the heavenly angels, for they had much to relate to them at every visit, of their new discoveries of the beauties of nature in their lovely Eden home, and they had many questions to ask relative to many things which they could but indistinctly comprehend. (1SP 32.3)

The angels graciously and lovingly gave them the information they desired. They also gave them the sad history of Satan's rebellion and fall. They then distinctly informed them that the tree of knowledge was placed in the garden to be a pledge of their obedience and love to God; that the high and happy estate of the holy angels was to be retained upon condition of obedience; that they were similarly situated; that they could obey the law of God and be inexpressibly happy, or disobey, and lose their high estate, and be plunged into hopeless despair. (1SP 33.1)

They told Adam and Eve that God would not compel them to obey–that he had not removed from them power to go contrary to his will; that they were moral agents, free to obey or disobey. There was but one prohibition that God had seen fit to lay upon them as yet. If they should transgress the will of God, they would surely die. They told Adam and Eve that the most exalted angel, next in order to Christ, refused obedience to the law of God which he had ordained to govern heavenly beings; that this rebellion had caused war in Heaven which resulted in the rebellious being expelled therefrom, and every angel was driven out of Heaven who united with him in questioning the authority of the great Jehovah; and that this fallen foe was now an enemy to all that concerned the interest of God and his dear Son. (1SP 33.2)

They told them that Satan purposed to do them harm, and it was necessary for them to be guarded, for they might come in contact with the fallen foe; but he could not harm them while they yielded obedience to God's command; for, if necessary, every angel from Heaven would come to their help rather than that he should in any way do them harm. But if they disobeyed the command of God, then Satan would have power to ever annoy, perplex, and trouble, them. If they remained steadfast against the first insinuations of Satan, they were as secure as the heavenly angels. But if they yielded to the tempter, He who spared not the exalted angels, would not spare them. They must suffer the penalty of their transgression; for the law of God was as sacred as himself, and he required implicit obedience from all in Heaven and on earth. (1SP 34.1)

The angels cautioned Eve not to separate from her husband in her employment; for she might be brought in contact with this fallen foe. If separated from each other, they would be in greater danger than if both were together. The angels charged them to closely follow the instructions God had given them in reference to the tree of knowledge; for in perfect obedience they were safe, and this fallen foe could then have no power to deceive them. God would not permit Satan to follow the holy pair with continual temptations. He could have access to them only at the tree of knowledge of good and evil. (1SP 34.2)

Adam and Eve assured the angels that they should never transgress the express command of God; for it was their highest pleasure to do his will. The angels united with Adam and Eve in holy strains of harmonious music; and as their songs pealed forth from blissful Eden, Satan heard the sound of their strains of joyful adoration to the Father and Son. And as Satan heard it, his envy, hatred, and malignity, increased, and he expressed his anxiety to his followers to incite them (Adam and Eve) to disobedience, and at once bring down the wrath of God upon them, and change their songs of praise to hatred, and curses to their Maker. (1SP 34.3)

Satan assumes the form of a serpent, and enters Eden. The serpent was a beautiful

Chapter 3 - The Temptation and Fall (1SP 35.1)

creature, with wings; and while flying through the air, his appearance was bright, resembling burnished gold. He did not go upon the ground, but went from place to place through the air, and ate fruit like man. Satan entered into the serpent, and took his position in the tree of knowledge, and commenced leisurely eating of the fruit. (1SP 35.1)

Eve, unconsciously at first, separated from her husband in her employment. When she became aware of the fact, she felt that there might be danger; but again she thought herself secure, even if she did not remain close by the side of her husband. She had wisdom and strength to know if evil came, and to meet it. This the angels had cautioned her not to do. Eve found herself gazing with mingled curiosity and admiration upon the fruit of the forbidden tree. She saw it was very lovely, and was reasoning with herself why God had so decidedly prohibited their eating or touching it. Now was Satan's opportunity. He addressed her as though he was able to divine her thoughts: "Yea, hath God said, Ye shall not eat of every tree of the garden?" Thus, with soft and pleasant words, and with musical voice, he addressed the wondering Eve. She was startled to hear a serpent speak. He extolled her beauty and exceeding loveliness, which was not displeasing to Eve. But she was amazed, for she knew that to the serpent God had not given the power of speech. (1SP 35.2)

Eve's curiosity was aroused. Instead of fleeing from the spot, she listened to hear a serpent talk. It did not occur to her mind that it might be that fallen foe, using the serpent as a medium. It was Satan that spoke, not the serpent. Eve was beguiled, flattered, infatuated. Had she met a commanding personage, possessing a form like the angels, and resembling them, she would have been upon her guard. But that strange voice should have driven her to her husband's side to inquire of him why another should thus freely address her. But she enters into a controversy with the serpent. She answers his question, "We may eat of the fruit of the trees of the garden. But of the fruit of the tree which is in the midst of the garden, God hath said, Ye shall not eat of it, neither shall ye touch it, lest ye die." The serpent answers, "Ye shall not surely die; for God doth know that in the day ye eat thereof, then your eyes shall be opened, and ye shall be as gods, knowing good and evil." (1SP 36.1)

Satan would convey the idea that by eating of the forbidden tree, they would receive a new and more noble kind of knowledge than they had hitherto attained. This has been his special work with great success ever since his fall, to lead men to pry into the secrets of the Almighty, and not to be satisfied with what God has revealed, and not careful to obey that which he has commanded. He would lead them to disobey God's commands, and then make them believe that they are entering a wonderful field of knowledge. This is purely supposition, and a miserable deception. They fail to understand what God has revealed, and disregard his explicit commandments, and aspire after wisdom, independent of God, and seek to understand that which he has been pleased to withhold from mortals. They are elated with their ideas of progression, and charmed with their own vain philosophy; but grope in midnight darkness relative to true knowledge. They are ever learning, and never able to come to the knowledge of the truth. (1SP 36.2)

It was not the will of God that this sinless pair should have any knowledge of evil. He had freely given them the good, but withheld the evil. Eve thought the words of the serpent wise, and she received the broad assertion, "Ye shall not surely die; for God doth know that in the day ye eat thereof then your eyes shall be opened, and ye shall be as gods knowing good and evil"–making God a liar. Satan boldly insinuates that God had deceived them to keep them from being exalted in knowledge equal with himself. God said, If ye eat "ye shall surely die." The serpent said, If ye eat "ye shall not surely die." (1SP 37.1)

The tempter assured Eve that as soon as she ate of the fruit she would receive a new and superior knowledge that would make her equal with God. He called her attention to himself. He ate freely of the tree and found it not only perfectly harmless, but delicious and exhilarating; and told her that it was because of its wonderful properties to impart wisdom and power that God had prohibited them from tasting or even touching it; for he knew its wonderful qualities. He stated that by eating of the fruit of the tree forbidden them was the reason he had attained the power of speech. He intimated that God would not carry out his word. It was merely a threat to intimidate them and keep them from great good. He further told them that they could not die. Had they not eaten of the tree of life which perpetuates immortality? He said that God was deceiving them to keep them from a higher state of felicity and more exalted happiness. The tempter plucked the fruit and passed it to Eve. She took it in her hand. Now, said the tempter, you were prohibited from even touching it lest you die. He told her that she would realize no more sense of evil and death in eating than in touching or handling the fruit. Eve was emboldened because she felt not the immediate signs of God's displeasure. She thought the words of the tempter all wise and correct. She ate, and was delighted with the fruit. It seemed delicious to her taste, and she imagined that she realized in herself the wonderful effects of the fruit. (1SP 37.2)

She then plucked for herself of the fruit and ate, and imagined she felt the quickening power of a new and elevated existence as the result of the exhilarating influence of the forbidden fruit. She was in a strange and unnatural excitement as she sought her husband, with her hands filled with the forbidden fruit. She related to him the wise discourse of the serpent, and wished to conduct him at once to the tree of knowledge. She told him she had eaten of the fruit, and instead of her feeling any sense of death, she realized a pleasing, exhilarating influence. As soon as Eve had disobeyed, she became a powerful medium through which to occasion the fall of her husband. (1SP 38.1)

I saw a sadness come over the countenance of Adam. He appeared afraid and astonished. A struggle appeared to be going on in his mind. He told Eve he was quite certain that this was the foe that they had been warned against; and if so, that she must die. She assured him she felt no ill effects, but rather a very pleasant influence, and entreated him to eat. (1SP 39.1)

Adam quite well understood that his companion had transgressed the only prohibition laid upon them as a test of their fidelity and love. Eve reasoned that the serpent said they should not surely die, and his words must be true, for she felt no signs of God's displeasure, but a pleasant influence, as she imagined the angels felt. Adam regretted that Eve had left his side; but now the deed was done. He must be separated from her whose society he had loved so well. How could he have it thus? His love for Eve was strong. And in utter discouragement he resolved to share her fate. He reasoned that Eve was a part of himself; and if she must die, he would die with her; for he could not bear the thought of separation from her. He lacked faith in his merciful and benevolent Creator. He did not think that God, who had formed him out of the dust of the ground into a living, beautiful form, and had created Eve to be his companion, could supply her place. After all, might not the words of this wise serpent be correct? Eve was before him, just as lovely and beautiful, and apparently as innocent, as before this act of disobedience. She expressed greater, higher love for him than before her disobedience, as the effects of the fruit she had eaten. He saw in her no signs of death. She had told him of the happy influence of the fruit, of her ardent love for him, and he decided to brave the consequences. He seized the fruit and quickly ate it, and, like Eve, felt not immediately its ill effects. (1SP 39.2)

Eve had thought herself capable of deciding between right and wrong. The flattering hope of entering a higher state of knowledge had led her to think that the serpent was her especial friend, possessing a great interest in her welfare. Had she sought her husband, and they had related to their Maker the words of the serpent, they would have been delivered at once from his artful temptation. (1SP 40.1)

God instructed our first parents in regard to the tree of knowledge, and they were fully informed relative to the fall of Satan, and the danger of listening to his suggestions. He did not deprive them of the power of eating the forbidden fruit. He left them as free moral agents to believe his word, obey his commandments and live, or believe the tempter, disobey and perish. They both ate, and the great wisdom they obtained was the knowledge of sin, and a sense of guilt. The covering of light about them soon disappeared, and under a sense of guilt, and loss of their divine covering, a shivering seized them, and they tried to cover their exposed forms. The Lord would not have them investigate the fruit of the tree of knowledge, for then they would be exposed to Satan masked. He knew that they would be perfectly safe if they touched not the fruit. (1SP 40.2)

Our first parents chose to believe the words, as they thought, of a serpent; yet he had given them no tokens of his love. He had done nothing for their happiness and benefit; while God had given them everything that was good for food, and pleasant to the sight. Everywhere the eye

Chapter 3 - The Temptation and Fall (1SP 40.3)

might rest was abundance and beauty; yet Eve was deceived by the serpent, to think that there was something withheld which would make them wise, even as God. Instead of believing and confiding in God, she basely distrusted his goodness, and cherished the words of Satan. (1SP 40.3)

After Adam's transgression he at first imagined that he felt the rising to a new and higher existence. But soon the thought of his transgression terrified him. The air that had been of a mild and even temperature, seemed to chill them. The guilty pair had a sense of sin. They felt a dread of the future, a sense of want, a nakedness of soul. The sweet love, and peace, and happy, contented bliss, seemed removed from them, and in its place a want of something came over them that they never experienced before. They then for the first turned their attention to the external. They had not been clothed, but were draped in light as were the heavenly angels. This light which had enshrouded them departed. To relieve the sense of lack and nakedness which they realized, their attention was directed to seek a covering for their forms; for how could they meet the eye of God and angels unclothed? (1SP 41.1)

Their crime is now before them in its true light. Their transgression of God's express command assumes a clearer character. Adam censured Eve's folly in leaving his side, and being deceived by the serpent. They both flattered themselves that God, who had given them everything to make them happy, might yet excuse their disobedience, because of his great love to them, and that their punishment would not be so dreadful, after all. (1SP 41.2)

Satan exulted in his success. He had now tempted the woman to distrust God, to question his wisdom, and to seek to penetrate his all-wise plans. And through her he had also caused the overthrow of Adam, who, in consequence of his love for Eve, disobeyed the command of God, and fell with her. (1SP 42.1)

The news of man's fall spread through Heaven–every harp was hushed. The angels cast their crowns from their heads in sorrow. All Heaven was in agitation. The angels were grieved at the base ingratitude of man, in return for the rich bounties God had provided. A council was held to decide what must be done with the guilty pair. The angels feared that they would put forth the hand, and eat of the tree of life, and thus perpetuate a life of sin. (1SP 42.2)

The Lord visited Adam and Eve, and made known to them the consequence of their disobedience. As they hear God's majestic approach, they seek to hide themselves from his inspection, whom they delighted, while in their innocence and holiness, to meet. "And the Lord God called unto Adam, and said unto him, Where art thou? And he said, I heard thy voice in the garden, and I was afraid because I was naked, and I hid myself. And he said, Who told thee that thou wast naked? Hast thou eaten of the tree whereof I commanded thee that thou shouldest not eat?" This question was asked by the Lord, not because he needed information, but for the conviction of the guilty pair. How didst thou become ashamed and fearful? Adam acknowledged his transgression, not because he was penitent for his great disobedience, but to cast reflection upon God. "The woman whom thou gavest to be with me, she gave me of the tree, and I did eat." The woman was then addressed: "What is this that thou hast done?" Eve answered, "The serpent beguiled me, and I did eat." The Lord then addressed the serpent: "Because thou hast done this, thou art cursed above all cattle, and above every beast of the field: upon thy belly shalt thou go, and dust shalt thou eat all the days of thy life." As the serpent had been exalted above the beasts of the field, he should be degraded beneath them all, and be detested by man, inasmuch as he was the medium through which Satan acted. "And unto Adam he said, Because thou hast hearkened unto the voice of thy wife, and hast eaten of the tree of which I commanded thee, saying, Thou shalt not eat of it, cursed is the ground for thy sake; in sorrow shalt thou eat of it all the days of thy life; thorns also and thistles shall it bring forth to thee; and thou shalt eat the herb of the field. In the sweat of thy face shalt thou eat bread till thou return unto the ground." (1SP 42.3)

God cursed the ground because of their sin in eating of the tree of knowledge, and declared, "In sorrow shalt thou eat of it all the days of thy life." He had apportioned them the good, but withheld the evil. Now God declares that they shall eat of it, that is, they should be acquainted with evil all the days of their life. (1SP 43.1)

The race from that time forward was to be afflicted by Satan's temptations. A life of perpetual toil and anxiety was appointed unto

Adam, instead of the happy, cheerful labor he had hitherto enjoyed. They should be subject to disappointment, grief and pain, and finally come to dissolution. They were made of the dust of the earth, and unto dust should they return. (1SP 43.2)

They were informed that they would have to lose their Eden home. They had yielded to Satan's deception and believed the word of Satan, that God would lie. By their transgression they had opened a way for Satan to gain access to them more readily, and it was not safe for them to remain in the garden of Eden, lest in their state of sin, they gain access to the tree of life, and perpetuate a life of sin. They entreated to be permitted to remain, although they acknowledged that they had forfeited all right to blissful Eden. They promised that they would in the future yield to God implicit obedience. They were informed that in their fall from innocence to guilt, they gained no strength but great weakness. They had not preserved their integrity while they were in a state of holy, happy innocence, and they would have far less strength to remain true and loyal in a state of conscious guilt. They were filled with keenest anguish and remorse. They now realized that the penalty of sin was death. (1SP 44.1)

Angels were commissioned to immediately guard the way of the tree of life. It was Satan's studied plan that Adam and Eve should disobey God, receive his frown, and then partake of the tree of life, that they might perpetuate a life of sin. But holy angels were sent to debar their way to the tree of life. Around these angels flashed beams of light on every side, which had the appearance of glittering swords. (1SP 44.2)

Chapter 4
The Plan of Salvation

Sorrow filled Heaven, as it was realized that man was lost, and the world that God created was to be filled with mortals doomed to misery, sickness, and death, and there was no way of escape for the offender. The whole family of Adam must die. I saw the lovely Jesus, and beheld an expression of sympathy and sorrow upon his countenance. Soon I saw him approach the exceeding bright light which enshrouded the Father. Said my accompanying angel, He is in close converse with his Father. The anxiety of the angels seemed to be intense while Jesus was communing with his Father. Three times he was shut in by the glorious light about the Father, and the third time he came from the Father his person could be seen. His countenance was calm, free from all perplexity and trouble, and shone with benevolence and loveliness, such as words cannot express. He then made known to the angelic host that a way of escape had been made for lost man. He told them that he had been pleading with his Father, and had offered to give his life a ransom, and take the sentence of death upon himself, that through him man might find pardon; that through the merits of his blood, and obedience to the law of God, they could have the favor of God, and be brought into the beautiful garden, and eat of the fruit of the tree of life. **(1SP 45.1)**

At first the angels could not rejoice, for their commander concealed nothing from them, but opened before them the plan of salvation. Jesus told them that he would stand between the wrath of his Father and guilty man, that he would bear iniquity and scorn, and but few would receive him as the Son of God. Nearly all would hate and reject him. He would leave all his glory in Heaven, appear upon earth as a man, humble himself as a man, become acquainted by his own experience with the various temptations with which man would be beset, that he might know how to succor those who should be tempted; and that finally, after his mission as a teacher should be accomplished, he would be delivered into the hands of men, and endure almost every cruelty and suffering that Satan and his angels could inspire wicked men to inflict; that he should die the cruelest of deaths, hung up between the heavens and the earth as a guilty sinner; that he should suffer dreadful hours of agony, which even angels could not look upon, but would vail their faces from the sight. Not merely agony of body would he suffer; but mental agony, that with which bodily suffering could in no wise be compared. The weight of the sins of the whole world would be upon him. He told them he would die, and rise again the third day, and should ascend to his Father to intercede for wayward, guilty man. **(1SP 45.2)**

The angels prostrated themselves before him. They offered their lives. Jesus said to them that he should by his death save many; that the life of an angel could not pay the debt. His life alone could be accepted of his Father as a ransom for man. Jesus also told them that they should have a part to act, to be with him, and at different times strengthen him. That he should take man's fallen nature, and his strength would not be even equal with theirs. And they should be witnesses of his humiliation and great sufferings. And as they should witness his sufferings, and the hate of men towards him, they would be stirred with the deepest emotions, and through their love for him, would wish to rescue and deliver him from his murderers; but that they must not interfere to prevent anything they should behold; and that they should act a part in his resurrection; that the plan of salvation was devised, and his Father had accepted the plan. **(1SP 46.1)**

With a holy sadness Jesus comforted and cheered the angels, and informed them that hereafter those whom he should redeem would be with him, and ever dwell with him; and that by his death he should ransom many, and destroy him who had the power of death. And his Father would give him the kingdom, and the greatness of the kingdom under the whole heaven, and he should possess it forever and ever. Satan and sinners should be destroyed, never more to disturb Heaven, or the purified new earth. Jesus bade the heavenly host be reconciled to the plan that his Father accepted, and rejoice that fallen man could be exalted again through his death, to obtain favor with God and enjoy Heaven. (1SP 47.1)

Then joy, inexpressible joy, filled Heaven. And the heavenly host sung a song of praise and adoration. They touched their harps and sung a note higher than they had done before, for the great mercy and condescension of God in yielding up his dearly Beloved to die for a race of rebels. Praise and adoration were poured forth for the self-denial and sacrifice of Jesus; that he would consent to leave the bosom of his Father, and choose a life of suffering and anguish, and die an ignominious death to give his life for others. (1SP 47.2)

Said the angel, Think ye that the Father yielded up his dearly beloved Son without a struggle? No, no. It was even a struggle with the God of Heaven, whether to let guilty man perish, or to give his beloved Son to die for them. Angels were so interested for man's salvation that there could be found among them those who would yield their glory, and give their life for perishing man. But, said my accompanying angel, That would avail nothing. The transgression was so great that an angel's life would not pay the debt. Nothing but the death and intercessions of his Son would pay the debt, and save lost man from hopeless sorrow and misery. (1SP 48.1)

But the work of the angels was assigned them, to ascend and descend with strengthening balm from glory to soothe the Son of God in his sufferings, and administer unto him. Also, their work would be to guard and keep the subjects of grace from the evil angels, and the darkness constantly thrown around them by Satan. I saw that it was impossible for God to alter or change his law, to save lost, perishing man; therefore he suffered his beloved Son to die for man's transgression. (1SP 48.2)

Satan again rejoiced with his angels that he could, by causing man's fall, pull down the Son of God from his exalted position. He told his angels that when Jesus should take fallen man's nature, he could overpower him, and hinder the accomplishment of the plan of salvation. (1SP 48.3)

I was then shown Satan as he was, a happy, exalted angel. Then I was shown him as he now is. He still bears a kingly form. His features are still noble, for he is an angel fallen. But the expression of his countenance is full of anxiety, care, unhappiness, malice, hate, mischief, deceit, and every evil. That brow which was once so noble, I particularly noticed. His forehead commenced from his eyes to recede backward. I saw that he had demeaned himself so long that every good quality was debased, and every evil trait was developed. His eyes were cunning and sly, and showed great penetration. His frame was large; but the flesh hung loosely about his hands and face. As I beheld him, his chin was resting upon his left hand. He appeared to be in deep thought. A smile was upon his countenance, which made me tremble, it was so full of evil and Satanic slyness. This smile is the one he wears just before he makes sure of his victim; and as he fastens the victim in his snare, this smile grows horrible. (1SP 48.4)

In humility and inexpressible sadness, Adam and Eve left the lovely garden wherein they had been so happy until they disobeyed the command of God. The atmosphere was changed. It was no longer unvarying as before the transgression. God clothed them with coats of skins to protect them from the sense of chilliness and then of heat to which they were exposed. (1SP 49.1)

All Heaven mourned on account of the disobedience and fall of Adam and Eve, which brought the wrath of God upon the whole human race. They were cut off from communing with God, and were plunged in hopeless misery. The law of God could not be changed to meet man's necessity; for in God's arrangement it was never to lose its force, nor give up the smallest part of its claims. (1SP 49.2)

The angels of God were commissioned to visit the fallen pair and inform them that although they could no longer retain possession of their holy estate, their Eden home, because of their transgression of the law of God, yet their case was not altogether hopeless. They were then informed that the Son of God, who had conversed with them in Eden, had been moved with pity as he viewed their hopeless condition, and had volunteered to take upon himself the punishment due to them, and die for them that man might yet live, through faith in the atonement Christ proposed to make for him.

Chapter 4 - The Plan of Salvation (1SP 49.3)

Through Christ a door of hope was opened, that man, notwithstanding his great sin, should not be under the absolute control of Satan. Faith in the merits of the Son of God would so elevate man that he could resist the devices of Satan. Probation would be granted him in which, through a life of repentance, and faith in the atonement of the Son of God, he might be redeemed from his transgression of the Father's law, and thus be elevated to a position where his efforts to keep his law could be accepted. (1SP 49.3)

The angels related to them the grief that was felt in Heaven, as it was announced that they had transgressed the law of God, which had made it expedient for Christ to make the great sacrifice of his own precious life. (1SP 50.1)

When Adam and Eve realized how exalted and sacred was the law of God, the transgression of which made so costly a sacrifice necessary to save them and their posterity from utter ruin, they plead to die themselves, or to let them and their posterity endure the penalty of their transgression, rather than that the beloved Son of God should make this great sacrifice. The anguish of Adam was increased. He saw that his sins were of so great magnitude as to involve fearful consequences. And must it be that Heaven's honored Commander, who had walked with him, and talked with him, while in his holy innocence, whom angels honored and worshiped, must be brought down from his exalted position to die because of his transgression[?] Adam was informed that an angel's life could not pay the debt. The law of Jehovah, the foundation of his government in Heaven and upon earth, was as sacred as God himself; and for this reason the life of an angel could not be accepted of God as a sacrifice for its transgression. His law was of more importance in his sight than the holy angels around his throne. The Father could not abolish nor change one precept of his law to meet man in his fallen condition. But the Son of God, who had in unison with the Father created man, could make an atonement for man acceptable to God, by giving his life a sacrifice, and bearing the wrath of his Father. Angels informed Adam that, as his transgression had brought death and wretchedness, life and immortality would be brought to light through the sacrifice of Jesus Christ. (1SP 50.2)

To Adam were revealed future, important events, from his expulsion from Eden to the flood, and onward to the first advent of Christ upon the earth. His love for Adam and his posterity would lead the Son of God to condescend to take human nature, and thus elevate, through his own humiliation, all who would believe on him. Such a sacrifice was of sufficient value to save the whole world; but only a few would avail themselves of the salvation brought to them through such a wonderful sacrifice. The many would not comply with the conditions required of them that they might be partakers of his great salvation. They would prefer sin and transgression of the law of God, rather than repentance and obedience, relying by faith upon the merits of the sacrifice offered. This sacrifice was of such infinite value as to make a man who should avail himself of it, more precious than fine gold, even a man than the golden wedge of Ophir. (1SP 51.1)

Adam was carried down through successive generations, and saw the increase of crime, of guilt and defilement, because man would yield to his naturally strong inclinations to transgress the holy law of God. He was shown the curse of God resting more and more heavily upon the human race, upon the cattle, and upon the earth, because of man's continued transgression. He was shown that iniquity and violence would steadily increase; yet amid all the tide of human misery and woe, there would ever be a few who would preserve the knowledge of God, and would remain unsullied amid the prevailing moral degeneracy. Adam was made to comprehend what sin is–the transgression of the law. He was shown that moral, mental, and physical degeneracy would result to the race, from transgression, until the world would be filled with human misery of every type. (1SP 52.1)

The days of man were shortened by his own course of sin in transgressing the righteous law of God. The race was finally so greatly depreciated that they appeared inferior, and almost valueless. They were generally incompetent to appreciate the mystery of Calvary, the grand and elevated facts of the atonement and the plan of salvation, because of the indulgence of the carnal mind. Yet, notwithstanding the weakness, and enfeebled mental, moral and physical, powers of the human race, Christ, true to the purpose for which he left Heaven, continues his interest in the feeble, depreciated, degenerate specimens of humanity, and invites them to hide their weakness and great deficiencies in him. If they will come unto him, he will supply all their needs. (1SP 52.2)

When Adam, according to God's special directions, made an offering for sin, it was to him a most painful ceremony. His hand must be raised to take life, which God alone could give, and make an offering for sin. It was the first time he had witnessed death. As he looked upon the bleeding victim, writhing in the agonies of death, he was to look forward by faith to the Son of God, whom the victim prefigured, who was to die man's sacrifice. (1SP 53.1)

This ceremonial offering, ordained of God, was to be a perpetual reminder to Adam of his guilt, and also a penitential acknowledgment of his sin. This act of taking life gave Adam a deeper and more perfect sense of his transgression, which nothing less than the death of God's dear Son could expiate. He marveled at the infinite goodness and matchless love which would give such a ransom to save the guilty. As Adam was slaying the innocent victim, it seemed to him that he was shedding the blood of the Son of God by his own hand. He knew that if he had remained steadfast to God, and true to his holy law, there would have been no death of beast nor of man. Yet in the sacrificial offerings, pointing to the great and perfect offering of God's dear Son, there appeared a star of hope to illuminate the dark and terrible future, and relieve it of its utter hopelessness and ruin. (1SP 53.2)

In the beginning, the head of each family was considered ruler and priest of his own household. Afterward, as the race multiplied upon the earth, men of divine appointment performed this solemn worship of sacrifice for the people. The blood of beasts was to be associated in the minds of sinners with the blood of the Son of God. The death of the victim was to evidence to all that the penalty of sin was death. By the act of sacrifice, the sinner acknowledged his guilt, and manifested his faith, looking forward to the great and perfect sacrifice of the Son of God, which the offering of beasts prefigured. Without the atonement of the Son of God there could be no communication of blessing, or salvation from God to man. God was jealous for the honor of his law. The transgression of that law caused a fearful separation between God and man. To Adam in his innocency was granted communion, direct, free and happy, with his Maker. After his transgression, God would communicate to man through Christ and angels. (1SP 53.3)

*****

Chapter 5
Cain and Abel

Cain and Abel, the sons of Adam, were very unlike in character. Abel feared God. Cain cherished rebellious feelings, and murmured against God because of the curse pronounced upon Adam, and because the ground was cursed for his sin. These brothers had been instructed in regard to the provision made for the salvation of the human race. They were required to carry out a system of humble obedience, showing their reverence for God, and their faith and dependence upon the promised Redeemer, by slaying the firstlings of the flock, and solemnly presenting them with the blood, as a burnt-offering to God. This sacrifice would lead them to continually keep in mind their sin, and the Redeemer to come, who was to be the great sacrifice for man. (1SP 54.1)

Cain brought his offering unto the Lord with murmuring and infidelity in his heart in regard to the promised Sacrifice. He was unwilling to strictly follow the plan of obedience, and procure a lamb and offer it with the fruit of the ground. He merely took of the fruit of the ground, and disregarded the requirement of God. God had made known to Adam that without shedding of blood there could be no remission of sin. Cain was not particular to bring even the best of the fruits. Abel advised his brother not to come before the Lord without the blood of a sacrifice. Cain being the eldest, would not listen to his brother. He despised his counsel, and with doubt and murmuring in regard to the necessity of the ceremonial offerings, he presented his offering. But God did not accept it. (1SP 55.1)

Abel brought of the firstlings of his flock, and of the fat as God had commanded; and in full faith of the Messiah to come, and with humble reverence, he presented the offering. God had respect unto his offering. A light flashes from Heaven and consumes the offering of Abel. Cain sees no manifestation that his is accepted. He is angry with the Lord, and with his brother. God condescends to send an angel to Cain to converse with him. (1SP 55.2)

The angel inquires of him the reason of his anger, and informs him that if he does well, and follows the directions God has given, he will accept him, and respect his offering. But if he will not humbly submit to God's arrangements, and believe and obey him, he cannot accept his offering. The angel tells Cain that it was no injustice on the part of God, or partiality shown to Abel; but that it was on account of his own sin, and disobedience of God's express command, why he could not respect his offering–and if he would do well he would be accepted of God, and his brother should listen to him, and he should take the lead, because he was the eldest. But even after being thus faithfully instructed, Cain did not repent. Instead of censuring and abhorring himself for his unbelief, he still complains of the injustice and partiality of God. And in his jealousy and hatred he contends with Abel, and reproaches him. Abel meekly points out his brother's error, and shows him that the wrong is in himself. But Cain hates his brother from the moment that God manifests to him the tokens of his acceptance. His brother Abel seeks to appease his wrath by contending for the compassion of God in saving the lives of their parents, when he might have brought upon them immediate death. He tells Cain that God loved them, or he would not have given his Son, innocent and holy, to suffer the wrath which man by his disobedience deserved to suffer. While Abel justifies the plan of God, Cain becomes enraged, and his anger increases and burns against Abel, until in his rage he slays him. God inquires of Cain for his brother, and Cain utters a guilty falsehood: "I know not; am I my brother's keeper?" God informs Cain that he knew in regard to his sin–that he was acquainted with his every act, and even the thoughts of his heart, and says to him, "Thy brother's blood crieth unto me from the ground. And now art thou cursed from the earth which hath opened her mouth to receive

Chapter 5 - Cain and Abel (1SP 59.1)

thy brother's blood from thy hand. When thou tillest the ground, it shall not henceforth yield unto thee her strength. A fugitive and a vagabond shalt thou be in the earth." (1SP 55.3)

The curse upon the ground at first had been felt but lightly; but now a double curse rested upon it. Cain and Abel represent the two classes, the righteous and the wicked, the believers and unbelievers, which should exist from the fall of man to the second coming of Christ. Cain's slaying his brother Abel, represents the wicked who will be envious of the righteous, and will hate them because they are better than themselves. They will be jealous of the righteous, and will persecute and put them to death because their right-doing condemns their sinful course. (1SP 57.1)

Adam's life was one of sorrow, humility, and continual repentance. As he taught his children and grand-children the fear of the Lord, he was often bitterly reproached for his sin which resulted in so much misery upon his posterity. When he left the beautiful Eden, the thought that he must die, thrilled him with horror. He looked upon death as a dreadful calamity. He was first made acquainted with the dreadful reality of death in the human family by his own son Cain slaying his brother Abel. Filled with the bitterest remorse for his own transgression, and deprived of his son Abel, and looking upon Cain as his murderer, and knowing the curse God pronounced upon him, bowed down Adam's heart with grief. Most bitterly did he reproach himself for his first great transgression. He entreated pardon from God through the promised Sacrifice. Deeply had he felt the wrath of God for his crime committed in Paradise. He witnessed the general corruption which afterward finally provoked God to destroy the inhabitants of the earth by a flood. The sentence of death pronounced upon him by his Maker, which at first appeared so terrible to him, after he had lived some hundreds of years, looked just and merciful in God, to bring to an end a miserable life. (1SP 57.2)

As Adam witnessed the first signs of decaying nature in the falling leaf, and in the drooping flowers, he mourned more deeply than men now mourn over their dead. The drooping flowers were not so deep a cause of grief, because more tender and delicate; but the tall, noble, sturdy trees to cast off their leaves, to decay, presented before him the general dissolution of beautiful nature, which God had created for the especial benefit of man. (1SP 58.1)

To his children, and to their children, to the ninth generation, he delineated the perfections of his Eden home; and also his fall and its dreadful results, and the load of grief brought upon him on account of the rupture in his family, which ended in the death of Abel. He related to them the sufferings God had brought him through, to teach him the necessity of strictly adhering to his law. He declared to them that sin would be punished in whatever form it existed. He entreated them to obey God, who would deal mercifully with them if they should love and fear him. (1SP 58.2)

Angels held communication with Adam after his fall, and informed him of the plan of salvation, and that the human race was not beyond redemption. Although a fearful separation had taken place between God and man, yet provision had been made through the offering of his beloved Son by which man might be saved. But their only hope was through a life of humble repentance, and faith in the provision made. All those who could thus accept Christ as their only Saviour, should be again brought into favor with God through the merits of his Son. (1SP 58.3)

Adam was commanded to teach his descendants the fear of the Lord, and, by his example and humble obedience, teach them to highly regard the offerings which typified a Saviour to come. Adam carefully treasured what God had revealed to him, and handed it down by word of mouth to his children and children's children. By this means the knowledge of God was preserved. There were some righteous upon the earth who knew and feared God even in Adam's day. The Sabbath was observed before the fall. Because Adam and Eve disobeyed God's command, and ate of the forbidden fruit, they were expelled from Eden; but they observed the Sabbath after their fall. They had experienced the bitter fruits of disobedience, and learned that every transgressor of God's commands will sooner or later learn that God means just what he says, and that he will surely punish the transgressor. (1SP 59.1)

Those who venture to lightly esteem the day upon which Jehovah rested, the day which he sanctified and blessed, the day which he has commanded to be kept holy, will yet know that

Chapter 5 - Cain and Abel (1SP 59.2)

death is the reward of the transgressor. On account of the special honors God conferred upon the seventh day, he required his people to number by sevens lest they should forget their Creator who made the heavens and the earth in six days and rested on the seventh. (1SP 59.2)

The descendants of Cain were not careful to respect the day upon which God rested. They chose their own time for labor and for rest, regardless of Jehovah's special command. There were two distinct classes upon the earth. One class were in open rebellion against God's law, while the other class obeyed his commandments, and revered his Sabbath. (1SP 60.1)

*****

Chapter 6
Seth and Enoch

Seth was a worthy character, and was to take the place of Abel in right doing. Yet he was a son of Adam like sinful Cain, and inherited from the nature of Adam no more natural goodness than did Cain. He was born in sin; but by the grace of God, in receiving the faithful instructions of his father Adam, he honored God in doing his will. He separated himself from the corrupt descendants of Cain, and labored, as Abel would have done had he lived, to turn the minds of sinful men to revere and obey God. (1SP 60.2)

Enoch was a holy man. He served God with singleness of heart. He realized the corruptions of the human family, and separated himself from the descendants of Cain, and reproved them for their great wickedness. There were those upon the earth who acknowledged God, who feared and worshiped him. Yet righteous Enoch was so distressed with the increasing wickedness of the ungodly, that he would not daily associate with them, fearing that he should be affected by their infidelity, and that his thoughts might not ever regard God with that holy reverence which was due his exalted character. His soul was vexed as he daily witnessed their trampling upon the authority of God. He chose to be separate from them, and spent much of his time in solitude, which he devoted to reflection and prayer. He waited before God, and prayed to know his will more perfectly, that he might perform it. God communed with Enoch through his angels, and gave him divine instruction. He made known to him that he would not always bear with man in his rebellion–that his purpose was to destroy the sinful race by bringing a flood of waters upon the earth. (1SP 60.3)

The pure and lovely garden of Eden, from which our first parents were driven, remained until God purposed to destroy the earth by a flood. God had planted that garden, and especially blessed it; and in his wonderful providence he withdrew it from the earth, and will return it to the earth again, more gloriously adorned than before it was removed from the earth. God purposed to preserve a specimen of his perfect work of creation free from the curse wherewith he had cursed the earth. (1SP 61.1)

The Lord opened more fully to Enoch the plan of salvation, and by the spirit of prophecy carried him down through the generations which should live after the flood, and showed him the great events connected with the second coming of Christ and the end of the world. (1SP 61.2)

Enoch was troubled in regard to the dead. It seemed to him that the righteous and the wicked would go to the dust together, and that would be their end. He could not clearly see the life of the just beyond the grave. In prophetic vision he was instructed in regard to the Son of God, who was to die man's sacrifice, and was shown the coming of Christ in the clouds of Heaven, attended by the angelic host, to give life to the righteous dead, and ransom them from their graves. He also saw the corrupt state of the world at the time when Christ should appear the second time–that there would be a boastful, presumptuous, self-willed generation arrayed in rebellion against the law of God, and denying the only Lord God and our Lord Jesus Christ, and trampling upon his blood, and despising his atonement. He saw the righteous crowned with glory and honor, while the wicked were separated from the presence of the Lord, and consumed with fire. (1SP 61.3)

Enoch faithfully rehearsed to the people all that God had revealed to him by the spirit of prophecy. Some believed his words, and turned from their wickedness to fear and worship God. Such often sought Enoch in his places of retirement, and he instructed them, and prayed for them that God would give them a knowledge of his will. At length he chose certain periods for retirement, and would not suffer the people to find him, for they interrupted his holy meditation and communion with God. He did not exclude himself at all times from the society of those who loved him and listened to his words

Chapter 6 - Seth and Enoch (1SP 62.1)

of wisdom; neither did he separate himself wholly from the corrupt. He met with the good and bad at stated times, and labored to turn the ungodly from their evil course, and instruct them in the knowledge and fear of God. He taught those who had the knowledge of God to serve him more perfectly. He would remain with them as long as he could benefit them by his godly conversation and holy example, and then would withdraw himself from all society–from the just, the scoffing and idolatrous, to remain in solitude, hungering and thirsting for communion with God, and that divine knowledge which he alone could give him. (1SP 62.1)

Enoch continued to grow more heavenly while communing with God. His face was radiant with a holy light which would remain upon his countenance while instructing those who would hear his words of wisdom. His heavenly and dignified appearance struck the people with awe. The Lord loved Enoch because he steadfastly followed him, and abhorred iniquity, and earnestly sought heavenly knowledge that he might do his will perfectly. He yearned to unite himself still more closely to God, whom he feared, reverenced, and adored. God would not permit Enoch to die as other men, but sent his angels to take him to Heaven without seeing death. In the presence of the righteous and the wicked, Enoch was removed from them. Those who loved him thought that God might have left him in some of his places of retirement; but after seeking him diligently, and being unable to find him, reported that he was not, for God took him. (1SP 63.1)

The Lord here teaches a lesson of the greatest importance by the translation of Enoch, a descendant of fallen Adam, that all would be rewarded, who by faith would rely upon the promised Sacrifice, and faithfully obey his commandments. Two classes are here again represented which were to exist until the second coming of Christ–the righteous and the wicked, the rebellious and the loyal. God will remember the righteous, who fear him. On account of his dear Son, he will respect and honor them, and give them everlasting life. But the wicked, who trample upon his authority, he will cut off and destroy from the earth, and they will be as though they had not been. (1SP 63.2)

After Adam's fall from a state of perfect happiness to a state of misery and sin, there was danger of man's becoming discouraged, and inquiring, "What profit is it that we have kept his ordinances, and walked mournfully before the Lord," since a heavy curse is resting upon the human race, and death is the portion of us all? But the instructions which God gave to Adam, and which were repeated by Seth, and fully exemplified by Enoch, cleared away the darkness and gloom, and gave hope to man, that as through Adam came death, through Jesus, the promised Redeemer, would come life and immortality. (1SP 64.1)

In the case of Enoch, the desponding faithful were taught that, although living among a corrupt and sinful people, who were in open and daring rebellion against God, their Creator, yet if they would obey him, and have faith in the promised Redeemer, they could work righteousness like the faithful Enoch, be accepted of God, and finally exalted to his heavenly throne. (1SP 64.2)

Enoch, separating himself from the world, and spending much of his time in prayer and in communion with God, represents God's loyal people in the last days who will be separate from the world. Unrighteousness will prevail to a dreadful extent upon the earth. Men will give themselves up to follow every imagination of their corrupt hearts, and carry out their deceptive philosophy, and rebel against the authority of high Heaven. (1SP 64.3)

God's people will separate themselves from the unrighteous practices of those around them, and will seek for purity of thought, and holy conformity to his will, until his divine image will be reflected in them. Like Enoch they will be fitting for translation to Heaven. While they endeavor to instruct and warn the world, they will not conform to the spirit and customs of unbelievers, but will condemn them by their holy conversation and godly example. Enoch's translation to Heaven just before the destruction of the world by a flood, represents the translation of all the living righteous from the earth previous to its destruction by fire. The saints will be glorified in the presence of those who have hated them for their loyal obedience to God's righteous commandments. (1SP 65.1)

Enoch instructed his family in regard to the flood. Methuselah, the son of Enoch, listened to the preaching of his grandson, Noah, who faithfully warned the inhabitants of the old world that a flood of waters was coming upon the earth. Methuselah and his sons, and grandsons, lived in the time of the building of the ark. They, with some others, received instruction from Noah, and assisted him in building the ark. **(1SP 65.2)**

Seth was of more noble stature than Cain or Abel, and resembled Adam more than any of his other sons. The descendants of Seth had separated themselves from the wicked descendants of Cain. They cherished the knowledge of God's will, while the ungodly race of Cain had no respect for God and his sacred commandments. But when men multiplied upon the earth, the descendants of Seth saw that the daughters of the descendants of Cain were very beautiful, and they departed from God and displeased him by taking wives as they chose of the idolatrous race of Cain. **(1SP 65.3)**

*****

Chapter 7
The Flood

Those who honored and feared to offend God, at first felt the curse but lightly; while those who turned from God and trampled upon his authority, felt the effects of the curse more heavily, especially in stature and nobleness of form. The descendants of Seth were called the sons of God–the descendants of Cain, the sons of men. As the sons of God mingled with the sons of men, they became corrupt, and by intermarriage with them, lost, through the influence of their wives, their peculiar, holy character, and united with the sons of Cain in their idolatry. Many cast aside the fear of God, and trampled upon his commandments. But there were a few that did righteousness, who feared and honored their Creator. Noah and his family were among the righteous few. (1SP 66.1)

The wickedness of man was so great, and increased to such a fearful extent, that God repented that he had made man upon the earth; for he saw that the wickedness of man was great, and that every imagination of the thoughts of his heart was only evil continually. (1SP 66.2)

The curse did not change at once the appearance of the earth. It was still rich in the bounty God had provided for it. There were gold and silver in abundance. The race of men then living was of very great stature, and possessed wonderful strength. The trees were vastly larger, and far surpassing in beauty and perfect proportions anything mortals can now look upon. The wood of these trees was of fine grain and hard substance–in this respect more like stone. It required much more time and labor, even of that powerful race, to prepare the timber for building, than it requires in this degenerate age to prepare trees that are now growing upon the earth, even with the present weaker strength men now possess. These trees were of great durability, and would know nothing of decay for very many years. (1SP 66.3)

A heavy, double curse, first in consequence of Adam's transgression, and second, because of the murder committed by Cain, was resting upon the earth; yet the mountains and hills were still lovely. Upon the highest elevations grew majestic trees, rising to a lofty height, their branches spreading to a great distance on every side, while the plains were covered with verdure, and appeared like a vast garden of flowers. Some of the hills were covered with trees of beauty, and vines climbing the stately trees were loaded with grapes, while beautiful flowers filled the air with their fragrance. But notwithstanding the richness and beauty of the earth, yet, when compared with its state before the curse was pronounced upon it, there was manifest evidence of sure and certain decay. (1SP 67.1)

The people used the gold, silver, precious stones, and choice wood, in building houses for themselves, each striving to excel the other. They beautified and adorned their houses and lands with the most ingenious works, and provoked God by their wicked deeds. They formed images to worship, and taught their children to regard these pieces of workmanship made with their own hands, as gods, and to worship them. They did not choose to think of God, the creator of the heavens and the earth, and rendered no grateful thanks to him who had provided them all the things which they possessed. They even denied the existence of the God of Heaven, and gloried in, and worshiped, the works of their own hands. They corrupted themselves with those things which God had placed upon the earth for man's benefit. They prepared for themselves beautiful walks, overhung with fruit trees of every description. Under these majestic and lovely trees, with their wide-spread branches, which were green from the commencement of the year to its close, they placed their idols of worship. Whole groves, because of the shelter of their branches, were dedicated to their idol gods, and made attractive for the people to resort to for their idolatrous worship. (1SP 67.2)

Instead of doing justice to their neighbors,

Chapter 7 - The Flood (1SP 71.1)

they carried out their own unlawful wishes. They had a plurality of wives, which was contrary to God's wise arrangement. In the beginning, God gave to Adam one wife–showing to all who should live upon the earth, his order and law in that respect. The transgression and fall of Adam and Eve brought sin and wretchedness upon the human race, and man followed his own carnal desires, and changed God's order. The more men multiplied wives to themselves, the more they increased in wickedness and unhappiness. If any one chose to take the wives, or cattle, or anything belonging to his neighbor, he did not regard justice or right, but if he could prevail over his neighbor by reason of strength, or by putting him to death, he did so, and exulted in his deeds of violence. They loved to destroy the lives of animals. They used them for food, and this increased their ferocity and violence, and caused them to look upon the blood of human beings with astonishing indifference. (1SP 68.1)

But if there was one sin above another which called for the destruction of the race by the flood, it was the base crime of amalgamation of man and beast which defaced the image of God, and caused confusion everywhere. God purposed to destroy by a flood that powerful, long-lived race that had corrupted their ways before him. He would not suffer them to live out the days of their natural life, which would be hundreds of years. It was only a few generations back when Adam had access to that tree which was to prolong life. After his disobedience he was not suffered to eat of the tree of life and perpetuate a life of sin. In order for man to possess an endless life he must continue to eat of the fruit of the tree of life. Deprived of that tree, his life would gradually wear out. (1SP 69.1)

More than one hundred years before the flood the Lord sent an angel to faithful Noah to make known to him that he would no longer have mercy upon the corrupt race. But he would not have them ignorant of his design. He would instruct Noah, and make him a faithful preacher to warn the world of its coming destruction, that the inhabitants of the earth might be left without excuse. Noah was to preach to the people, and also to prepare an ark as God should direct him for the saving of himself and family. He was not only to preach, but his example in building the ark was to convince all that he believed what he preached. (1SP 69.2)

Noah and his family were not alone in fearing and obeying God. But Noah was the most pious and holy of any upon the earth, and was the one whose life God preserved to carry out his will in building the ark and warning the world of its coming doom. Methuselah, the grandfather of Noah, lived until the very year of the flood; and there were others who believed the preaching of Noah, and aided him in building the ark, who died before the flood of waters came upon the earth. Noah, by his preaching and example in building the ark, condemned the world. God gave all who chose an opportunity to repent and turn to him. But they believed not the preaching of Noah. They mocked at his warnings, and ridiculed the building of that immense vessel on dry land. Noah's efforts to reform his fellow-men did not succeed. But for more than one hundred years he persevered in his efforts to turn men to repentance and to God. Every blow struck upon the ark was preaching to the people. Noah directed, he preached, he worked, while the people looked on in amazement, and regarded him as a fanatic. (1SP 70.1)

God gave Noah the exact dimensions of the ark, and explicit directions in regard to the construction of it in every particular. In many respects it was not made like a vessel, but prepared like a house, the foundation like a boat which would float upon water. There were no windows in the sides of the ark. It was three stories high, and the light they received was from a window in the top. The door was in the side. The different apartments prepared for the reception of different animals were so made that the window in the top gave light to all. The ark was made of the cypress or gopher wood, which would know nothing of decay for hundreds of years. It was a building of great durability, which no wisdom of man could invent. God was the designer, and Noah his master-builder. (1SP 70.2)

After Noah had done all in his power to make every part of the work correct, it was impossible that it could of itself withstand the violence of the storm which God in his fierce anger was to bring upon the earth. The work of completing the building was a slow process. Every piece of timber was closely fitted, and every seam covered with pitch. All that men could do was done to make the work perfect; yet, after all, God alone could preserve the building upon the angry, heaving billows, by his miraculous power. (1SP 71.1)

Chapter 7 - The Flood (1SP 71.2)

A multitude at first apparently received the warning of Noah, yet did not fully turn to God with true repentance. There was some time given them before the flood was to come, in which they were to be placed upon probation–to be proved and tried. They failed to endure the trial. The prevailing degeneracy overcame them, and they finally joined others who were corrupt, in deriding and scoffing at faithful Noah. They would not leave off their sins, but continued in polygamy, and in the indulgence of their corrupt passions. (1SP 71.2)

The period of their probation was drawing near its close. The unbelieving, scoffing inhabitants of the world were to have a special sign of God's divine power. Noah had faithfully followed the instructions God had given to him. The ark was finished exactly as God had directed. He had laid in store immense quantities of food for man and beast. And after this was accomplished, God commanded the faithful Noah, "Come thou, and all thy house, into the ark, for thee have I seen righteous before me." Angels were sent to collect from the forest and field the beasts which God had created. Angels went before these animals and they followed, two and two, male and female, and clean beasts by sevens. These beasts, from the most ferocious, down to the most gentle and harmless, peacefully and solemnly marched into the ark. The sky seemed clouded with birds of every description. They came flying to the ark, two and two, male and female, and the clean birds by sevens. The world looked on with wonder–some with fear, but they had become so hardened by rebellion that this most signal manifestation of God's power had but a momentary influence upon them. For seven days these animals were coming into the ark, and Noah was arranging them in the places prepared for them. (1SP 71.3)

And as the doomed race beheld the sun shining in its glory, and the earth clad in almost its Eden beauty, they drove away their rising fears by boisterous merriment; and by their deeds of violence seemed to be encouraging upon themselves the visitation of the already awakened wrath of God. (1SP 72.1)

Everything was now ready for the closing of the ark, which could not have been done by Noah from within. An angel is seen by the scoffing multitude descending from Heaven, clothed with brightness like the lightning. He closes that massive outer door, and then takes his course upward to Heaven again. Seven days were the family of Noah in the ark before the rain began to descend upon the earth. In this time they were arranging for their long stay while the waters should be upon the earth. And these were days of blasphemous merriment by the unbelieving multitude. They thought because the prophecy of Noah was not fulfilled immediately after he entered the ark, that he was deceived, and that it was impossible that the world could be destroyed by a flood. Previous to this there had been no rain upon the earth. A mist had risen from the waters, which God caused to descend at night like dew, reviving vegetation and causing it to flourish. (1SP 72.2)

Notwithstanding the solemn exhibition they had witnessed of God's power–of the unnatural occurrence of the beasts' leaving the forests and fields, and going into the ark, and the angel of God clothed with brightness, and terrible in majesty, descending from Heaven and closing the door; yet they hardened their hearts, and continued to revel and sport over the signal manifestations of divine power. But upon the eighth day the heavens gathered blackness. The muttering thunders, and vivid lightning flashes, began to terrify man and beast. The rain descended from the clouds above them. This was something they had never witnessed, and their hearts began to faint with fear. The beasts were roving about in the wildest terror, and their discordant voices seemed to moan out their own destiny and the fate of man. The storm increased in violence until water seemed to come from heaven like mighty cataracts. The boundaries of rivers broke away, and the waters rushed to the valleys. The foundations of the great deep also were broken up. Jets of water would burst up from the earth with indescribable force, throwing massive rocks hundreds of feet into the air, and then they would bury themselves deep in the earth. (1SP 73.1)

The people first beheld the destruction, of the works of their hands. Their splendid buildings, their beautifully-arranged gardens and groves, where they had placed their idols, were destroyed by lightning from heaven. Their ruins were scattered everywhere. They had erected altars in groves, and consecrated them to their idols, whereon they offered human sacrifices. These which God detested were torn down in his wrath before them, and they were made to tremble before the power of the living God, the

Maker of the heavens and the earth, and they were made to know that it was their abominations and horrible, idolatrous sacrifices, which had called for their destruction. (1SP 74.1)

The violence of the storm increased, and there were mingled with the warring of the elements, the wailings of the people who had despised the authority of God. Trees, buildings, rocks, and earth, were hurled in every direction. The terror of man and beast was beyond description. And even Satan himself, who was compelled to be amid the warring elements, feared for his own existence. He had delighted to control so powerful a race, and wished them to live to practice their abominations, and increase their rebellion against the God of Heaven. He uttered imprecations against God, charging him with injustice and cruelty. Many of the people, like Satan, blasphemed God, and if they could have carried out their rebellion, would have torn him from the throne of justice. While many were blaspheming and cursing their Creator, others were frantic with fear, stretching their hands toward the ark, pleading for admittance. But this was impossible. God had closed the door, the only entrance, and shut Noah in, and the ungodly out. He alone could open the door. Their fear and repentance came too late. They were compelled to know that there was a living God who was mightier than man, whom they had defied and blasphemed. They called upon him earnestly, but his ear was not open to their cry. Some in their desperation sought to break into the ark, but that firm-made structure resisted all their efforts. Some clung to the ark until borne away with the furious surging of the waters, or their hold was broken off by rocks and trees that were hurled in every direction. Those who had slighted the warning of Noah, and ridiculed that faithful preacher of righteousness, repented too late of their unbelief. The ark was severely rocked and tossed about. The beasts within expressed, by their varied noises, the wildest terror, yet amid all the warring of the elements, the surging of the waters, and the hurling about of trees and rocks, the ark rode safely. Angels that excel in strength guided the ark and preserved it from harm. Every moment during that frightful storm of forty days and forty nights the preservation of the ark was a miracle of almighty power. (1SP 74.2)

The animals exposed to the tempest rushed toward man, choosing the society of human beings, as though expecting help of them. Some of the people would bind their children and themselves upon powerful beasts, knowing that they would be tenacious for life, and would climb the highest points to escape the rising water. The storm does not abate its fury–the waters increase faster than at first. Some fasten themselves to lofty trees upon the highest points of land, but these trees are torn up by the roots, and carried with violence through the air, and appear as though angrily hurled, with stones and earth, into the swelling, boiling billows. Upon the loftiest heights human beings and beasts would strive to hold their position until all were hurled together into the foaming waters, which nearly reached the highest points of land. The loftiest heights are at length reached, and man and beast alike perish by the waters of the flood. (1SP 75.1)

Anxiously did Noah and his family watch the decrease of the waters. He desired to go forth upon the earth again. He sent out a raven which flew back and forth to and from the ark. He did not receive the information he desired, and he sent forth a dove which, finding no rest, returned to the ark again. After seven days the dove was sent forth again, and when the olive leaf was seen in its mouth, there was great rejoicing by this family of eight, which had so long been shut up in the ark. Again an angel descends and opens the door of the ark. Noah could remove the top, but he could not open the door which God had shut. God spoke to Noah through the angel who opened the door, and bade the family of Noah go forth out of the ark, and bring forth with them every living thing. (1SP 76.1)

Noah did not forget God who had so graciously preserved them, but immediately erected an altar and took of every clean beast, and of every clean fowl, and offered burnt offerings on the altar, showing his faith in Christ the great sacrifice, and manifesting his gratitude to God for their wonderful preservation. The offering of Noah came up before God like a sweet savor. He accepted the offering, and blessed Noah and his family. Here a lesson is taught all who should live upon the earth, that for every manifestation of God's mercy and love toward them, the first act of all should be to render to him grateful thanks and humble worship. (1SP 76.2)

And lest man should be terrified with gathering clouds, and falling rains, and should be in continual dread, fearing another flood, God

Chapter 7 - The Flood (1SP 77.1)

graciously encourages the family of Noah by a promise. "And I will establish my covenant with you; neither shall all flesh be cut off any more by the waters of a flood; neither shall there any more be a flood to destroy the earth. And God said, This is the token of the covenant which I make between me and you and every living creature that is with you, for perpetual generations. I do set my bow in the cloud, and it shall be for a token of a covenant between me and the earth. And it shall come to pass, when I bring a cloud over the earth, that the bow shall be seen in the cloud. And the bow shall be in the cloud; and I will look upon it, that I may remember the everlasting covenant between God and every living creature of all flesh that is upon the earth." (1SP 77.1)

What a condescension on the part of God! What compassion for erring man, to place the beautiful, variegated rainbow in the clouds, a token of the covenant of the great God with man! This rainbow was to evidence the fact to all generations that God destroyed the inhabitants of the earth by a flood, because of their great wickedness. It was his design that as the children of after generations should see the bow in the cloud, and should inquire the reason of this glorious arch that spanned the heavens, that their parents could explain to them the destruction of the old world by a flood, because the people gave themselves up to all manner of wickedness, and that the hands of the Most High had bended the bow, and placed it in the clouds, as a token that he would never bring again a flood of waters on the earth. This symbol in the clouds was to confirm the belief of all, and establish their confidence in God; for it was a token of divine mercy and goodness to man; that although God had been provoked to destroy the earth by the flood, yet his mercy still encompasseth the earth. God says when he looketh upon the bow in the cloud, he will remember. He would not have us understand that he would ever forget; but he speaks to man in his own language, that man may better understand him. (1SP 77.2)

A rainbow is represented in Heaven round about the throne, also above the head of Christ, as a symbol of God's mercy encompassing the earth. When man, by his great wickedness, provokes the wrath of God, Christ, man's intercessor, pleads for him, and points to the rainbow in the cloud, as evidence of God's great mercy and compassion for erring man; also the rainbow above the throne and upon his head, emblematical of the glory and mercy from God resting there for the benefit of repentant man. (1SP 78.1)

Every species of animals which God had created was preserved in the ark. The confused species which God did not create, which were the result of amalgamation, were destroyed by the flood. Since the flood, there has been amalgamation of man and beast, as may be seen in the almost endless varieties of species of animals, and in certain races of men. (1SP 78.2)

After Noah had come forth from the ark, he looked around upon the powerful and ferocious beasts which he brought out of the ark, and then upon his family numbering eight, and was greatly afraid that they would be destroyed by the beasts. But the Lord sent his angel to say to Noah, "The fear of you, and the dread of you, shall be upon every beast of the earth, and upon every fowl of the air, upon all that moveth upon the earth, and upon all the fishes of the sea; into your hands are they delivered. Every moving thing that liveth shall be meat for you; even as the green herb have I given you all things." (1SP 78.3)

Previous to this time God had given man no permission to eat animal food. Every living substance upon the face of the earth upon which man could subsist had been destroyed; therefore God gave Noah permission to eat of the clean beasts which he had taken with him into the ark. God said to Noah, "Every moving thing that liveth shall be meat for you, even as the green herb have I given you all things." As God had formerly given them the herb of the ground and fruit of the field, now, in the peculiar circumstances in which they are placed, he permits them to eat animal food. Yet I saw that the flesh of animals was not the most healthful article of food for man. (1SP 79.1)

The whole surface of the earth was changed at the flood. A third dreadful curse now rested upon it in consequence of man's transgression. The beautiful trees and shrubbery bearing flowers were destroyed, yet Noah preserved seed and took it with him into the ark, and God by his miraculous power preserved a few of the different kinds of trees and shrubs alive for future generations. Soon after the flood, trees and plants seemed to spring out of the very rocks. In God's providence seeds were scattered and driven into the crevices of the rocks, and there securely hid for the future use of man. (1SP 79.2)

The waters had been fifteen cubits above the highest mountains. The Lord remembered Noah, and as the waters decreased, he caused the ark to rest upon the top of a cluster of mountains, which God in his power had preserved and made to stand fast all through that violent storm. These mountains were but a little distance apart, and the ark moved about and rested upon one, then another, of these mountains, and was no more driven upon the boundless ocean. This gave great relief to Noah and all within the ark. As the mountains and hills appeared, they were in a broken, rough condition, and all around them appeared like a sea of roiled water or soft mud. (1SP 80.1)

In the time of the flood the people, and beasts also, gathered to the highest points of land, and as the waters returned from off the earth, dead bodies were left upon high mountains and upon the hills, as well as upon the plains. Upon the surface of the earth were the bodies of men and beasts. But God would not have these to remain upon the face of the earth to decompose and pollute the atmosphere, therefore he made of the earth a vast burying ground. He caused a powerful wind to pass over the earth for the purpose of drying up the waters, which moved them with great force– in some instances carrying away the tops of the mountains like mighty avalanches, forming huge hills and high mountains where there were none to be seen before, and burying the dead bodies with trees, stones, and earth. These mountains and hills increased in size and became more irregular in shape by collections of stones, ledges, trees, and earth, which were driven upon and around them. The precious wood, stone, silver and gold, that had made rich and adorned the world before the flood, and which the inhabitants had idolized, was sunk beneath the surface of the earth. The waters which had broken forth with such great power, had moved earth and rocks, and heaped them upon earth's treasures, and in many instances formed mountains above them to hide them from the sight and search of men. (1SP 80.2)

God saw that the more he enriched and prospered sinful man, the more he corrupted his way before him. These treasures, which should have led man to glorify the bountiful giver, had been worshiped instead of God, while the giver had been rejected. (1SP 81.1)

The beautiful, regular-shaped mountains had disappeared. Stones, ledges, and ragged rocks, appeared upon some parts of the earth which were before out of sight. Where had been hills and mountains, no traces of them were visible. Where had been beautiful plains covered with verdure and lovely plants, hills and mountains were formed of stones, trees, and earth, above the bodies of men and beasts. The whole surface of the earth presented an appearance of disorder. Some parts of the earth were more disfigured than the others. Where once had been earth's richest treasures of gold, silver, and precious stones, were seen the heaviest marks of the curse. And upon countries which were not inhabited, and those portions of the earth where there had been the least crime, the curse rested more lightly. (1SP 81.2)

Before the flood there were immense forests. The trees were many times larger than any trees which we now see. They were of great durability. They would know nothing of decay for hundreds of years. At the time of the flood, these forests were torn up or broken down and buried in the earth. In some places large quantities of these immense trees were thrown together and covered with stones and earth by the commotions of the flood. They have since petrified and become coal, which accounts for the large coal beds which are now found. This coal has produced oil. God causes large quantities of coal and oil to ignite and burn. Rocks are intensely heated, limestone is burned, and iron ore melted. Water and fire under the surface of the earth meet. The action of water upon the limestone adds fury to the intense heat, and causes earthquakes, volcanoes, and fiery issues. The action of fire and water upon the ledges of rocks and ore causes loud explosions which sound like muffled thunder. These wonderful exhibitions will be more numerous and terrible just before the second coming of Christ and the end of the world, as signs of its speedy destruction. (1SP 81.3)

Coal and oil are generally to be found where there are no burning mountains or fiery issues. When fire and water under the surface of the earth meet, the fiery issues cannot give sufficient vent to the heated elements beneath. The earth is convulsed, the ground heaves, and rises into swells or waves, and there are heavy sounds like

Chapter 7 - The Flood (1SP 82.1)

thunder under ground. The air is heated, and suffocating. The earth quickly opens, and I saw villages, cities and burning mountains carried down together into the earth. (1SP 82.1)

God controls all these elements; they are his instruments to do his will; he calls them into action to serve his purpose. These fiery issues have been, and will be, his agents to blot out from the earth very wicked cities. Like Korah, Dathan and Abiram, they go down alive into the pit. These are evidences of God's power. Those who have beheld these burning mountains pouring forth fire, and flame, and a vast amount of melted ore, drying up rivers and causing them to disappear, have been struck with terror at the grandeur of the scene. They have been filled with awe as though they were beholding the infinite power of God. (1SP 82.2)

These manifestations bear the special marks of God's power, and are designed to cause the people of the earth to tremble before him, and to silence those who, like Pharaoh, would proudly say, "Who is the Lord, that I should obey his voice?" Isaiah refers to these exhibitions of God's power where he exclaims, "Oh! that thou wouldest rend the heavens, that thou wouldest come down, that the mountains might flow down at thy presence, as when the melting fire burneth, the fire causeth the waters to boil, to make thy name known to thine adversaries, that the nations may tremble at thy presence! When thou didst terrible things which we looked not for, thou camest down, the mountains flowed down at thy presence." *Isaiah 64:1-3.* (1SP 83.1)

"The Lord is slow to anger, and great in power, and will not at all acquit the wicked. The Lord hath his way in the whirlwind and in the storm, and the clouds are the dust of his feet. He rebuketh the sea and maketh it dry, and drieth up all the rivers. Bashan languisheth, and Carmel, and the flower of Lebanon languisheth. The mountains quake at him, and the hills melt, and the earth is burned at his presence, yea, the world, and all that dwell therein. Who can stand before his indignation? and who can abide in the fierceness of his anger? His fury is poured out like fire, and the rocks are thrown down by him." *Nahum 1:3-6.* (1SP 83.2)

"Bow thy heavens, O Lord, and come down: touch the mountains, and they shall smoke. Cast forth lightning, and scatter them: shoot out thine arrows, and destroy them." *Psalm 144:5, 6.*

(1SP 84.1)

Greater wonders than have yet been seen will be witnessed by those upon the earth a short period previous to the coming of Christ. "And I will show wonders in heaven above, and signs in the earth beneath; blood, and fire, and vapor of smoke." "And there were voices, and thunders, and lightnings; and there was a great earthquake, such as was not since men were upon the earth, so mighty an earthquake, and so great." "And every island fled away, and the mountains were not found. And there fell upon men a great hail out of heaven, every stone about the weight of a talent; and men blasphemed God because of the plague of the hail; for the plague thereof was exceeding great." (1SP 84.2)

The bowels of the earth were the Lord's arsenal, from which he drew forth the weapons he employed in the destruction of the old world. Waters in the bowels of the earth gushed forth, and united with the waters from heaven, to accomplish the work of destruction. Since the flood, God has used both water and fire in the earth as his agents to destroy wicked cities. (1SP 84.3)

In the day of the Lord, just before the coming of Christ, God will send lightnings from heaven in his wrath, which will unite with fire in the earth. The mountains will burn like a furnace, and will pour forth terrible streams of lava, destroying gardens and fields, villages and cities; and as they pour their melted ore, rocks and heated mud, into the rivers, will cause them to boil like a pot, and send forth massive rocks, and scatter their broken fragments upon the land with indescribable violence. Whole rivers will be dried up. The earth will be convulsed, and there will be dreadful eruptions and earthquakes everywhere. God will plague the wicked inhabitants of the earth until they are destroyed from off it. The saints are preserved in the earth in the midst of these dreadful commotions, as Noah was preserved in the ark at the time of the flood. (1SP 84.4)

*****

Chapter 8
Disguised Infidelity

I was then carried back to the creation, and was shown that the first week, in which God performed the work of creation in six days and rested on the seventh day, was just like every other week. The great God, in his days of creation and day of rest, measured off the first cycle as a sample for successive weeks till the close of time. "These are the generations of the heavens and of the earth when they were created." God gives us the productions of his work at the close of each literal day. Each day was accounted of him a generation, because every day he generated or produced some new portion of his work. On the seventh day of the first week God rested from his work, and then blessed the day of his rest, and set it apart for the use of man. The weekly cycle of seven literal days, six for labor and the seventh for rest, which has been preserved and brought down through Bible history, originated in the great facts of the first seven days. (1SP 85.1)

When God spake his law with an audible voice from Sinai, he introduced the Sabbath by saying, "Remember the Sabbath-day to keep it holy." He then declares definitely what shall be done on the six days, and what shall not be done on the seventh. He then, in giving the reason for thus observing the week, points them back to his example on the first seven days of time. "For in six days the Lord made heaven and earth, the sea and all that in them is, and rested the seventh day, wherefore the Lord blessed the Sabbath-day and hallowed it." This reason appears beautiful and forcible when we understand the record of creation to mean literal days. The first six days of each week are given to man in which to labor, because God employed the same period of the first week in the work of creation. The seventh day God has reserved as a day of rest, in commemoration of his rest during the same period of time after he had performed the work of creation in six days. (1SP 86.1)

But the infidel supposition that the events of the first week required seven vast, indefinite periods for their accomplishment, strikes directly at the foundation of the Sabbath of the fourth commandment. It makes indefinite and obscure that which God has made very plain. It is the worst kind of infidelity; for with many who profess to believe the record of creation, it is infidelity in disguise. It charges God with commanding men to observe the week of seven literal days in commemoration of seven indefinite periods, which is unlike his dealings with mortals, and is an impeachment of his wisdom. (1SP 86.2)

Infidel geologists claim that the world is very much older than the Bible record makes it. They reject the Bible record because of those things which are to them evidences from the earth itself that the world has existed tens of thousands of years. And many who profess to believe the Bible record are at a loss to account for wonderful things which are found in the earth, with the view that creation week was only seven literal days, and that the world is now only about six thousand years old. These, to free themselves from difficulties thrown in their way by infidel geologists, adopt the view that the six days of creation were six vast, indefinite periods, and the day of God's rest was another indefinite period; making senseless the fourth commandment of God's holy law. Some eagerly receive this position; for it destroys the force of the fourth commandment, and they feel a freedom from its claims upon them. They have limited ideas of the size of men, animals, and trees, before the flood, and of the great changes which then took place in the earth. (1SP 87.1)

Bones of men and animals are found in the earth, in mountains and in valleys, showing that much larger men and beasts once lived upon the earth. I was shown that very large, powerful animals existed before the flood, which do not now exist. Instruments of warfare are sometimes found; also petrified wood. Because the bones of

Chapter 8 - Disguised Infidelity (1SP 87.2)

human beings and of animals found in the earth are much larger than those of men and animals now living, or that have existed for many generations past, some conclude that the world is older than we have any scriptural record of, and was populated long before the record of creation, by a race of beings vastly superior in size to men now upon the earth. (1SP 87.2)

I have been shown that, without Bible history, geology can prove nothing. Relics found in the earth do give evidence of a state of things differing in many respects from the present. But the time of their existence, and how long a period these things have been in the earth, are only to be understood by Bible history. It may be innocent to conjecture beyond Bible history, if our suppositions do not contradict the facts found in the sacred Scriptures. But when men leave the word of God in regard to the history of creation, and seek to account for God's creative works upon natural principles, they are upon a boundless ocean of uncertainty. Just how God accomplished the work of creation in six literal days, he has never revealed to mortals. His creative works are just as incomprehensible as his existence. (1SP 88.1)

"Great is the Lord, and greatly to be praised; and his greatness is unsearchable." (1SP 88.2)

"Which doeth great things past finding out; yea, and wonders without number." (1SP 88.3)

"Which doeth great things, and unsearchable; marvelous things without number." (1SP 88.4)

"God thundereth marvelously with his voice; great things doeth he, which we cannot comprehend." (1SP 88.5)

"Oh! the depth of the riches both of the wisdom and knowledge of God! how unsearchable are his judgments, and his ways past finding out! For who hath known the mind of the Lord? or who hath been his counselor?" (1SP 88.6)

The word of God is given as a lamp unto our feet, and a light unto our path. Those who cast his word behind them, and seek by their own blind philosophy to trace out the wonderful mysteries of Jehovah, will stumble in darkness. A guide has been given to mortals whereby they may trace Jehovah and his works as far as will be for their good. Inspiration, in giving us the history of the flood, has explained wonderful mysteries that geology, independent of inspiration, never could. (1SP 89.1)

It has been the special work of Satan to lead fallen man to rebel against God's government, and he has succeeded too well in his efforts. He has tried to obscure the law of God, which in itself is very plain. He has manifested a special hate against the fourth precept of the decalogue, because it defines the living God, the maker of the heavens and the earth. The plainest precepts of Jehovah are turned from, to receive infidel fables. (1SP 89.2)

Man will be left without excuse. God has given sufficient evidence upon which to base faith, if he wishes to believe. In the last days, the earth will be almost destitute of true faith. Upon the merest pretense, the word of God will be considered unreliable, while human reasoning will be received, though it be in opposition to plain Scripture facts. Men will endeavor to explain from natural causes the work of creation, which God has never revealed. But human science cannot search out the secrets of the God of Heaven, and explain the stupendous works of creation, which were a miracle of almighty power, any sooner than it can show how God came into existence. (1SP 89.3)

"The secret things belong unto the Lord our God; but those things which are revealed belong unto us and to our children forever." Men, professing to be ministers of God, raise their voices against the investigation of prophecy, and tell the people that the prophecies, especially of Daniel and John, are obscure, and that we cannot understand them. But some of the very men who oppose the investigation of prophecy because it is obscure, eagerly receive the suppositions of geologists, which dispute the Mosaic record. But if God's revealed will is so difficult to be understood, certainly men should not rest their faith upon mere suppositions in regard to that which he has not revealed. God's ways are not as our ways, neither are his thoughts as our thoughts. Human science can never account for his wondrous works. God so ordered that men, beasts, and trees, many times larger than those now upon the earth, and other things, should be buried in the earth at the time of the flood, and there be preserved to evidence to man that the inhabitants of the old world perished by a flood. God designed that the discovery of these things in the earth should establish the faith of men in inspired history. But men, with their vain reasoning, make a wrong use of these things which God designed should lead them to exalt him. They fall into the same error as did the people before the flood–those things which God gave them as a benefit, they turned into a curse, by making a wrong use of them. (1SP 90.1)

Chapter 9
The Tower of Babel

Some of the descendants of Noah soon began to apostatize. A portion followed the example of Noah, and obeyed God's commandments; others were unbelieving and rebellious, and even these did not believe alike in regard to the flood. Some disbelieved in the existence of God, and in their own minds accounted for the flood from natural causes. Others believed that God existed, and that he destroyed the antediluvian race by a flood; and their feelings, like Cain, rose in rebellion against God, because he destroyed the people from the earth, and cursed the earth the third time by a flood. (1SP 91.1)

Those who were enemies of God felt daily reproved by the righteous conversation and godly lives of those who loved, obeyed, and exalted God. The unbelieving consulted among themselves, and agreed to separate from the faithful, whose righteous lives were a continual restraint upon their wicked course. They journeyed a distance from them, and selected a large plain wherein to dwell. They built them a city, and then conceived the idea of building a large tower to reach unto the clouds, that they might dwell together in the city and tower, and be no more scattered. They reasoned that they would secure themselves in case of another flood, for they would build their tower to a much greater height than the waters prevailed in the time of the flood, and all the world would honor them, and they would be as gods, and rule over the people. This tower was calculated to exalt its builders, and was designed to turn the attention of others who should live upon the earth from God to join with them in their idolatry. Before the work of building was accomplished, people dwelt in the tower. Rooms were splendidly furnished, decorated and devoted to their idols. Those who did not believe in God, imagined if their tower could reach unto the clouds, they would be able to discover reasons for the flood. (1SP 91.2)

They exalted themselves against God. But he would not permit them to complete their work. They had built their tower to a lofty height, when the Lord sent two angels to confound them in their work. Men had been appointed for the purpose of receiving word from the workmen at the top of the tower, calling for material for their work, which the first would communicate to the second, and he to the third, until the word reached those upon the ground. As the word was passing from one to another in its descent, the angels confounded their language, and when the word reached the workmen upon the ground, material was called for which had not been required. And after the laborious process of getting the material to the workmen at the top of the tower, it was not that which they wished for. Disappointed and enraged, they reproached those whom they supposed were at fault. After this, there was no harmony in their work. Angry with one another, and unable to account for the misunderstanding, and strange words among them, they left the work and separated from each other, and scattered abroad in the earth. Up to this time, men had spoken but one language. Lightning from heaven, as a token of God's wrath, broke off the top of their tower, casting it to the ground. Thus God would show to rebellious man that he is supreme. (1SP 92.1)

*****

Chapter 10
Abraham

The Lord selected Abraham to carry out his will. He was directed to leave his idolatrous nation, and separate from his kindred. The Lord had revealed himself to Abraham in his youth, and gave him understanding, and preserved him from idolatry. He designed to make him an example of faith, and true devotion, for his people who should afterward live upon the earth. His character was marked for integrity, generosity, and hospitality. He commanded respect as a mighty prince among the people. His reverence and love for God, and his strict obedience in performing his will, gained for him the respect of his servants and neighbors. His godly example and righteous course, united with his faithful instructions to his servants and all his household, led them to fear, love, and reverence, the God of Abraham. The Lord appeared to Abraham, and promised him that his seed should be like the stars of heaven for number. He also made known to him, through the figure of the horror of great darkness which came upon him, the long, servile bondage of his descendants in Egypt. (1SP 93.1)

In the beginning, God gave to Adam one wife, thus showing his order. He never designed that man should have a plurality of wives. Lamech was the first who departed in this respect from God's wise arrangement. He had two wives, which created discord in his family. The envy and jealousy of both made Lamech unhappy. When men began to multiply upon the face of the earth, and daughters were born unto them, they took them wives of all which they chose. This was one of the great sins of the inhabitants of the old world, which brought the wrath of God upon them. This custom was practiced after the flood, and became so common that even righteous men fell into the practice, and had a plurality of wives. Yet it was no less sin because they became corrupted, and departed in this thing from God's order. (1SP 93.2)

The Lord said of Noah and his family who were saved in the ark, "For thee have I seen righteous before me in this generation." Noah had but one wife; and their united family discipline was blessed of God. Because Noah's sons were righteous, they were preserved in the ark with their righteous father. God has not sanctioned polygamy in a single instance. It was contrary to his will. He knew that the happiness of man would be destroyed by it. Abraham's peace was greatly marred by his unhappy marriage with Hagar. (1SP 94.1)

After Abraham's separation from Lot, the Lord said to him, "Lift up now thine eyes and look from the place where thou art, northward, and southward, and eastward, and westward; for all the land which thou seest, to thee will I give it, and to thy seed forever. And I will make thy seed as the dust of the earth; so that if a man can number the dust of the earth, then shall thy seed also be numbered." "The word of the Lord came unto Abram in a vision, saying, Fear not, Abram, I am thy shield, and thy exceeding great reward." "And Abram said, Behold, to me thou hast given no seed; and lo, one born in my house is mine heir." (1SP 94.2)

As Abraham had no son, he at first thought that his trusty servant, Eliezer, should become his son by adoption, and his heir. But God informs Abraham that his servant shall not be his son and heir, but that he should really have a son. "And he brought him forth abroad, and said, Look now toward heaven, and tell me the stars, if thou be able to number them; and he said unto him, So shall thy seed be." (1SP 95.1)

If Abraham and Sarah had waited in confiding faith for the fulfillment of the promise that they should have a son, much unhappiness would have been avoided. They believed that it would be just as God had promised, but could not believe that Sarah, in her old age, would have a son. Sarah suggested a plan whereby she thought the promise of God could be fulfilled.

Chapter 10 - Abraham (1SP 95.2)

She entreated Abraham to take Hagar as his wife. In this they both lacked faith, and a perfect trust in the power of God. By hearkening to the voice of Sarah, and taking Hagar as his wife, Abraham failed to endure the test of his faith in God's unlimited power, and brought upon himself, and upon Sarah, much unhappiness. The Lord intended to prove the firm faith and reliance of Abraham upon the promises he had made him. **(1SP 95.2)**

Hagar was proud and boastful, and carried herself haughtily before Sarah. She flattered herself that she was to be the mother of the great nation God had promised to make of Abraham. And Abraham was compelled to listen to complaints from Sarah in regard to the conduct of Hagar, charging Abraham with wrong in the matter. Abraham is grieved, and tells Sarah that Hagar is her servant, and that she can have the control of her, but refuses to send her away, for she is to be the mother of his child through whom he thinks the promise is to be fulfilled. He informs Sarah that he should not have taken Hagar for his wife if it had not been her special request. Abraham was also compelled to listen to Hagar's complaints of abuse from Sarah. Abraham is in perplexity. If he seeks to redress the wrongs of Hagar, he increases the jealousy and unhappiness of Sarah, his first and much-loved wife. Hagar fled from the face of Sarah. An angel of God meets her, and comforts her, and also reproves her for her haughty conduct, in bidding her return to her mistress, and submit herself under her hands. **(1SP 95.3)**

After the birth of Ishmael, the Lord manifested himself again to Abraham, and said unto him, "I will establish my covenant between me and thee, and thy seed after thee, in their generations, for an everlasting covenant." Again the Lord repeated by his angel his promise to give Sarah a son, and that she should be a mother of many nations. Abraham did not yet understand the promise of God. His mind immediately rests upon Ishmael, as though through him would come the many nations promised, and he exclaims, in his affection for his son, "Oh, that Ishmael might live before thee!" **(1SP 96.1)**

Again the promise is more definitely repeated to Abraham: "Sarah thy wife shall bear thee a son indeed; and thou shalt call his name Isaac; and I will establish my covenant with him for an everlasting covenant, and with his seed after him." Angels are sent the second time to Abraham on their way to destroy Sodom, and they repeat the promise more distinctly that Sarah shall have a son. **(1SP 96.2)**

After the birth of Isaac, the great joy manifested by Abraham and Sarah caused Hagar to be very jealous. Ishmael had been instructed by his mother that he was to be especially blessed of God, as the son of Abraham, and to be heir to that which was promised to him. Ishmael partook of his mother's feelings, and was angry because of the joy manifested at the birth of Isaac. He despised Isaac because he thought that he was preferred before him. Sarah saw the disposition manifested by Ishmael against her son Isaac, and she was greatly moved. She related to Abraham the disrespectful conduct of Ishmael to her, and to her son Isaac, and said to him, "Cast out this bondwoman, and her son, for the son of this bondwoman shall not be heir with my son, even with Isaac." **(1SP 97.1)**

Abraham is greatly distressed. Ishmael is his son, beloved by him. How can he send him away! He prays to God in his perplexity, for he knows not what course to take. The Lord informs Abraham, through his angels, to listen to the voice of Sarah his wife, and that he should not let his affections for his son, or for Hagar, prevent his compliance with her wishes. For this was the only course he could pursue to restore harmony and happiness again to his family. Abraham has the consoling promise from the angel, that Ishmael, although separated from his father's house, should not die, nor be forsaken of God; that he should be preserved because he was the son of Abraham. God also promises to make of Ishmael a great nation. **(1SP 97.2)**

Abraham was of a noble, benevolent disposition, which was manifested in his pleading so earnestly for the people of Sodom. His strong spirit suffered much. He was bowed with grief, and his paternal feelings were deeply moved as he sends away Hagar and his son Ishmael to wander as strangers in a strange land. **(1SP 98.1)**

If God had sanctioned polygamy, he would not have thus directed Abraham to send away Hagar and her son. He would teach all a lesson in this, that the rights and happiness of the marriage relation are to be ever respected and guarded, even at a great sacrifice. Sarah was the first and only true wife of Abraham. She was entitled to rights, as a wife and mother, which no other could have in the family. She reverenced her husband, calling him lord; but she was jealous lest his affections should be divided with Hagar. God did not rebuke Sarah for the course she pursued. Abraham was reproved by the angels for distrusting God's power, which had led him to take Hagar as his wife, and to think that through her the promise would be fulfilled. (1SP 98.2)

Again the Lord saw fit to test the faith of Abraham by a most fearful trial. If he had endured the first test, and had patiently waited for the promise to be fulfilled in Sarah, and had not taken Hagar as his wife, he would not have been subjected to the closest test that was ever required of man. The Lord bade Abraham, "Take now thy son, thine only son Isaac, whom thou lovest, and get thee unto the land of Moriah; and offer him there for a burnt-offering upon one of the mountains which I will tell thee of." (1SP 98.3)

Abraham did not disbelieve God, and hesitate, but early in the morning he took two of his servants, and Isaac his son, and the wood for the burnt-offering, and went unto the place of which God had told him. He did not reveal the true nature of his journey to Sarah, knowing that her affection for Isaac would lead her to distrust God, and withhold her son. Abraham did not suffer paternal feelings to control him, and lead him to rebel against God. The command of God was calculated to stir the depths of his soul. "Take now thy son." Then, as though to probe the heart a little deeper, he adds, "thine only son Isaac, whom thou lovest;" that is, the only son of promise, "and offer him as a burnt-offering." (1SP 99.1)

Three days this father traveled with his son, having sufficient time to reason, and doubt God if he was disposed to doubt. But he did not distrust God. He did not now reason that the promise would be fulfilled through Ishmael; for God plainly told him that through Isaac should the promise be fulfilled. (1SP 99.2)

Abraham believed that Isaac was the son of promise. He also believed that God meant just what he said when he bade him to go offer him as a burnt-offering. He staggered not at the promise of God; but believed that God, who had in his providence given Sarah a son in her old age, and who had required him to take that son's life, could also give life again, and bring up Isaac from the dead. (1SP 99.3)

Abraham left the servants by the way, and proposed to go alone with his son to worship some distance from them. He would not permit his servants to accompany them, lest their love for Isaac might lead them to prevent him from carrying out what God had commanded him to do. He took the wood from the hands of his servants, and laid it upon the shoulders of his son. He also took the fire and the knife. He was prepared to execute the dreadful mission given him of God. Father and son walked on together. (1SP 99.4)

"And Isaac spake unto Abraham his father, and said, My father; and he said, Here am I, my son. And he said, Behold the fire and the wood; but where is the lamb for a burnt-offering? And Abraham said, My son, God will provide himself a lamb for a burnt-offering; so they went both of them together." Firmly walked on that stern, loving, suffering father by the side of his son. As they came to the place which God had pointed out to Abraham, he builds there an altar, and lays the wood in order, ready for the sacrifice, and then informs Isaac of the command of God to offer him as a burnt-offering. He repeats to him the promise that God several times made to him that through Isaac he should become a great nation, and that in performing the command of God in slaying him, God would fulfill his promise; for he was able to raise him from the dead. (1SP 100.1)

Isaac believed in God. He had been taught implicit obedience to his father, and he loved and reverenced the God of his father. He could have resisted his father if he had chosen to do so. But after affectionately embracing his father, he submitted to be bound and laid upon the wood. And as his father's hand is raised to slay his son, an angel of God who had marked all the faithfulness of Abraham on the way to Moriah, calls to him out of Heaven, and says, "Abraham, Abraham; and he said, Here am I. And he said, Lay not thine hand upon the lad, neither do thou anything unto him; for now I know that thou fearest God, seeing thou hast not withheld thy son, thine only son, from me. (1SP 100.2)

"And Abraham lifted up his eyes, and looked, and behold behind him a ram caught in a thicket by his horns; and Abraham went and took the ram, and offered him up for a

Chapter 10 - Abraham (1SP 101.1)

burnt-offering in the stead of his son." (1SP 101.1)

Abraham has now fully and nobly borne the test, and by his faithfulness redeemed his lack of perfect trust in God, which lack led him to take Hagar as his wife. After the exhibition of Abraham's faith and confidence, God renews his promise to him. "And the angel of the Lord called unto Abraham out of Heaven the second time, and said, By myself I have sworn, saith the Lord, for because thou hast done this thing, and hast not withheld thy son, thine only son, that in blessing I will bless thee, and in multiplying I will multiply thy seed as the stars of the heaven, and as the sand which is upon the sea shore; and thy seed shall possess the gate of his enemies. And in thy seed shall all the nations of the earth be blessed; because thou hast obeyed my voice." (1SP 101.2)

*****

Chapter 11
Isaac

The Canaanites were idolaters, and the Lord had commanded that his people should not intermarry with them, lest they should be led into idolatry. Abraham was old, and he expected soon to die. Isaac was yet unmarried. Abraham was afraid of the corrupting influence surrounding Isaac, and was anxious to have a wife selected for him who would not lead him from God. He committed this matter to his faithful, experienced servant who ruled over all that he had. Abraham required his servant to make a solemn oath to him before the Lord, that he would not take a wife for Isaac of the Canaanites, but that he would go unto Abraham's kindred, who believed in the true God, and select a wife for Isaac. He charged him to beware, and not take Isaac to the country from which he came; for they were nearly all affected with idolatry. If he could not find a wife for Isaac who would leave her kindred and come where he was, then he should be clear of the oath which he had made. (1SP 101.3)

This important matter was not left with Isaac, for him to select for himself, independent of his father. Abraham tells his servant that God will send his angel before him to direct him in his choice. The servant to whom this mission was intrusted started on his long journey. As he entered the city where Abraham's kindred dwelt, he prayed earnestly to God to direct him in his choice of a wife for Isaac. He asked that certain evidence might be given him, that he should not err in the matter. He rested by a well which was a place of the greatest gathering. Here he particularly noticed the engaging manners and courteous conduct of Rebekah; and all the evidence he had asked of God he received that Rebekah was the one whom God had been pleased to select to become Isaac's wife. She invited the servant to her father's house. He then related to Rebekah's father and her brother the evidences he had received from the Lord that Rebekah should become the wife of his master's son Isaac. Abraham's servant then said to them, "And now if ye will deal kindly and truly with my master, tell me; and if not, tell me; that I may turn to the right hand or to the left." The father and brother answered, "The thing proceedeth from the Lord; we cannot speak unto thee bad or good. Behold, Rebekah is before thee; take her, and go, and let her be thy master's son's wife, as the Lord hath spoken. And it came to pass, that, when Abraham's servant heard their words, he worshiped the Lord, bowing himself to the earth." (1SP 102.1)

After all had been arranged, the consent of the father and brother had been obtained, then Rebekah was consulted whether she would go with the servant of Abraham a great distance from her father's family, to become the wife of Isaac. She believed from the circumstances that had taken place, that God's hand had selected her to be Isaac's wife, "and she said, I will go." (1SP 103.1)

Marriage contracts were then generally made by the parents, yet no compulsion was used to make them marry those they could not love. But the children had confidence in the judgment of their parents, and followed their counsel, and bestowed their affections upon those whom their God-fearing, experienced parents chose for them. It was considered a crime to follow a course contrary to this. (1SP 103.2)

What a contrast to the course now pursued by many children! Instead of showing reverence and due honor for their parents, by consulting them, and having the advantages of their experienced judgment in choosing for them, they move hastily in the matter, and are controlled by impulse rather than by the judgment of their parents and the fear of God. It is often the case that they contract marriage without even the knowledge of their parents. And, in many instances, their lives are imbittered by hasty marriages, because the son-in-law or the daughter-in-law feels under no obligation to

Chapter 11 - Isaac (1SP 103.3)

make their parents happy. (1SP 103.3)

Young men and women sometimes manifest great independence upon the subject of marriage, as though the Lord had nothing to do with them, or they with the Lord, in that matter; and that it was purely a matter of their own, which neither God nor their parents should in any wise control. They seem to think that the bestowal of their affections is a matter in which self alone should be consulted. Such make a serious mistake; and a few years of marriage experience generally teaches them that it is a miserable mistake. This is the great reason of so many unhappy marriages, in which there is so little true, generous love, and so little exercise of noble forbearance, toward each other. These often behave in their own homes more like pettish children, than the dignified, affectionate husband and wife. (1SP 104.1)

Isaac had been trained in the fear of God to a life of obedience. And when he was forty years old, he submitted to have the God-fearing, experienced servant of his father choose for him. He believed that God would direct in regard to his obtaining a wife. (1SP 104.2)

Children now from fifteen to twenty generally consider themselves competent to make their own choice, without the consent of their parents. And they would look with astonishment, if it should be proposed to them to move in the fear of God and make the matter a subject of prayer. Isaac's case is left on record, as an example for children to imitate in after generations, especially those who profess to fear God. (1SP 104.3)

The course which Abraham pursued in the education of Isaac, that caused him to love a life of noble obedience, is recorded for the benefit of parents, and should lead them to command their households after them. They should instruct their children to yield to, and respect, their authority. And they should feel that a responsibility rests upon them to guide the affections of their children, that they may be placed upon persons who their judgment would teach them would be suitable companions for their sons and their daughters. It is a sad fact that Satan controls the affections of the young to a great extent. And some parents feel that the affections should not be guided or restrained. The course pursued by Abraham is a rebuke to all such. (1SP 105.1)

*****

Chapter 12
Jacob and Esau

God knows the end from the beginning. He knew, before the birth of Jacob and Esau, just what characters they would both develop. He knew that Esau would not have a heart to obey him. He answered the troubled prayer of Rebekah, and informed her that she would have two children, and the elder should serve the younger. He presented the future history of her two sons before her, that they would be two nations, the one greater than the other, and the elder should serve the younger. The first-born was entitled to peculiar advantages and special privileges, which belonged to no other members of the family. (1SP 105.2)

Isaac loved Esau better than Jacob, because Esau provided him venison. He was pleased with his bold, courageous spirit manifested in hunting wild beasts. Jacob was the favorite son of his mother, because his disposition was mild, and better calculated to make his mother happy. Jacob had learned from his mother what God had taught her, that the elder should serve the younger, and his youthful reasoning led him to conclude that this promise could not be fulfilled while Esau had the privileges which were conferred on the first-born. And when Esau came in from the field, faint with hunger, Jacob improved the opportunity to turn Esau's necessity to his own advantage, and proposed to feed him with pottage, if he would renounce all claim to his birthright; and Esau sold his birthright to Jacob. (1SP 106.1)

Esau took two idolatrous wives, which was a great grief to Isaac and Rebekah. Notwithstanding this, Isaac loved Esau better than Jacob. And when he thought that he was about to die, he requested Esau to prepare him meat, that he might bless him before he died. Esau did not tell his father that he had sold his birthright to Jacob, and confirmed it with an oath. Rebekah heard the words of Isaac, and she remembered the words of the Lord, "The elder shall serve the younger," and she knew that Esau had lightly regarded his birthright and sold it to Jacob. She persuaded Jacob to deceive his father, and by fraud receive the blessing of his father, which she thought could not be obtained in any other way. Jacob was at first unwilling to practice this deception, but finally consented to his mother's plans. (1SP 106.2)

Rebekah was acquainted with Isaac's partiality for Esau, and was satisfied that reasoning would not change his purpose. Instead of trusting in God, the disposer of events, she manifested her lack of faith by persuading Jacob to deceive his father. Jacob's course in this was not approbated by God. Rebekah and Jacob should have waited for God to bring about his own purposes, in his own way, and in his own time, instead of trying to bring about the foretold events by the aid of deception. If Esau had received the blessing of his father, which was bestowed upon the first-born, his prosperity could have come from God alone; and he would have blessed him with prosperity, or brought upon him adversity, according to his course of action. If he should love and reverence God, like righteous Abel, he would be accepted and blessed of God. If like wicked Cain he had no respect for God, nor for his commandments, but followed his own corrupt course, he would not receive a blessing from God, but would be rejected of God, as was Cain. If Jacob's course should be righteous, if he should love and fear God, he would be blessed of God, and the prospering hand of God would be with him, even if he did not obtain the blessings and privileges generally bestowed upon the first-born. (1SP 107.1)

Rebekah repented in bitterness for the wrong counsel which she gave to Jacob, for it was the means of separating him from her forever. He was compelled to flee for his life from the wrath of Esau, and his mother never saw his face again. Isaac lived many years after he gave Jacob the blessing, and was convinced, by the course of Esau and Jacob, that the blessing rightly belonged

Chapter 12 - Jacob and Esau (1SP 107.2)

to Jacob. (1SP 107.2)

The circumstances of Esau's selling his birthright represent the unrighteous, who consider the redemption purchased for them by Christ of little value, and sacrifice their heirship to Heaven for perishable treasures. Many are controlled by their appetite, and rather than to deny an unhealthy appetite, will sacrifice high and valuable considerations. If one must be yielded, the gratification of a depraved appetite, or the high and heavenly blessings which God promises only to the self-denying and God-fearing, the clamors of appetite, as in the case of Esau, will generally prevail, and for self-gratification, God and Heaven will be virtually despised. Even professed Christians will use tea, coffee, snuff, tobacco and spirits, all of which benumb the finer sensibilities of the soul. If you tell them they cannot have Heaven, and these hurtful indulgences, and that they should deny their appetites, and cleanse themselves from all filthiness of the flesh and spirit, perfecting holiness in the fear of the Lord, they are offended, look sorrowful, and conclude that if the way is so strait that they cannot indulge in their gross appetites, they will not walk any longer in it. (1SP 108.1)

Especially will the corrupt passions control the mind of those who value Heaven of so little worth. Health will be sacrificed, the mental faculties enfeebled, and Heaven will be sold for these pleasures, as Esau sold his birthright. Esau was a reckless person. He made a solemn oath that Jacob should have his birthright. This case is left on record as a warning to others. As Esau learned that Jacob had obtained the blessing which would have belonged to him, had he not rashly sold it, he was greatly distressed. He repented of his rash act, when it was too late to remedy the matter. Thus it will be with sinners in the day of God, who have bartered away their heirship to Heaven for selfish gratifications and hurtful lusts. They will then find no place for repentance, although they may seek it, like Esau, carefully and with tears. (1SP 108.2)

Jacob was not happy in his marriage relation, although his wives were sisters. He formed the marriage contract with Laban for his daughter Rachel, whom he loved. After he had served seven years for Rachel, Laban deceived him and gave him Leah. When Jacob realized the deception that had been practiced upon him, and that Leah had acted her part in deceiving him, he could not love Leah. Laban wished to retain the faithful services of Jacob a greater length of time, therefore deceived him by giving him Leah, instead of Rachel. Jacob reproved Laban for thus trifling with his affections, in giving him Leah, whom he had not loved. Laban entreated Jacob not to put away Leah, for this was considered a great disgrace, not only to the wife, but to the whole family. Jacob was placed in a most trying position; but he decided to still retain Leah, and also marry her sister. Leah was loved in a much less degree than Rachel. Laban was selfish in his dealings with Jacob. He only thought of advantaging himself by the faithful labors of Jacob. He would have left the artful Laban long before, but he was afraid of encountering Esau. He heard the complaint of Laban's sons, saying, "Jacob hath taken away all that was our father's; and of that which was our father's hath he gotten all this glory. And Jacob beheld the countenance of Laban, and, behold, it was not toward him as before." (1SP 109.1)

Jacob was distressed. He knew not which way to turn. He carries his case to God, and intercedes for direction from him. The Lord mercifully answers his distressed prayer. "And the Lord said unto Jacob, Return unto the land of thy fathers, and to thy kindred; and I will be with thee. And Jacob sent and called Rachel and Leah to the field unto his flock, and said unto them, I see your father's countenance, that it is not toward me as before; but the God of my father hath been with me. And ye know that with all my power I have served your father. And your father hath deceived me, and changed my wages ten times; but God suffered him not to hurt me." Jacob related to them the dream given him of God, to leave Laban and go unto his kindred. Rachel and Leah expressed their dissatisfaction of their father's proceedings. As Jacob rehearsed his wrongs to them, and proposed to leave Laban, Rachel and Leah said to Jacob, "Is there yet any portion or inheritance for us in our father's house? Are we not counted of him strangers? for he hath sold us, and hath quite devoured also our money. For all the riches which God hath taken from our father, that is ours, and our children's; now then, whatsoever God hath said unto thee, do." (1SP 110.1)

It was customary anciently for the bridegroom to pay a sum of money, according to his circumstances, to the father of his wife. If he had no money, or anything of value, his labor

Chapter 12 - Jacob and Esau **(1SP 113.2)**

was accepted for a stated length of time before he could obtain the daughter as his wife. This custom was considered a safeguard to the marriage contract. Fathers did not consider it safe to trust the happiness of their daughters to men who had not made sufficient provisions to take care of a family. If they had not ability to manage business, to acquire cattle or lands, they were afraid that their lives would be worthless. But that the truly worthy should not become discouraged, a provision was made to test the worth of those who had nothing of value to pay for a wife. They were permitted to labor for the father whose daughter they loved. Their labors were engaged for a certain length of time, regulated by the value of the dowry required for their daughter. In doing this, marriages were not hasty, and there was opportunity to test the depth of affections of the suitor. If he was faithful in his services, and was otherwise considered worthy, the daughter was given him as his wife. And, generally, all the dowry the father had received was given to his daughter at her marriage. **(1SP 110.2)**

What a contrast to the course now pursued by parents and children! There are many unhappy marriages because of so much haste. Two unite their interests at the marriage altar, by most solemn vows before God, without previously weighing the matter, and devoting time to sober reflection and earnest prayer. Many move from impulse. They have no thorough acquaintance with the dispositions of each other. They do not realize that the happiness of their life is at stake. If they move wrong in this matter, and their married life proves unhappy, it cannot be taken back. If they find they are not calculated to make each other happy, they must endure it the best they can. In some instances the husband proves to be too indolent to provide for a family, and his wife and children suffer. If the ability of such had been proved, as was the custom anciently, before marriage, much misery would have been saved. In the case of Rachel and Leah, Laban selfishly kept the dowry which should have been given to them. They have reference to this when they say, "He hath sold us, and hath quite devoured also our money." **(1SP 111.1)**

In the absence of Laban, Jacob took his family and all that he had, and left Laban. After he had pursued his journey three days, Laban learned that he had left him, and he was very angry. And he pursued after him, determined to bring him back by force. But the Lord had pity upon Jacob, and as Laban was about to overtake him, gave him a dream not to speak good or bad to Jacob. That is, he should not force him to return, or urge him by flattering inducements. When Laban met Jacob, he inquired why he had stolen away unawares, and carried away his daughters as captives taken with the sword. Laban tells him, "It is in the power of my hand to do you hurt; but the God of your fathers spake unto me yesternight, saying, Take thou heed that thou speak not to Jacob either good or bad." Jacob then rehearsed to Laban the ungenerous course he had pursued toward him, that he had only studied his own advantage. He appeals to Laban as to the uprightness of his conduct while with him, and says, "That which was torn of beasts I brought not unto thee; I bare the loss of it; of my hand didst thou require it, whether stolen by day, or stolen by night. Thus I was; in the day the drought consumed me, and the frost by night; and my sleep departed from mine eyes." **(1SP 112.1)**

A shepherd's life was one of diligence. He was obliged to watch his flocks day and night. Wild beasts were common, and often bold, and would do great injury to flocks of sheep and cattle that were not guarded by a faithful shepherd. Although Jacob had a number of servants to aid him in tending the flocks owned by himself and Laban, yet the responsibility of the whole matter rested upon him. And in some seasons of the year he was obliged to be with the flocks himself, day and night, to protect them in the driest season of the year, that they should not perish with thirst; and in the coldest part of the season, to save them from becoming chilled with the heavy night frosts. Their flocks were also in danger of being stolen by unprincipled shepherds, who wished to enrich themselves by stealing their neighbor's cattle. **(1SP 113.1)**

A shepherd's life was one of constant care. He was not qualified for a shepherd unless he was merciful, and possessed courage and perseverance. Jacob was chief shepherd, and had shepherds under him who were termed servants. The chief shepherd called these servants, to whom he intrusted the care of the flock, to a strict account if they were not found in a flourishing condition. If there were any of the cattle missing, the chief shepherd suffered the loss. **(1SP 113.2)**

The relation of Christ to his people is

Chapter 12 - Jacob and Esau (1SP 113.3)

compared to a shepherd. He saw, after the fall, his sheep in a pitiable condition, exposed to sure destruction. He left the honors and glory of his Father's house to become a shepherd, to save the miserable, wandering sheep, who were ready to perish. His winning voice was heard calling them to his fold, a safe and sure retreat from the hand of robbers; also a shelter from the scorching heat, and a protection from the chilling blasts. His care was continually exercised for the good of his sheep. He strengthened the weak, nourished the suffering, and gathered the lambs of the flock in his arms, and carried them in his bosom. His sheep love him. He goeth before his sheep, and they hear his voice, and follow him. "And a stranger will they not follow, but will flee from him; for they know not the voice of strangers." Christ says, "I am the good Shepherd. The good shepherd giveth his life for the sheep. But he that is an hireling, and not the shepherd, whose own the sheep are not, seeth the wolf coming, and leaveth the sheep, and fleeth; and the wolf catcheth them, and scattereth the sheep. The hireling fleeth because he is an hireling, and careth not for the sheep. I am the good Shepherd, and know my sheep, and am known of mine." (1SP 113.3)

Christ is the chief shepherd. He has intrusted the care of his flock to under shepherds. He requires these shepherds to have the same interest for his sheep which he has ever manifested, and to ever feel the responsibility of the charge he has intrusted to them. Ministers, who are called of God to labor in word and doctrine, are Christ's shepherds. He has appointed them under himself to oversee and tend his flock. He has solemnly commanded these to be faithful shepherds, to feed the flock with diligence, to follow his example, to strengthen the weak, nourish the fainting, and shield them from devouring beasts. He points them to his example of love for his sheep. To secure their deliverance, he laid down his life for them. If they imitate his self-denying example, the flock will prosper under their care. They will manifest a deeper interest than Jacob, who was a faithful shepherd over the sheep and cattle of Laban. They will be constantly laboring for the welfare of the flock. They will not be merely hirelings, of whom Jesus speaks, who possess no particular interest in the sheep; who, in time of danger or trial, flee and leave the sheep. A shepherd who labors merely for the wages he obtains, cares only for himself, and is continually studying his own interest and ease, instead of the welfare of his flock. (1SP 114.1)

Says Peter, "Feed the flock of God which is among you, taking the oversight thereof, not by constraint, but willingly; not for filthy lucre, but of a ready mind; neither as being lords over God's heritage, but being ensamples to the flock." Says Paul, "Take heed therefore unto yourselves, and to all the flock over which the Holy Ghost hath made you overseers, to feed the church of God, which he hath purchased with his own blood." (1SP 115.1)

All those professing to be shepherds, who feel that to minister in word and doctrine, and bear the burdens and have the care which every faithful shepherd should have, is a disagreeable task, are reproved by the apostle: "Not by constraint, but willingly; not for filthy lucre, but of a ready mind." All such unfaithful shepherds, the chief Shepherd would willingly release. The church of God is purchased with the blood of Christ, and every shepherd should realize that the sheep under his care cost a priceless sum. They should be diligent in their labor, and persevering in their efforts to keep the flock in a healthy, flourishing condition. They should consider the sheep intrusted to their care of the highest value, and realize that they will be called to render a strict account of their ministry. And if they are found faithful, they will receive a rich reward. "And when the chief Shepherd shall appear, ye shall receive a crown of glory that fadeth not away." (1SP 115.2)

Jacob says, "Thus have I been twenty years in thy house. I served thee fourteen years for thy two daughters, and six years for thy cattle; and thou hast changed my wages ten times. Except the God of my father, the God of Abraham, and the fear of Isaac, had been with me, surely thou hadst sent me away now empty. God hath seen mine affliction, and the labor of my hands, and rebuked thee yesterday." (1SP 116.1)

Laban then assured Jacob that he had an interest for his daughters and their children, that he could not harm them. He proposed to make a covenant between them. And Laban said, "Now, therefore, come thou, let us make a covenant, I and thou; and let it be for a witness between me and thee. And Jacob took a stone, and set it up for a pillar. And Jacob said unto his brethren, Gather stones; and they took stones, and made an heap, and they did eat there upon the heap." (1SP 116.2)

Laban understood the wrong of polygamy, although it was alone through his artifice that Jacob had taken two wives. He well knew that it was the jealousy of Leah and Rachel that led them to give their maids to Jacob, which confused the family relation, and increased the unhappiness of his daughters. And now as his daughters are journeying at a great distance from him, and their interest is to be entirely separate from his own, he would guard, as far as possible, their happiness. Laban would not have Jacob bring still greater unhappiness upon himself, and upon Leah and Rachel, by taking other wives. And Laban said, "The Lord watch between me and thee, when we are absent one from another. If thou shalt afflict my daughters; or if thou shalt take other wives besides my daughters; no man is with us; see, God is witness betwixt me and thee." (1SP 116.3)

Jacob made a solemn covenant before the Lord, that he would not take other wives. "And Laban said to Jacob, Behold this heap, and behold this pillar, which I have cast betwixt me and thee; this heap be witness, and this pillar be witness, that I will not pass over this heap to thee, and that thou shalt not pass over this heap and this pillar unto me, for harm. The God of Abraham, and the God of Nahor, the God of their father, judge betwixt us. And Jacob swear by the fear of his father Isaac." (1SP 117.1)

As Jacob went on his way, the angels of God met him. And when he saw them, he said, "This is God's host." He saw the angels of God, in a dream, encamping around about him. Jacob sent a humble conciliatory message to his brother Esau. "And the messengers returned to Jacob, saying, We came to thy brother Esau, and also he cometh to meet thee, and four hundred men with him. Then Jacob was greatly afraid and distressed; and he divided the people that was with him, and the flocks, and herds, and the camels, into two bands; and said, if Esau come to the one company, and smite it, then the other company which is left shall escape. (1SP 117.2)

"And Jacob said, O God of my father Abraham, and God of my father Isaac, the Lord which saidst unto me, Return unto thy country, and to thy kindred, and I will deal well with thee; I am not worthy of the least of all the mercies, and of all the truth, which thou hast showed unto thy servant; for with my staff I passed over this Jordan, and now I am become two bands. Deliver me, I pray thee, from the hand of my brother, from the hand of Esau; for I fear him, lest he will come and smite me, and the mother with the children. And thou saidst, I will surely do thee good, and make thy seed as the sand of the sea, which cannot be numbered for multitude." (1SP 117.3)

*****

Chapter 13
Jacob and the Angel

Jacob's wrong, in receiving his brother's blessing by fraud, is again brought forcibly before him, and he is afraid that God will permit Esau to take his life. In his distress he prays to God all night. An angel was represented to me as standing before Jacob, presenting his wrong before him in its true character. As the angel turns to leave him, Jacob lays hold of him, and will not let him go. He makes supplications with tears. He pleads that he has deeply repented of his sins, and the wrongs against his brother, which have been the means of separating him from his father's house for twenty years. He ventures to plead the promises of God, and the tokens of his favor to him from time to time, in his absence from his father's house. All night Jacob wrestled with the angel, making supplication for a blessing. The angel seemed to be resisting his prayer, by continually calling his sins to his remembrance, at the same time endeavoring to break away from him. Jacob was determined to hold the angel, not only by physical strength, but by the power of living faith. In his distress Jacob referred to the repentance of his soul, the deep humility he had felt for his wrongs. The angel regarded his prayer with seeming indifference, continually making efforts to release himself from the grasp of Jacob. He might have exercised his supernatural power, and forced himself from Jacob's grasp, but he did not choose to do this. But when he saw that he prevailed not against Jacob, to convince him of his supernatural power he touched his thigh, which was immediately out of joint. But Jacob would not give up his earnest efforts for bodily pain. His object was to obtain a blessing; and pain of body was not sufficient to divert his mind from his object. His determination was stronger in the last moments of the conflict than at the beginning. His faith grew more earnest and persevering until the very last, even till the breaking of the day. He would not let go his hold of the angel until he blessed him. "And he said, Let me go, for the day breaketh. And he said, I will not let thee go, except thou bless me." The angel then inquired, "What is thy name? And he said, Jacob. And he said, Thy name shall be called no more Jacob, but Israel; for as a prince hast thou power with God, and with men, and hast prevailed." **(1SP 118.1)**

Jacob's persevering faith prevailed. He held fast the angel until he obtained the blessing he desired, and the assurance of the pardon of his sins. His name was then changed from Jacob, the supplanter, to Israel, which signifies a prince of God. "And Jacob asked him and said, Tell me, I pray thee, thy name. And he said, Wherefore is it that thou dost ask after my name? And he blessed him there. And Jacob called the name of the place Peniel; for I have seen God face to face, and my life is preserved." It was Christ that was with Jacob through the night, with whom he wrestled, and whom he perseveringly held until he blessed him. **(1SP 119.1)**

The Lord heard the supplications of Jacob, and changed the purposes of Esau's heart. He did not sanction any wrong course which Jacob pursued. His life had been one of doubt, perplexity, and remorse, because of his sin, until his earnest wrestling with the angel, and the evidence he there obtained that God had pardoned his sins. **(1SP 120.1)**

"Yea, he had power over the angel, and prevailed. He wept, and made supplication unto him. He found him in Bethel, and there he spake with us, even the Lord God of hosts. The Lord is his memorial." **(1SP 120.2)**

Esau was marching against Jacob with an army, for the purpose of killing his brother. But while Jacob was wrestling with the angel that night, another angel was sent to move upon the heart of Esau in his sleeping hours. In his dream he saw Jacob an exile from his father's house for twenty years, because he was afraid of his life. And he marked his sorrow to find his mother dead. He saw in his dream Jacob's humility, and angels of God around about him. He dreamed

Chapter 13 - Jacob and the Angel (1SP 123.1)

that when they met he had no mind to harm him. When Esau awoke, he related his dream to his four hundred men, and told them that they must not injure Jacob, for the God of his father was with him. And when they should meet Jacob, not one of them should do him harm. "And Jacob lifted up his eyes, and looked, and behold, Esau came, and with him four hundred men." "And he passed over before them, and bowed himself to the ground seven times, until he came near to his brother. And Esau ran to meet him, and embraced him, and fell on his neck, and kissed him; and they wept." Jacob entreated Esau to accept a peace-offering, which Esau declined, but Jacob urged him: "Take, I pray thee, my blessing that is brought to thee; because God hath dealt graciously with me, and because I have enough. And he urged him, and he took it." (1SP 120.3)

Jacob and Esau represent two classes: Jacob, the righteous; and Esau, the wicked. Jacob's distress when he learned that Esau was marching against him with four hundred men, represents the trouble of the righteous as the decree goes forth to put them to death, just before the coming of the Lord. As the wicked gather about them, they will be filled with anguish; for, like Jacob, they can see no escape for their lives. The angel placed himself before Jacob, and he took hold of the angel, and held him, and wrestled with him all night. So also will the righteous, in their time of trouble and anguish, wrestle in prayer with God, as Jacob wrestled with the angel. Jacob in his distress prayed all night for deliverance from the hand of Esau. The righteous in their mental anguish will cry to God day and night for deliverance from the hand of the wicked who surround them. (1SP 121.1)

Jacob confessed his unworthiness: "I am not worthy of the least of all the mercies, and of all the truth, which Thou hast showed unto thy servant." The righteous in their distress will have a deep sense of their unworthiness, and with many tears will acknowledge their utter unworthiness, and, like Jacob, will plead the promises of God through Christ, made to just such dependent, helpless, repenting sinners. (1SP 121.2)

Jacob took firm hold of the angel in his distress, and would not let him go. As he made supplication with tears, the angel reminded him of his past wrongs, and endeavored to escape from Jacob, to test and prove him. So will the righteous, in the day of their anguish, be tested, proved, and tried, to manifest their strength of faith, their perseverance and unshaken confidence in the power of God to deliver them. (1SP 122.1)

Jacob would not be turned away. He knew that God was merciful, and he appealed to his mercy. He pointed back to his past sorrow for, and repentance of, his wrongs, and urged his petition for deliverance from the hand of Esau. Thus his importuning continued all night. As he reviewed his past wrongs, he was driven almost to despair. But he knew that he must have help from God or perish. He held the angel fast, and urged his petition with agonizing, earnest cries, until he prevailed. Thus will it be with the righteous. As they review the events of their past lives, their hopes will almost sink. But as they realize that it is a case of life or death, they will earnestly cry unto God, and appeal to him in regard to their past sorrow for, and humble repentance of, their many sins, and then will refer to his promise, "Let him take hold of my strength, that he may make peace with me, and he shall make peace with me." Thus will their earnest petitions be offered to God day and night. (1SP 122.2)

God would not have heard the prayer of Jacob, and mercifully saved his life, if he had not previously repented of his wrongs in obtaining the blessing by fraud. (1SP 122.3)

The righteous, like Jacob, will manifest unyielding faith and earnest determination, which will take no denial. They will feel their unworthiness, but will have no concealed wrongs to reveal. If they had sins, unconfessed and unrepented of, to appear then before them, while tortured with fear and anguish, with a lively sense of all their unworthiness, they would be overwhelmed. Despair would cut off their earnest faith, and they could not have confidence to plead with God thus earnestly for deliverance, and their precious moments would be spent in confessing hidden sins, and bewailing their hopeless condition. (1SP 123.1)

Those professed believers who come up to the time of trouble unprepared, will, in their despair, confess their sins before all in words of burning anguish, while the wicked exult over their distress. The case of all such is hopeless. When Christ stands up, and leaves the most holy place, then the time of trouble commences, and

Chapter 13 - Jacob and the Angel (1SP 123.2)

the case of every soul is decided, and there will be no atoning blood to cleanse from sin and pollution. As Jesus leaves the most holy, he speaks in tones of decision and kingly authority: "He that is unjust, let him be unjust still; and he which is filthy, let him be filthy still; and he that is righteous, let him be righteous still; and he that is holy, let him be holy still. And behold, I come quickly; and my reward is with me, to give every man according as his work shall be." (1SP 123.2)

Those who have delayed a preparation for the day of God, cannot obtain it in the time of trouble, or at any future period. The righteous will not cease their earnest, agonizing cries for deliverance. They cannot bring to mind any particular sins; but in their whole life they can see but little good. Their sins had gone beforehand to judgment, and pardon had been written. Their sins had been borne away into the land of forgetfulness, and they could not bring them to remembrance. Certain destruction threatens them, and, like Jacob, they will not suffer their faith to grow weak because their prayers are not immediately answered. Though suffering the pangs of hunger, they will not cease their intercessions. They lay hold of the strength of God, as Jacob laid hold of the angel; and the language of their soul is, "I will not let thee go except thou bless me." The saints at length prevail, like Jacob, and are gloriously delivered by the voice of God. (1SP 123.3)

That season of distress and anguish will require an effort of earnestness and determined faith that can endure delay and hunger, and will not fail under weakness, though severely tried. The period of probation is the time granted to all to prepare for the day of God. If any neglect the preparation, and heed not the faithful warnings given, they will be without excuse. Jacob's earnest, persevering wrestling with the angel, should be an example for Christians. Jacob prevailed because he was persevering and determined. All who desire the blessing of God, as did Jacob, and will lay hold of the promises as he did, and be as earnest and persevering as he was, will succeed as he succeeded. Why there is so little exercise of true faith, and so little of the weight of truth resting upon many professed believers, is because they are indolent in spiritual things. They are unwilling to make exertions, to deny self, to agonize before God, to pray long and earnestly for the blessing, and therefore they do not obtain it. That faith which will live through the time of trouble must be daily in exercise now. Those who do not make strong efforts now to exercise persevering faith, will be wholly unprepared to exercise that faith which will enable them to stand in the day of trouble. (1SP 124.1)

The sons of Jacob were not all righteous. They were affected in some degree with idolatry. God did not sanction the cruel, revengeful conduct of Jacob's sons to the Shechemites. Jacob was ignorant of their purpose, until their work of cruelty was accomplished. He reproved his sons, and told them that they had troubled him, to make him despised among the inhabitants of the land. And because of this their wrong, the surrounding nations would manifest their indignation by destroying him and his house. In his distress Jacob again calls upon God. "And God said unto Jacob, Arise, go up to Bethel, and dwell there, and make there an altar unto God, that appeared unto thee when thou fleddest from the face of Esau thy brother. Then Jacob said unto his household, and to all that were with him, Put away the strange gods that are among you, and be clean, and change your garments, and let us arise, and go up to Bethel, and I will make there an altar unto God, who answered me in the day of my distress, and was with me in the way which I went. And they gave unto Jacob all the strange gods which were in their hand, and all their earrings which were in their ears, and Jacob hid them under the oak which was by Shechem." And the family of Jacob never found them again. "And they journeyed; and the terror of God was upon the cities that were round about them, and they did not pursue after the sons of Jacob." (1SP 125.1)

Jacob was humbled, and required his family to humble themselves, and to lay off all their ornaments, for he was to make an atonement for their sins, by offering a sacrifice unto God, that he might be entreated for them, and not leave them to be destroyed by other nations. God accepted the efforts of Jacob to remove the wrong from his family, and appeared unto him, and blessed him, and renewed that promise made to him, because his fear was before him. "And Jacob set up a pillar in the place where he talked with him, even a pillar of stone." (1SP 126.1)

*****

Chapter 14
Joseph and his Brethren

Joseph listened to his father's instructions, and feared the Lord. He was more obedient to his father's righteous teachings than any of his brethren. He treasured his instructions, and, with integrity of heart, loved to obey God. He was grieved at the wrong conduct of some of his brethren, and meekly entreated them to pursue a righteous course, and leave off their wicked acts. This only imbittered them against him. His hatred of sin was such that he could not endure to see his brethren sinning against God. He laid the matter before his father, hoping that his authority might reform them. This exposure of their wrongs enraged his brethren against him. They had observed their father's strong love for Joseph, and were envious at him. Their envy grew into hatred, and finally to murder. (1SP 126.2)

The angel of God instructed Joseph in dreams which he innocently related to his brethren: "For, behold, we were binding sheaves in the field, and lo, my sheaf arose, and also stood upright; and behold, your sheaves stood round about, and made obeisance to my sheaf. And his brethren said to him, Shalt thou indeed reign over us? or shalt thou indeed have dominion over us? And they hated him yet the more for his dreams, and for his words. (1SP 127.1)

"And he dreamed yet another dream, and told it his brethren, and said, Behold I have dreamed a dream more; and behold, the sun, and the moon, and the eleven stars made obeisance to me. And he told it to his father, and to his brethren, and his father rebuked him, and said unto him, What is this dream that thou hast dreamed? Shall I and thy mother and thy brethren indeed come to bow down ourselves to thee to the earth? And his brethren envied him; but his father observed the saying." (1SP 127.2)

Jacob appeared to regard the dreams of his son with indifference. But he had been often instructed by the Lord in dreams himself, and he believed that the Lord was teaching Joseph in the same manner. He reproved Joseph, that his true feelings might not be discovered by his envious brothers. (1SP 127.3)

Jacob's sons were shepherds, and fed their flocks where they could find the best pastures. In traveling from place to place with their cattle, they often wandered quite a distance from their father's house, so that they did not see their father for several months at a time. In his anxiety for them, he sent Joseph to see if they were all well. With the true interest of a brother, Joseph searched for his brethren, where his father supposed he would find them, but they were not there. A certain man found him wandering in the field in search of his brethren, and directed him to Dothan. This was a long journey for Joseph. But he cheerfully performed it, because he loved his brethren, and also wished to relieve the anxiety of his father. But he was illy repaid for his love to them, and obedience to his father. (1SP 127.4)

"And when they saw him afar off, even before he came near unto them, they conspired against him to slay him. And they said one to another, Behold, this dreamer cometh. Come now therefore, and let us slay him, and cast him into some pit; and we will say, Some evil beast hath devoured him; and we shall see what will become of his dreams. And Reuben heard it, and he delivered him out of their hands, and said, Let us not kill him. And Reuben said unto them, Shed no blood, but cast him into this pit that is in the wilderness, and lay no hand upon him; that he might rid him out of their hands, to deliver him to his father again." (1SP 128.1)

Joseph, unsuspicious of what was to befall him, approached his brethren with gladness of heart to greet them after his long, wearisome journey. His brothers rudely repulsed him. He told them his errand, but they answered him not. Joseph was alarmed at their angry looks. Fear took the place of joy, and he instinctively shrank

Chapter 14 - Joseph and his Brethren (1SP 128.2)

with dread from their presence. They then took hold of him violently. They taunted him with the admonitions he had given them in the past, and accused him of relating his dreams to exalt himself above them in the mind of their father, that he might love him more than themselves. They accused him of hypocrisy. As they gave utterance to their envious feelings, Satan controlled their minds, and they had no sense of pity, and no feelings of love for their brother. They stripped him of his coat of many colors that he wore, which was a token of his father's love, and which had excited their envious feelings. (1SP 128.2)

Joseph was weary and hungry, yet they gave him neither rest nor food. "And they took him, and cast him into a pit; and the pit was empty, there was no water in it." As Judah thought of Joseph lying in the pit, suffering a lingering death by starvation, he was troubled. For a short time, he, with others of his brethren, seemed to possess a satanic frenzy. But after they had begun to accomplish their wicked purposes to the helpless, innocent Joseph, some of them were ill at ease. They did not feel that satisfaction they thought they should have to see Joseph perish. Judah was the first to express his feelings. He "said unto his brethren, What profit is it if we slay our brother, and conceal his blood? Come, and let us sell him to the Ishmaelites, and let not our hand be upon him; for he is our brother, and our flesh; and his brethren were content. Then there passed by Midianites, merchantmen; and they drew and lifted up Joseph out of the pit, and sold Joseph to the Ishmaelites for twenty pieces of silver; and they brought Joseph into Egypt." (1SP 129.1)

The thought of being sold as a slave was more dreadful to Joseph than to die. He manifested the deepest anguish, and appealed first to one of his brethren, then to another, for compassion. Some of their hearts were moved with pity, but through fear of derision from the rest, kept silent. They all thought they had gone too far to repent of their acts; for Joseph might expose them to their father, and he would be exceedingly angry with them for their treatment of his much-loved Joseph. They steeled their hearts against his distress, and would not listen to his entreaties for his father's sake to let him go, but sold him as a slave. (1SP 129.2)

Reuben went away from his brethren, that they might not learn his purpose in regard to Joseph. He advised them to put him in the pit, and designed to return and take him to his father. "And Reuben returned unto the pit, and, behold, Joseph was not in the pit; and he rent his clothes. And he returned unto his brethren, and said, The child is not; and I, whither shall I go?" His brethren told him that they had sold Joseph. (1SP 130.1)

"And they took Joseph's coat, and killed a kid of the goats, and dipped the coat in the blood; and they sent the coat of many colors, and they brought it to their father, and said, This have we found; know now whether it be thy son's coat or no." They caused their father intense anguish, as he pictured to himself the violent death his son must have suffered by being torn in pieces by wild beasts. His sons had not imagined that their father's grief would be so deep. All his children tried to comfort him, but he refused to refrain from his grief. He declared to his children that he would go down into his grave mourning. (1SP 130.2)

Joseph's brethren flattered themselves that they were taking a sure course to prevent the fulfillment of Joseph's strange dreams. But the Lord controlled events, and caused the cruel course of Joseph's brethren to bring about the fulfillment of the dreams which they were laboring to frustrate. (1SP 130.3)

Joseph was greatly afflicted to be separated from his father, and his bitterest sorrow was in reflecting upon his father's grief. But God did not leave Joseph to go into Egypt alone. Angels prepared the way for his reception. Potiphar, an officer of Pharaoh, captain of the guard, bought him of the Ishmaelites. And the Lord was with Joseph, and he prospered him, and gave him favor with his master, so that all he possessed he intrusted to Joseph's care. "And he left all that he had in Joseph's hand; and he knew not ought he had, save the bread which he did eat." It was considered an abomination for a Hebrew to prepare food for an Egyptian. (1SP 131.1)

When Joseph was tempted to deviate from the path of right, to transgress the law of God and prove untrue to his master, he firmly resisted, and gave evidence of the elevating power of the fear of God, in his answer to his master's wife. After speaking of the great confidence of his master in him, by intrusting all that he had with him, he exclaims, "How then can I do this great wickedness, and sin against God?" He would not be persuaded to deviate

Chapter 14 - Joseph and his Brethren (1SP 134.1)

from the path of righteousness, and trample upon God's law, by any inducements or threats. And when he was accused, and a base crime was falsely laid to his charge, he did not sink in despair. In the consciousness of innocence and right, he still trusted in God. And God, who had hitherto supported him, did not forsake him. He was bound with fetters, and kept in a gloomy prison. Yet God turned even this misfortune into a blessing. He gave him favor with the keeper of the prison, and to Joseph was soon committed the charge of all the prisoners. (1SP 131.2)

Here is an example to all generations who should live upon the earth. Although they may be exposed to temptations, yet they should ever realize that there is a defense at hand, and it will be their own fault if they are not preserved. God will be a present help, and his Spirit a shield. Although surrounded with the severest temptations, there is a source of strength to which they can apply and resist them. How fierce was the assault upon Joseph's morals. It came from one of influence, the most likely to lead astray. Yet how promptly and firmly was it resisted. He suffered for his virtue and integrity; for she who would lead him astray, revenged herself upon the virtue she could not subvert, and by her influence caused him to be cast into prison, by charging him with a foul wrong. Here Joseph suffered because he would not yield his integrity. He had placed his reputation and interest in the hands of God. And although he was suffered to be afflicted for a time, to prepare him to fill an important position, yet God safely guarded that reputation that was blackened by a wicked accuser, and afterward, in his own good time, caused it to shine. God made even the prison the way to his elevation. Virtue will in time bring its own reward. The shield which covered Joseph's heart, was the fear of God, which caused him to be faithful and just to his master, and true to God. He despised that ingratitude which would lead him to abuse his master's confidence, although his master might never learn the fact. The grace of God he called to his aid, and then fought with the tempter. He nobly says, "How then can I do this great wickedness, and sin against God?" He came off conqueror. (1SP 132.1)

Amid the snares to which all are exposed, they need strong and trustworthy defenses on which to rely. Many, in this corrupt age, have so small a supply of the grace of God, that in many instances their defense is broken down by the first assault, and fierce temptations take them captives. The shield of grace can preserve all unconquered by the temptations of the enemy, though surrounded with the most corrupting influences. By firm principle and unwavering trust in God, their virtue and nobleness of character can shine; and, although surrounded with evil, no taint need be left upon their virtue and integrity. And if, like Joseph, they suffer calumny and false accusations, Providence will overrule all the enemy's devices for good, and God will, in his own time, exalt as much higher, as for awhile they were debased by wicked revenge. (1SP 133.1)

The part which Joseph acted in connection with the scenes of the gloomy prison, was that which raised him finally to prosperity and honor. God designed that he should obtain an experience by temptations, adversity, and hardships, to prepare him to fill an exalted position. (1SP 133.2)

While he was confined in prison, Pharaoh became offended with two of his officers, the chief baker and the chief butler, and they were put in the prison where Joseph was bound. "And the captain of the guard charged Joseph with them, and he served them; and they continued a season in ward." Joseph made his life useful even while in prison. His exemplary conduct, humble deportment, and faithfulness, obtained for him the confidence of all in the prison, and those who were connected with it. He did not spend his time in mourning over the injustice of his accusers, which had deprived him of his liberty. (1SP 133.3)

One morning, as Joseph brought food to the king's officers, he observed that they were looking very sad. He kindly inquired, "Wherefore look ye so sadly today? And they said unto him, We have dreamed a dream, and there is no interpreter of it. And Joseph said unto them, Do not interpretations belong to God? Tell me them, I pray you." Then the butler related to Joseph his dream, which he interpreted, that the butler would be restored to the king's favor, and deliver Pharaoh's cup into his hand as he had formerly done. The butler was satisfied with the interpretation, and his mind was at once relieved. (1SP 134.1)

Joseph told the chief butler that in three days he would be no more a prisoner. He felt

Chapter 14 - *Joseph and his Brethren* (1SP 134.2)

very grateful to Joseph because of the interest he had manifested for him, and the kind treatment he had received at his hands; and, above all, for helping him when in great distress of mind, by interpreting his dream. Then Joseph, in a very touching manner, alluded to his captivity, and entreated him, "But think on me when it shall be well with thee, and shew kindness, I pray thee, unto me, and make mention of me unto Pharaoh, and bring me out of this house; for indeed I was stolen away out of the land of the Hebrews; and here also have I done nothing that they should put me into the dungeon. When the chief baker saw that the interpretation was good," he took courage and made known his dream. As soon as he related his dream, Joseph looked sad. He understood its terrible meaning. Joseph possessed a kind, sympathizing heart, yet his high sense of duty led him to give the truthful, yet sad, interpretation to the chief baker's dream. He told him that the three baskets upon his head meant three days; and that, as in his dream, the birds ate the baked meats out of the upper basket, so they would eat his flesh as he hung upon a tree. (1SP 134.2)

"And it came to pass the third day, which was Pharaoh's birthday, that he made a feast unto all his servants; and he lifted up the head of the chief butler and of the chief baker among his servants. And he restored the chief butler unto his butlership again; and he gave the cup into Pharaoh's hand: but he hanged the chief baker, as Joseph had interpreted to them. Yet did not the chief butler remember Joseph, but forgat him." The butler was guilty of the sin of ingratitude. After he had obtained relief from his anxiety, by the cheering interpretation of Joseph, he thought that he should, if brought again into the king's favor, certainly remember the captive Joseph, and speak in his favor to the king. He had seen the interpretation of the dream exactly fulfilled, yet in his prosperity he forgot Joseph in his affliction and confinement. Ingratitude is regarded by the Lord as among the most aggravating sins. And although abhorred by God and man, yet it is of daily occurrence. (1SP 135.1)

Two years longer Joseph remained in his gloomy prison. The Lord gave Pharaoh remarkable dreams. In the morning the king was troubled because he could not understand them. He called for the magicians of Egypt, and the wise men. The king thought that they would soon help him to understand these dreams, for they had a reputation for solving difficulties. The king related his dreams to them, but was greatly disappointed to find that with all their magic and boasted wisdom, they could not explain them. The perplexity and distress of the king increased. As the chief butler saw his distress, all at once Joseph came into his mind, and at the same time a conviction of his forgetfulness and ingratitude. "Then spake the chief butler unto Pharaoh, saying, I do remember my faults this day." He then related to the king the dreams which he and the chief baker had, which troubled them as the dreams which now troubled the king, and said, "And there was there with us a young man, an Hebrew, servant to the captain of the guard; and we told him, and he interpreted to us our dreams; to each man according to his dream he did interpret. And it came to pass, as he interpreted to us, so it was; me he restored unto mine office, and him he hanged." (1SP 135.2)

It was humiliating to Pharaoh to turn away from the magicians and wise men of his kingdom to a Hebrew servant. But his learned and wise men failed him, and he now will condescend to accept the humble services of a slave, if his troubled mind can obtain relief. (1SP 136.1)

"Then Pharaoh sent and called Joseph, and they brought him hastily out of the dungeon; and he shaved himself, and changed his raiment, and came in unto Pharaoh. And Pharaoh said unto Joseph, I have dreamed a dream, and there is none that can interpret it; and I have heard say of thee, that thou canst understand a dream to interpret it. And Joseph answered Pharaoh, saying, It is not in me; God shall give Pharaoh an answer of peace." (1SP 136.2)

Joseph's answer to the king shows his strong faith and humble trust in God. He modestly disclaims all honor of possessing in himself superior wisdom to interpret. He tells the king that his knowledge is not greater than that of those whom he has consulted. "It is not in me." God alone can explain these mysteries. "And Pharaoh said unto Joseph, In my dream, behold, I stood upon the bank of the river; and behold, there came up out of the river seven kine, fat-fleshed and well-favored; and they fed in a meadow; and behold, seven other kine came up after them, poor and very ill-favored and lean-fleshed, such as I never saw in all the land of Egypt for badness. And the lean and the

Chapter 14 - Joseph and his Brethren (1SP 139.1)

ill-favored kine did eat up the first seven fat kine; and when they had eaten them up, it could not be known that they had eaten them; but they were still ill-favored, as at the beginning. So I awoke. (1SP 136.3)

"And I saw in my dream, and behold, seven ears came up in one stalk, full and good; and, behold, seven ears, withered, thin, and blasted with the east wind, sprung up after them; and the thin ears devoured the seven good ears: and I told this unto the magicians; but there was none that could declare it to me. (1SP 137.1)

"And Joseph said unto Pharaoh, The dream of Pharaoh is one. God hath shewed Pharaoh what he is about to do. The seven good kine are seven years; and the seven good ears are seven years; the dream is one. And the seven thin and ill-favored kine that came up after them are seven years; and the seven empty ears blasted with the east wind shall be seven years of famine." (1SP 137.2)

Joseph told the king that there would be seven years of great plenty. Everything would grow in great abundance. Fields and gardens would yield more plentifully than formerly. Fruits and grains would yield abundantly. And these seven years of abundance were to be followed by seven years of famine. The years of plenty would be given that he might prepare for the coming years of famine. "And the plenty shall not be known in the land by reason of that famine following; for it shall be very grievous. And for that the dream was doubled unto Pharaoh twice, it is because the thing is established by God, and God will shortly bring it to pass. Now therefore let Pharaoh look out a man discreet and wise, and set him over the land of Egypt." (1SP 137.3)

The king believed all that Joseph said. He believed that God was with him, and was impressed with the fact that he was the most suitable man to be placed in authority at the head of affairs. He did not despise him because he was a Hebrew slave. He saw that he possessed an excellent spirit. "And Pharaoh said unto his servants, Can we find such a one as this is, a man in whom the Spirit of God is? And Pharaoh said unto Joseph, Forasmuch as God hath shewed thee all this, there is none so discreet and wise as thou art. Thou shalt be over my house, and according unto thy word shall all my people be ruled; only in the throne will I be greater than thou." (1SP 138.1)

Although Joseph was exalted as a ruler over all the land, yet he did not forget God. He knew that he was a stranger in a strange land, separated from his father and his brethren, which often caused him sadness, but he firmly believed that God's hand had overruled his course, to place him in an important position. And depending on God continually, he performed all the duties of his office, as ruler over the land of Egypt with faithfulness. "And in the seven plenteous years the earth brought forth by handfuls. And he gathered up all the food of the seven years which were in the land of Egypt, and laid up the food in the cities, the food of the field which was round about every city, laid he up in the same. And Joseph gathered corn as the sand of the sea, very much, until he left numbering; for it was without number." (1SP 138.2)

Joseph traveled throughout all the land of Egypt, giving command to build immense store-houses, and using his clear head and excellent judgment to aid in the preparations to secure food, necessary for the long years of famine. At length the seven years of plenteousness in the land of Egypt ended. "And the seven years of dearth began to come, according as Joseph had said; and the dearth was in all lands; but in all the land of Egypt there was bread. And when all the land of Egypt was famished, the people cried to Pharaoh for bread. And Pharaoh said unto all the Egyptians, Go unto Joseph; what he saith to you, do. And the famine was over all the face of the earth, and Joseph opened all the store-houses, and sold unto the Egyptians; and the famine waxed sore in the land of Egypt." (1SP 139.1)

The famine was severe in the land of Canaan. Jacob and his sons were troubled. Their supply of food was nearly exhausted, and they looked forward to the future with perplexity. They talked despondingly to one another in regard to being able to supply their families with food. Want and starvation stared them in the face. At length Jacob heard of the wonderful provisions which the king of Egypt had made; that he was instructed of God in a dream seven years before the famine to lay up large supplies for the seven years of famine which were to follow, and that all the countries journeyed to Egypt to buy corn. He said unto his sons, "Why do ye look one upon another? And he said,

Chapter 14 - Joseph and his Brethren (1SP 139.2)

Behold, I have heard that there is corn in Egypt. Get you down thither, and buy for us from thence, that we may live, and not die. And Joseph's ten brethren went down to buy corn in Egypt. But Benjamin, Joseph's brother, Jacob sent not with his brethren; for he said, Lest peradventure mischief befall him." (1SP 139.2)

Jacob's sons came with the crowd of buyers to purchase corn of Joseph; and they "bowed down themselves before him with their faces to the earth." And Joseph knew his brethren, but he appeared not to know them, and spake roughly unto them. "And he said unto them, Whence come ye? And they said, From the land of Canaan to buy food." "And Joseph remembered the dreams which he dreamed of them, and said unto them, Ye are spies; to see the nakedness of the land ye are come." (1SP 140.1)

They assured Joseph that their only errand into Egypt was to buy food. Joseph again charges them with being spies. He wished to learn if they possessed the same haughty spirit they had when he was with them; and he was anxious to draw from them some information in regard to his father and Benjamin. They feel humbled in their adversity, and manifest grief, rather than anger, at the suspicions of Joseph. They assure him that they are no spies, but the sons of one man; that they are twelve brethren; that the youngest is now with their father, and one is not. His father and Benjamin are the very ones Joseph wishes to learn in regard to. He professes to doubt the truthfulness of their story, and tells them that he will prove them, and that they shall not go forth from Egypt until their youngest brother come hither. He proposes to keep them in confinement until one shall go and bring their brother, to prove their words, whether there was any truth in them. If they would not consent to this, he would regard them as spies. (1SP 140.2)

The sons of Jacob felt unwilling to consent to this arrangement. It would require some time for one to go to their father, to get Benjamin, and their families would suffer for food. And then again, who among them would undertake the journey alone, leaving their brethren in a prison? How could that one meet his father? They saw his distress at the supposed death of Joseph, and he would feel that he was deprived of all his sons. As they conversed with one another in this manner, Joseph heard them. They said, further, It may be we shall lose our lives, or be made slaves. And if one go back to our father for Benjamin, and bring him here, he may be made a slave also, and our father will surely die. They decided to all remain, and suffer together, rather than to bring greater sorrow upon their father by the loss of his much-loved Benjamin. (1SP 141.1)

The three days of confinement were days of bitter sorrow with Jacob's sons. They reflected upon their past wrong course, especially their cruelty to Joseph. They knew if they were convicted of being spies, and they could not bring evidence to clear themselves, they would all have to die, or become slaves. They doubted whether any effort any one of them might make would cause their father to consent to have Benjamin go from him, after the cruel death, as he thought, Joseph had suffered. They sold Joseph as a slave, and they were fearful that God designed to punish them by suffering them to become slaves. Joseph considers that his father and the families of his brethren may be suffering for food, and he is convinced that his brethren have repented of their cruel treatment of him, and that they would in no case treat Benjamin as they had treated him. (1SP 141.2)

Joseph makes another proposition to his brethren. And he said unto them the third day, "This do, and live; for I fear God. If ye be true men, let one of your brethren be bound in the house of your prison: go ye, carry corn for the famine of your houses. But bring your youngest brother unto me; so shall your words be verified, and ye shall not die." They agree to accept this proposition of Joseph's, but express to one another little hope that their father will let Benjamin return with them. They accuse themselves, and one another, in regard to their treatment of Joseph. "And they said one to another, We are verily guilty concerning our brother, in that we saw the anguish of his soul, when he besought us, and we would not hear; therefore is this distress come upon us. And Reuben answered them, saying, Spake I not unto you, saying, Do not sin against the child; and ye would not hear? therefore, behold, also his blood is required. And they knew not that Joseph understood them; for he spake unto them by an interpreter. And he turned himself about from them, and wept; and returned to them again, and communed with them, and took from them Simeon, and bound him before their eyes." (1SP 142.1)

Joseph selected Simeon to be bound, because he was the instigator and principal actor in the cruelty of his brethren toward him. He then directed that his brethren should be liberally supplied with provision, and that every man's money should be placed in his sack. They pursued their homeward journey in sadness. As one of them opened his sack to feed his beast with provender, he found his money, just as he had brought it to Joseph. He told his brethren, and they considered that a new evil would arise; and they were afraid, and said one to another, What is this that God hath done unto us? Shall we consider this as a token of good from the Lord, or has he suffered it to occur to punish us for our sins, and plunge us still deeper in affliction? They acknowledge that God has seen their sins, and has marked their wrongs, and that he is now visiting them for their transgressions. (1SP 142.2)

When they came to their father Jacob, they related to him all that had transpired, and said, "The man who is the Lord of the land spake roughly to us, and took us for spies of the country. And we said unto him, We are true men; we are no spies. We be twelve brethren, sons of our father; one is not, and the youngest is this day with our father in the land of Canaan." They told their father that he would not believe their word, and said, If ye are not spies, leave one of your brethren with me, and take food for your households; and when ye come again bring your youngest brother, and then I will release you your brother that is bound, and ye shall be at liberty to trade in the land. (1SP 143.1)

As they emptied their sacks, every man's money was found in his sack, and they were all afraid. Jacob was distressed, and said unto them, "Me have ye bereaved of my children; Joseph is not, and Simeon is not, and ye will take Benjamin away. All these things are against me." Reuben assured his father that if he would intrust Benjamin to his care, he would surely bring him again to his father; if not, he might slay his two sons. This rash speech did not relieve the mind of Jacob. He said, "My son shall not go down with you; for his brother is dead, and he is left alone. If mischief befall him by the way in the which ye go, then shall ye bring down my gray hairs with sorrow to the grave." (1SP 143.2)

Jacob's affections cling to Benjamin with all the strength of a mother's love. He shows how deeply he has felt the loss of Joseph. But want presses upon Jacob and his children, and their households are calling for food. Jacob requests his sons to go again into Egypt and buy food. Judah says to his father that he cannot go down unless Benjamin is with them; for "the man did solemnly protest unto us saying, Ye shall not see my face, except your brother be with you." Judah assures his father that he will be surety for his brother, that if he would send him with them they would go, and if he did not bring Benjamin back, he would bear the blame of it forever. (1SP 144.1)

He tells his father that while they had been lingering, because of his unwillingness to send Benjamin, they could have journeyed to Egypt and returned again. Jacob feels compelled to permit his son Benjamin to go with his brethren. He also sent a present to the ruler, hoping therewith to obtain his favor. He also directed his sons to take double money, and return the money found in their sacks; for it might have been placed there by mistake. He says to them, "Take also your brother, and arise, go again unto the man." (1SP 144.2)

As his sons were about to leave him to go on their doubtful journey, their aged father arose, and, while standing in their midst, raised his hands to heaven, and entreated the Lord to go with them, and pronounced upon them a gracious benediction. "And God Almighty give you mercy before the man, that he may send away your other brother, and Benjamin. If I be bereaved of my children, I am bereaved." (1SP 145.1)

"And the men took that present, and they took double money in their hand, and Benjamin, and rose up, and went down to Egypt, and stood before Joseph." And when Joseph saw Benjamin with them, he could scarcely restrain his brotherly feelings of love. He gave direction to make preparation for his brethren to dine with him. When they were taken into Joseph's house, they were afraid that it was for the purpose of calling them to account because of the money found in their sacks. And they thought that it might have been intentionally placed there for the purpose of finding occasion against them to make them slaves, and that they were brought into the ruler's house to better accomplish this object. They sought to make friends with the steward of the house, and made known to him that they had found their money in the mouths of their sacks, fearing that the ruler who had treated them so roughly would accuse them of wrong in regard to the matter. They informed the

Chapter 14 - *Joseph and his Brethren* (1SP 145.2)

steward that they had brought back the money found in their sacks, in full weight; also other money to buy food; and added, "We cannot tell who put our money in our sacks." (1SP 145.2)

"And he said, Peace be to you, fear not; your God, and the God of your father, hath given you treasure in your sacks. I had your money. And he brought Simeon out unto them." The words of the steward relieved their anxiety, and they thought God was indeed gracious unto them, as their father had entreated he would be. (1SP 146.1)

When Joseph came home, his brethren gave him the present in the name of their father, and they bowed themselves to him to the earth. "And he asked them of their welfare, and said, Is your father well, the old man of whom ye spake? Is he yet alive? And they answered, Thy servant our father is in good health, he is yet alive. And they bowed down their heads and made obeisance. And he lifted up his eyes, and saw his brother Benjamin, his mother's son, and said, Is this your younger brother, of whom ye spake unto me? And he said, God be gracious unto thee, my son. And Joseph made haste; for his bowels did yearn upon his brother: and he sought where to weep; and he entered into his chamber, and wept there. And he washed his face, and went out, and refrained himself, and said, Set on bread." (1SP 146.2)

Joseph did not eat at the same table with his brethren, for the Egyptians considered it an abomination for them to eat bread with the Hebrews. Joseph placed his brethren at the table, as was customary when their ages were known, commencing with the eldest, according to his birthright, arranging them in order down to the youngest, as though he perfectly knew their ages. His brethren were astonished at this act of Joseph, who they thought could have no knowledge of their ages. (1SP 146.3)

As he sent a portion of food to each of his brethren, he sent Benjamin five times as much as the others. He did this not only to show his particular regard for his brother Benjamin, but to prove them, and see if they regarded Benjamin with the same envious feelings they had him. They thought that Joseph did not understand their language, and were free to converse with one another in his presence; therefore Joseph had a good opportunity to learn the true state of their feelings without their knowledge. Joseph again commanded to provide his brethren with food, as much as they could carry, and to put every man's money in his sack's mouth, and to place his silver cup in the sack of the youngest. When his brethren were gone out of the city, Joseph sent his steward to overtake them, and inquire why they had rewarded evil for good, by taking the silver cup belonging to the king, whereby, indeed, he divineth. (1SP 147.1)

Kings and rulers had a cup from which they drank, which was considered a sure detective if any poisonous substance was placed in their drink. "And they said unto him, Wherefore saith my Lord these words? God forbid that thy servants should do according to this thing. Behold, the money which we found in our sacks' mouths, we brought again unto thee out of the land of Canaan; how then should we steal out of thy lord's house silver or gold? With whomsoever of thy servants it be found, both let him die, and we also will be my lord's bondmen. And he said, Not also let it be according unto your words; he with whom it is found shall be my servant; and ye shall be blameless. Then they speedily took down every man his sack to the ground, and opened every man his sack. And he searched, and began at the eldest, and left at the youngest; and the cup was found in Benjamin's sack." (1SP 147.2)

At this discovery all were greatly surprised; and, to express their great distress, they rent their garments, which was the custom when in great affliction. Benjamin was more amazed and confounded than his brethren. They returned into the city sorrowful and afraid. They thought that the hand of God was against them for their past wickedness. By their own promise, Benjamin was appointed to a life of slavery. And the fears of their father they thought would be fully realized. Mischief had befallen his much-loved Benjamin. (1SP 148.1)

Judah had pledged himself to be surety for Benjamin. "And Judah and his brethren came to Joseph's house; for he was yet there; and they fell before him on the ground. And Joseph said unto them, What deed is this that ye have done? wot ye not that such a man as I can certainly divine?" Joseph asked this question to draw forth from his brethren an acknowledgment of their past wrong course, that their true feelings might be more fully revealed. He did not claim any power of divination, but was willing his brethren should believe that he could read the secret acts of their

Chapter 14 - Joseph and his Brethren (1SP 151.1)

lives. "And Judah said, What shall we say unto my lord? what shall we speak? or how shall we clear ourselves? God hath found out the iniquity of thy servants. Behold, we are my lord's servants, both we, and he also with whom the cup is found." Judah told his brethren that God had found out their iniquity for selling their brother in Egypt, and was now returning upon them their transgressions, by permitting them to become slaves also. (1SP 148.2)

Joseph refused to accept them all, according to the word of Judah, as bondmen. "And he said, God forbid that I should do so; but the man in whose hand the cup is found, he shall be my servant; and as for you, get you up in peace unto your father." Judah spoke with Joseph aside from the rest, and related to him the reluctance of his father to let Benjamin come with them to Egypt, and that he pledged himself to become surety for Benjamin, that if he brought him not to his father, he would bear the blame forever. He eloquently plead in behalf of his father, relating his great grief at the loss of Joseph, and that Benjamin was all that was left of the mother which his father loved, and that if Benjamin should be separated from his father, he would die; for his life was bound up in the lad's life. Judah then nobly offered to become a slave instead of his brother; for he could not meet his father without Benjamin was with him. Said Judah, "Now therefore, I pray thee, let thy servant abide instead of the lad a bondman to my lord, and let the lad go up with his brethren." (1SP 149.1)

Joseph was satisfied. He had proved his brethren, and had seen in them the fruits of true repentance for their sins; and he was so deeply affected that he could no longer conceal his feelings, and requested to be left alone with his brethren. He then gave vent to his long-suppressed feelings, and wept aloud. "And Joseph said unto his brethren, I am Joseph; doth my father yet live? And his brethren could not answer him; for they were troubled at his presence." His brethren could not answer him for astonishment. They could not really believe that the ruler of Egypt was their brother Joseph whom they had envied, and would have murdered, but finally were satisfied to sell as a slave. All their ill treatment of their brother painfully passed before them, and especially his dreams, which they had despised, and had labored to prevent their fulfillment. They had acted their part in fulfilling these dreams. Repeatedly had they made obeisance to Joseph, according to his dream. And now they stood before him condemned and amazed. (1SP 149.2)

As Joseph saw the confusion of his brethren, he said to them, "Come near to me, I pray you. And they came near. And he said, I am Joseph your brother, whom ye sold into Egypt." He nobly sought to make this occasion as easy for his brethren as possible. He had no desire to increase their embarrassment by censuring them. He felt that they had suffered enough for their cruelty to him, and he endeavored to comfort them. He said to them, "Now therefore be not grieved, nor angry with yourselves, that ye sold me hither; for God did send me before you to preserve life. For these two years hath the famine been in the land; and yet there are five years, in the which there shall be neither earing nor harvest. And God sent me before you to preserve you a posterity in the earth, and to save your lives by a great deliverance. So now it was not you that sent me hither, but God; and he hath made me a father to Pharaoh, and Lord of all his house, and a ruler throughout all the land of Egypt. Haste ye, and go up to my father, and say unto him, Thus saith thy son Joseph, God hath made me Lord of all Egypt. Come down unto me, tarry not. And thou shalt dwell in the land of Goshen, and thou shalt be near unto me, thou, and thy children, and thy children's children, and thy flocks, and thy herds, and all that thou hast. And there will I nourish thee; for yet there are five years of famine; lest thou, and thy household, and all that thou hast, come to poverty. And behold, your eyes see, and the eyes of my brother Benjamin, that it is my mouth that speaketh unto you. And ye shall tell my father of all my glory in Egypt, and of all that ye have seen; and ye shall haste and bring down my father hither. And he fell upon his brother Benjamin's neck, and wept; and Benjamin wept upon his neck. Moreover, he kissed all his brethren, and wept upon them, and after that his brethren talked with him." (1SP 150.1)

They humbly confessed their wrongs which they had committed against Joseph, and entreated his forgiveness, and were greatly rejoiced to find that he was alive; for they had suffered remorse and great distress of mind since their cruelty toward him. And now as they knew that they were not guilty of his blood, their troubled minds were relieved. (1SP 151.1)

Chapter 14 - Joseph and his Brethren (1SP 151.2)

Joseph gladly forgave his brethren, and sent them away abundantly provided with provisions, and carriages, and everything necessary for the removal of their father's family, and their own, to Egypt. Joseph gave his brother Benjamin more valuable presents than to his other brethren. As he sent them away he charged them, "See that ye fall not out by the way." He was afraid that they might enter into a dispute, and charge upon one another the cause of their guilt in regard to their cruel treatment of himself. With joy they returned to their father, and told him, saying, "Joseph is yet alive, and he is governor over all the land of Egypt. And Jacob's heart fainted, for he believed them not. And they told him all the words of Joseph, which he had said unto them; and when he saw the wagons which Joseph had sent to carry him, the spirit of Jacob their father revived. And Israel said, It is enough; Joseph my son is yet alive. I will go and see him before I die." (1SP 151.2)

Jacob's sons then made their humiliating confessions to their father, of their wicked treatment of Joseph, and entreated his forgiveness. Jacob did not suspect his sons were guilty of such cruelty. But he saw that God had overruled it all for good, and he forgave and blessed his erring sons. He commenced his journey with gladness of heart, and when he came to Beersheba he offered grateful sacrifices, and entreated God to bless him, and make known to him if he was pleased with their moving into Egypt. Jacob wanted an evidence from God that he would go with them. "And God spake unto Israel in the visions of the night, and said, Jacob, Jacob. And he said, Here am I. And he said, I am God, the God of thy father. Fear not to go down into Egypt, for I will there make of thee a great nation. I will go down with thee into Egypt, and I will also surely bring thee up again; and Joseph shall put his hand upon thine eyes." (1SP 152.1)

The meeting of Joseph and his father was very affecting. Joseph left his chariot, and ran to meet his father on foot, and embraced him, and and they wept over each other. Jacob then expressed his willingness to die, since he had again seen his son Joseph, for whom he had so long mourned as dead. (1SP 152.2)

Joseph counseled his brethren, when Pharaoh should ask them of their occupation, to tell him frankly that they were shepherds, although such an occupation was regarded by the Egyptians as degrading. Joseph loved righteousness, and feared God. He did not wish his brethren to be exposed to temptation, therefore would not have them in the king's special services, amid the corrupting, idolatrous influence at court. If they should tell the king that they were shepherds, he would not seek to employ them in his service, and exalt them to some honorable position for Joseph's sake. When the king learned that they were shepherds, he gave Joseph permission to settle his father and his brethren in the best part of the country of Egypt. Joseph selected Goshen as a suitable place provided with good pastures, well watered. Here also they could worship God without being disturbed with the ceremonies attending the idolatrous worship of the Egyptians. The country round about Goshen was inhabited by the Israelites, until with power and mighty signs and wonders God brought his people out of Egypt. (1SP 153.1)

Joseph brought Jacob before Pharaoh, and introduced his much-honored father to the king. Jacob blessed Pharaoh for his kindness to his son Joseph. "And Pharaoh said unto Jacob, How old art thou? And Jacob said unto Pharaoh, The days of the years of my pilgrimage are an hundred and thirty years. Few and evil have the days of the years of my life been, and have not attained unto the days of the years of the life of my fathers in the days of their pilgrimage." (1SP 153.2)

Jacob told the king that his years had been few and evil; that is, he had seen much trouble, and suffered much perplexity, which had cut short his years. The life of Jacob had not been smooth and peaceful. The jealousy of his wives had brought a train of evils. Some of his children had grieved him, and made his life very bitter. But the last years of Jacob's life were more peaceful. His sons had reformed. (1SP 154.1)

As Jacob was about to die, his children gathered about him to receive his blessing, and to listen to his last words of advice to them. He forgave his children for all their unfilial conduct, and for their wicked treatment of Joseph, which had caused him many years of grief as he had reflected upon his supposed dreadful death. As he spoke with his children for the last time, the Spirit of the Lord rested upon him, and he uttered prophecies concerning them, which reached far in the future. While under the spirit of inspiration, he laid open before them their past lives, and their future history, revealing the purposes of God in regard to them. He showed them that God would by no means sanction cruelty, or wickedness. He commenced with the eldest. Although Reuben had no hand in selling Joseph, yet previous to that transaction he had grievously sinned. His course was corrupt, for he had transgressed the law of God. Jacob uttered his prophecy in regard to him: "Reuben, thou art my first-born, my might, and the beginning of my strength, the excellency of dignity and the excellency of power; unstable as water, thou shalt not excel." **(1SP 154.2)**

He then prophesied in regard to Simeon and Levi, who practiced deception to the Shechemites, and then, in a most cruel, revengeful manner, destroyed them. They were also the ones who were the most guilty in the case of Joseph. "Simeon and Levi are brethren; instruments of cruelty are in their habitations. O my soul, come not thou into their secret; unto their assembly, mine honor, be not thou united! for in their anger they slew a man, and in their self-will they digged down a wall. Cursed be their anger, for it was fierce; and their wrath, for it was cruel. I will divide them in Jacob, and scatter them in Israel." **(1SP 154.3)**

Jacob thus uttered the words of inspiration to his sorrowing sons, presenting before them the light in which God viewed their deeds of violence, and that he would visit them for their sins. His prophetic words in regard to his other sons were not as gloomy. **(1SP 155.1)**

In regard to Judah, Jacob's words of inspiration were more joyful. His prophetic eye looked hundreds of years in the future to the birth of Christ, and he said, "The scepter shall not depart from Judah, nor a lawgiver from between his feet, until Shiloh come; and unto him shall the gathering of the people be." **(1SP 155.2)**

Jacob predicted a cheerful future for most of his sons. Especially for Joseph he uttered words of eloquence of a happy character: "Joseph is a fruitful bough, even a fruitful bough by a well, whose branches run over the wall. The archers have sorely grieved him, and shot at him, and hated him; but his bow abode in strength, and the arms of his hands were made strong by the hands of the mighty God of Jacob. (From thence is the shepherd, the stone of Israel.)" "The blessings of thy father have prevailed above the blessings of my progenitors, unto the utmost bound of the everlasting hills; they shall be on the head of Joseph, and on the crown of the head of him that was separate from his brethren." **(1SP 155.3)**

Jacob was an affectionate father. The words he uttered to his children were not his, spoken because he had retained an unforgiving spirit on account of their wrongs. He had forgiven them. He had loved them to the last. He mourned deeply at the loss of Joseph, and when Simeon was retained in Egypt, he manifested grief, and expressed his anxious wish that his children should return safely from Egypt with their brother Simeon. He had no resentful feeling toward his sorrowing children. But God, by the spirit of prophecy, elevated the mind of Jacob above his natural feelings. In his last hours, angels were all around him, and the power of the grace of God shone upon him. His paternal feelings would have led him to utter, in his dying testimony, only expressions of love and tenderness. But under the influence of inspiration he uttered truth, although painful. **(1SP 156.1)**

After the death of Jacob, Joseph's brethren were filled with gloom and distress. They thought that Joseph had concealed his resentment, out of respect for their father; and now that he was dead, he would be revenged for the ill treatment he had suffered at their hands. "And when Joseph's brethren saw that their father was dead, they said, Joseph will peradventure hate us, and will certainly requite us all the evil which we did unto him. And they sent a messenger unto Joseph, saying, Thy father did command before he died, saying, So shall ye say unto Joseph, Forgive, I pray thee now, the trespass of thy brethren, and their sin; for they did unto thee evil; and now, we pray thee, forgive the trespass of the servants of the God of thy father. And Joseph wept when they spake unto him. And his brethren also went and fell down before his face; and they said, Behold we be thy servants. And Joseph said unto them, Fear not; for am I in the place of God? But as for you, ye thought evil against me; but God meant it unto good, to bring to pass, as it is this day, to save much people alive. Now therefore fear ye not; I will nourish you, and your little ones. And he comforted them, and spake kindly unto them." **(1SP 156.2)**

Joseph could not bear the thought that his brethren should think that he harbored a spirit of revenge toward them whom he cordially loved.

Chapter 14 - Joseph and his Brethren (1SP 157.1)

(1SP 157.1)

Joseph illustrates Christ. Jesus came to his own, but his own received him not. He was rejected and despised, because his acts were righteous, and his consistent, self-denying life was a continual rebuke upon those who professed piety, but whose lives were corrupt. Joseph's integrity and virtue were fiercely assailed; and she who would lead him astray could not prevail, therefore her hatred was strong against the virtue and integrity which she could not corrupt, and she testified falsely against him. The innocent suffered because of his righteousness. He was cast into prison because of his virtue. Joseph was sold to his enemies, by his own brethren, for a small sum of money. The Son of God was sold to his bitterest enemies by one of his own disciples. Jesus was meek and holy. His was a life of unexampled self-denial, goodness, and holiness. He was not guilty of any wrong; yet false witnesses were hired to testify against him. He was hated because he had been a faithful reprover of sin and corruption. Joseph's brethren stripped him of his coat of many colors. The executioners of Jesus cast lots for his seamless coat. (1SP 157.2)

Joseph's brethren purposed to kill him, but were finally content to sell him as a slave, to prevent his becoming greater than themselves. They thought they had placed him where they would be no more troubled with his dreams, and where there would not be a possibility of their fulfillment. But the very course which they pursued, God overruled to bring about that which they designed never should take place–that he should have dominion over them. (1SP 158.1)

The chief priests and elders were jealous of Christ, that he would draw the attention of the people away from themselves, to him. They knew that he was doing greater works than they ever had done, or ever could perform; and they knew that if he was suffered to continue his teachings, he would become higher in authority than they, and might become king of the Jews. They agreed together to prevent this by privately taking him, and hiring witnesses to testify falsely against him, that they might condemn him, and put him to death. They would not accept him as their king, but cried out, Crucify him! crucify him! The Jews thought that by taking the life of Christ, they could prevent his becoming king. But by murdering the Son of God, they were bringing about the very thing they sought to prevent. Joseph, by being sold by his brethren into Egypt, became a saviour to his father's family. Yet this fact did not lessen the guilt of his brethren. The crucifixion of Christ by his enemies, made him the Redeemer of mankind, the Saviour of the fallen race, and ruler over the whole world. The crime of his enemies was just as heinous as though God's providential hand had not controlled events for his own glory and the good of man. (1SP 158.2)

Joseph walked with God. He would not be persuaded to deviate from the path of righteousness, and transgress God's law, by any inducements or threats. And when he was imprisoned, and suffered because of his innocence, he meekly bore it without murmuring. His self-control, and patience in adversity, and his unwavering fidelity, are left on record for the benefit of all who should afterward live on the earth. When Joseph's brethren acknowledged their sin before him, he freely forgave them, and showed by his acts of benevolence and love that he harbored no resentful feelings for their former cruel conduct toward him. The life of Jesus, the Saviour of the world, was a pattern of benevolence, goodness, and holiness. Yet he was despised and insulted, mocked and derided, for no other reason than because of his righteous life, which was a constant rebuke to sin. His enemies would not be satisfied until he was given into their hands, that they might put him to a shameful death. He died for the guilty race; and, while suffering the most cruel torture, meekly forgave his murderers. He rose from the dead, ascended up to his father, and received all power and authority, and returned to the earth again to impart it to his disciples. He gave gifts unto men. And all who have ever come to him repentant, confessing their sins, he has received into his favor, and freely pardoned them. And if they remain true to him, he will exalt them to his throne, and make them his heirs to the inheritance which he has purchased with his own blood. (1SP 159.1)

The children of Israel were not slaves. They had never sold their cattle, their lands, and themselves, to Pharaoh for food, as many of the Egyptians had done. They had been granted a portion of land wherein to dwell, with their flocks and cattle, on account of the service Joseph had been to the kingdom. Pharaoh appreciated his wisdom in the management of all things connected with the kingdom, especially in the preparations for the long years of famine which came upon the land of Egypt. He felt that the whole kingdom was indebted for their prosperity to the wise management of Joseph; and, as a token of his gratitude, he said to Joseph, "The land of Egypt is before thee; in the best of the land make thy father and brethren to dwell; in the land of Goshen let them dwell; and if thou knowest any men of activity among them, then make them rulers over my cattle." "And Joseph placed his father and his brethren, and gave them a possession in the land of Egypt, in the best of the land, in the land of Rameses, as Pharaoh had commanded. And Joseph nourished his father, and his brethren, and all his father's household, with bread according to their families." (1SP 159.2)

No tax was required of Joseph's father and brethren by the king of Egypt, and Joseph was allowed the privilege of supplying them liberally with food. The king said to his rulers, Are we not indebted to the God of Joseph, and to him, for this liberal supply of food? Was it not because of his wisdom that we laid in so abundantly? While other lands are perishing, we have enough! His management has greatly enriched the kingdom. (1SP 160.1)

"And Joseph died, and all his brethren, and all that generation. And the children of Israel were fruitful, and increased abundantly, and multiplied, and waxed exceeding mighty; and the land was filled with them. Now there rose up a new king over Egypt, which knew not Joseph. And he said unto his people, Behold, the people of the children of Israel are more and mightier than we. Come on, let us deal wisely with them, lest they multiply, and it come to pass, that, when there falleth out any war, they join also unto our enemies, and fight against us, and so get them up out of the land." (1SP 160.2)

This new king of Egypt learned that the children of Israel were of great service to the kingdom. Many of them were able and understanding workmen, and he was not willing to lose their labor. This new king ranked the children of Israel with that class of slaves who had sold their flocks, their herds, their lands, and themselves, to the kingdom. "Therefore they did set over them taskmasters, to afflict them with their burdens. And they built for Pharaoh treasure-cities, Pithom, and Raamses. But the more they afflicted them, the more they multiplied and grew. And they were grieved because of the children of Israel. And the Egyptians made the children of Israel to serve with rigor. And they made their lives bitter with hard bondage, in mortar, and in brick, and in all manner of service in the field; all their service wherein they made them serve was with rigor." They compelled their women to work in the fields, as though they were slaves. Yet their numbers did not decrease. As the king and his rulers saw that they continually increased, they consulted together to compel them to accomplish a certain amount every day. They thought to subdue them with hard labor, and were angry because they could not decrease their numbers, and crush out their independent spirit. (1SP 161.1)

And because they failed to accomplish their purpose, they hardened their hearts to go still further. The king commanded that the male children should be killed as soon as they were born. Satan was the mover in these matters. He knew that a deliverer was to be raised up among the Hebrews to rescue them from oppression. He thought that if he could move the king to destroy the male children, the purpose of God would be defeated. The women feared God, and did not do as the king of Egypt commanded them, but saved the male children alive. The women dared not murder the Hebrew children; and because they obeyed not the command of the king, the Lord prospered them. As the king of Egypt was informed that his command had not been obeyed, he was very angry. He then made his command more urgent and extensive. He charged all his people to keep a strict watch, saying, "Every son that is born ye shall cast into the river, and every daughter ye shall save alive." (1SP 162.1)

*****

Chapter 15
Moses

When this cruel decree was in full force, Moses was born. His mother hid him as long as she could with any safety, and then prepared a little vessel of bulrushes, making it secure with pitch, that no water might enter the little ark, and placed it at the edge of the water, while his sister should be lingering around the water with apparent indifference. She was anxiously watching to see what would become of her little brother. Angels were also watching that no harm should come to the helpless infant, which had been placed there by an affectionate mother, and committed to the care of God by her earnest prayers mingled with tears. And these angels directed the footsteps of Pharaoh's daughter to the river, near the very spot where lay the innocent little stranger. Her attention was attracted to the little strange vessel, and she sent one of her waiting-maids to fetch it to her. And when she had removed the cover of this singularly-constructed little vessel, she saw a lovely babe, "and behold, the babe wept; and she had compassion on him." She knew that a tender Hebrew mother had taken this singular means to preserve the life of her much-loved babe, and she decided at once that it should be her son. The sister of Moses immediately came forward and inquired, "Shall I go, and call to thee a nurse of the Hebrew women, that she may nurse the child for thee? And Pharaoh's daughter said to her, Go." **(1SP 162.2)**

Joyfully sped the sister to her mother, and related to her the happy news, and conducted her with all haste to Pharaoh's daughter, where the child was committed to the mother to nurse, and she was liberally paid for the bringing up of her own son. Thankfully did this mother enter upon her now safe and happy task. She believed that God had preserved his life. Faithfully did she improve the precious opportunity of educating her son in reference to a life of usefulness. She was more particular in his instruction than in that of her other children; for she felt confident that he was preserved for some great work. By her faithful teachings she instilled into his young mind the fear of God, and love for truthfulness and justice. She did not rest here in her efforts, but earnestly prayed to God for her son that he might be preserved from every corrupting influence. She taught him to bow and pray to God, the living God, for he alone could hear him and help him in any emergency. She sought to impress his mind with the sinfulness of idolatry. She knew that he was to be soon separated from her influence, and given up to his adopted royal mother, to be surrounded with influences calculated to make him disbelieve in the existence of the Maker of the heavens and of the earth. **(1SP 163.1)**

The instructions he received from his parents were such as to fortify his mind, and shield him from being lifted up and corrupted with sin, and becoming proud amid the splendor and extravagance of court life. He had a clear mind, and an understanding heart, and never lost the pious impressions he received in his youth. His mother kept him as long as she could, but was obliged to separate from him when he was about twelve years old, and he then became the son of Pharaoh's daughter. **(1SP 164.1)**

Here Satan was defeated. By moving Pharaoh to destroy the male children, he thought to turn aside the purposes of God, and destroy the one whom God would raise up to deliver his people. But that very decree, appointing the Hebrew children to death, was the means God overruled to place Moses in the royal family, where he had advantages to become a learned man, and eminently qualified to lead his people from Egypt. Pharaoh expected to exalt his adopted grandson to the throne. He educated him to stand at the head of the armies of Egypt, and lead them to battle. Moses was a great favorite with Pharaoh's host, and was honored because he conducted warfare with superior skill and wisdom. "And Moses was learned in all the wisdom of the Egyptians, and was mighty in words and in deeds." The Egyptians regarded Moses as a remarkable character. (1SP 164.2)

Angels instructed Moses that God had chosen him to deliver the children of Israel. The rulers among the children of Israel were also taught by angels that the time for their deliverance was nigh, and that Moses was the man whom God would use to accomplish this work. Moses thought that the children of Israel would be delivered by warfare, and that he would stand at the head of the Hebrew host, to conduct the warfare against the Egyptian armies, and deliver his brethren from the yoke of oppression. Having this in view, Moses guarded his affections, that they might not be strongly placed upon his adopted mother, or upon Pharaoh, lest it should be more difficult for him to remain free to do the will of God. (1SP 165.1)

The splendor and pride displayed at the Egyptian court, and the flattery he received, could not make him forget his despised brethren in slavery. He would not be induced, even with the promise of wearing the crown of Egypt, to identify himself with the Egyptians, and engage with them in their idolatrous worship. He would not forsake his oppressed brethren, who he knew were God's chosen people. The king was interested in Moses, and he commanded that he should be instructed in the worship of the Egyptians. This work was committed to the priests, who officiated in the idolatrous feasts observed by the people in honor of their idol gods. But they could not, by any threats or promises of rewards, prevail upon Moses to engage with them in their heathenish ceremonies. He was threatened with the loss of the crown, and that he should be disowned by Pharaoh's daughter, unless he renounced his Hebrew faith. But he would not renounce his faith. He was firm to render homage to no object save God, the maker of the heavens and of the earth, to whom alone reverence and honor are due. He even reasoned with the priests and idolatrous worshipers upon their superstitious ceremonial worship of senseless objects. They could not answer him. His firmness in this respect was tolerated, because he was the king's adopted grandson, and was a universal favorite with the most influential in the kingdom. (1SP 165.2)

The Lord preserved Moses from being injured by the corrupting influences around him. The principles of truth, received in his youth from God-fearing parents, were never forgotten by him. And when he most needed to be shielded from the corrupting influences attending a life at court, then the lessons of his youth bore fruit. The fear of God was before him. And so strong was his love for his brethren, and so great was his respect for the Hebrew faith, that he would not conceal his parentage for the honor of being an heir of the royal family. (1SP 166.1)

When Moses was forty years old, "he went out unto his brethren, and looked on their burdens; and he spied an Egyptian smiting a Hebrew, one of his brethren. And he looked this way and that way, and when he saw that there was no man, he slew the Egyptian, and hid him in the sand. And when he went out the second day, behold, two men of the Hebrews strove together; and he said to him that did the wrong, Wherefore smitest thou thy fellow? And he said, Who made thee a prince and a judge over us? Intendest thou to kill me as thou killedst the Egyptian? And Moses feared, and said, Surely this thing is known. Now when Pharaoh heard this thing, he sought to slay Moses. But Moses fled from the face of Pharaoh, and dwelt in the land of Midian." (1SP 166.2)

The matter of Moses' killing the Egyptian was made known to the Egyptians by the envious Hebrew whom Moses reproved. And when it reached Pharaoh, it was greatly exaggerated. And the Egyptians told Pharaoh that Moses designed to make war with the Egyptians, and to overcome them, and rule himself as king. Pharaoh was exceedingly angry. He thought that this conduct of Moses meant much, and that there was no safety for his kingdom while he lived. He commanded that Moses should be slain. But he was not ignorant of Pharaoh's design, and he secretly left Egypt. The Lord directed his course, and he found a home with Jethro, a man that worshiped God. He was a shepherd, also priest of Midian. His daughters tended his flocks. But Jethro's flocks were soon placed under the care of Moses, who married Jethro's daughter, and remained in Midian forty years. (1SP 167.1)

Moses was too fast in slaying the Egyptian. He supposed that the people of Israel understood that God's special providence had raised him up to deliver them. But God did not design to deliver the children of Israel by warfare, as Moses thought; but by his own mighty power, that the glory might be ascribed to him alone.

Chapter 15 - Moses (1SP 167.2)

(1SP 167.2)

God overruled the act of Moses in slaying the Egyptian to bring about his purpose. He had in his providence brought Moses into the royal family of Egypt, where he had received a thorough education; and yet he was not prepared for God to intrust to him the great work he had raised him up to accomplish. Moses could not immediately leave the king's court, and the indulgences granted him as the king's grandson, to perform the special work of God. He must have time to obtain an experience, and be educated in the school of adversity and poverty. His father-in-law feared God, and was especially honored of all the people around him for his far-seeing judgment. His influence with Moses was great. (1SP 168.1)

While Moses was living in retirement, the Lord sent his angels to especially instruct him in regard to the future. Here he learned more fully the great lesson of self-control and humility. He kept the flocks of Jethro; and while he was performing his humble duties as a shepherd, God was preparing him to become a spiritual shepherd of his sheep, even of his people Israel. He had been fully qualified as a general, to stand at the head of armies; and now the Lord would have him learn the duties, and perform the offices, of a faithful shepherd of his people, to tenderly care for his erring, straying sheep. As Moses led the flock to the desert, and came to the mountain of God, even to Horeb, "the angel of the Lord appeared unto him in a flame of fire, out of the midst of a bush. And he looked, and behold, the bush burned with fire, and the bush was not consumed. And Moses said, I will now turn aside, and see this great sight, why the bush is not burned. And when the Lord saw that he turned aside to see, God called unto him out of the midst of the bush, and said, Moses, Moses. And he said, Here am I. And he said, Draw not nigh hither. Put off thy shoes from off thy feet, for the place whereon thou standest is holy ground. Moreover he said, I am the God of thy father, the God of Abraham, and God of Isaac, and the God of Jacob. And Moses hid his face; for he was afraid to look upon God. And the Lord said, I have surely seen the affliction of my people which are in Egypt, and have heard their cry by reason of their task-masters; for I know their sorrows; and I am come down to deliver them out of the hand of the Egyptians, and to bring them up out of that land unto a good land and a large, unto a land flowing with milk and honey; unto the place of the Canaanites, and the Hittites, and the Amorites, and the Perizzites, and the Hivites, and the Jebusites. Now therefore, behold, the cry of the children of Israel is come unto me; and I have also seen the oppression wherewith the Egyptians oppress them. Come now, therefore, and I will send thee unto Pharaoh, that thou mayest bring forth my people, the children of Israel, out of Egypt." (1SP 168.2)

The time had fully come when God would have Moses exchange the shepherd's staff for the rod of God, which he would make powerful in accomplishing signs and wonders, in delivering his people from oppression, and in preserving them when pursued by their enemies. "And Moses said unto God, Who am I, that I should go unto Pharaoh, and that I should bring forth the children of Israel out of Egypt? And he said, Certainly I will be with thee; and this shall be a token unto thee, that I have sent thee: When thou hast brought forth the people out of Egypt, ye shall serve God upon this mountain. And Moses said unto God, Behold, when I come unto the children of Israel, and shall say unto them, The God of your fathers hath sent me unto you, and they shall say to me, What is his name? what shall I say unto them? And God said unto Moses, I Am That I Am. And he said, Thus shalt thou say unto the children of Israel, I AM hath sent me unto you. And God said moreover unto Moses, Thus shalt thou say unto the children of Israel, The Lord God of your fathers, the God of Abraham, the God of Isaac, and the God of Jacob, hath sent me unto you. This is my name for ever, and this is my memorial unto all generations." (1SP 169.1)

Moses did not expect that this was the manner in which the Lord would use him to deliver Israel from Egypt. He thought that it would be by warfare. And when the Lord made known to him that he must stand before Pharaoh, and in his name demand him to let Israel go, he shrank from the task. (1SP 170.1)

The Pharaoh before whom he was to appear, was not the one who had decreed that he should be put to death. That king was dead, and another had taken the reins of government. Nearly all the Egyptian kings were called by the name of Pharaoh. Moses would have preferred to stand at the head of the children of Israel as their general, and make war with the Egyptians. But this was

Chapter 15 - Moses (1SP 173.1)

not God's plan. He would be magnified before his people, and teach not only them, but the Egyptians, that there is a living God, who has power to save, and to destroy. Moses was commanded first to assemble the elders of Israel, the most noble and righteous among them, who had long grieved because of their bondage, and say unto them, "The Lord God of your fathers, the God of Abraham, of Isaac, and of Jacob, appeared unto me, saying, I have surely visited you, and seen that which is done to you in Egypt; and I have said, I will bring you up out of the affliction of Egypt, unto the land of the Canaanites, and the Hittites, and the Amorites, and the Perizzites, and the Hivites, and the Jebusites, unto a land flowing with milk and honey. And they shall hearken to thy voice; and thou shalt come, thou and the elders of Israel, unto the king of Egypt, and ye shall say unto him, The Lord God of the Hebrews hath met with us; and now let us go, we beseech thee, three days' journey into the wilderness, that we may sacrifice to the Lord our God." (1SP 170.2)

The Lord also assured Moses that Pharaoh would not let Israel go. Yet his courage should not fail; for he would make this the occasion of manifesting his signs and wonders before the Egyptians, and before his people. "And I am sure that the king of Egypt will not let you go, no, not by a mighty hand. And I will stretch out my hand, and smite Egypt with all my wonders which I will do in the midst thereof; and after that he will let you go." (1SP 171.1)

The powerful works of God, which he wrought before the Egyptians for the deliverance of the Hebrews, would give them favor in the sight of the Egyptians, that when they should leave Egypt they should not go empty-handed; "but every woman shall borrow of her neighbor, and of her that sojourneth in her house, jewels of silver, and jewels of gold, and raiment; and ye shall put them upon your sons, and upon your daughters, and ye shall spoil the Egyptians." (1SP 171.2)

The Egyptians had made slaves of the children of Israel, when they were not slaves, and the Egyptians were not entitled to their labor. They had only allowed the children of Israel a sustenance, and had enriched themselves with the labor which they had extorted from them. They had oppressed them, and bound them down under heavy burdens, until God interposed in their behalf. And as they were to go from their oppressors, they would need for their long journey that which they could exchange for bread, and use as their circumstances should require. Therefore, God directed them to borrow of their neighbors, and of the stranger that sojourned with them; that is, the Egyptian that had been appointed over them to see that they performed a certain amount of labor each day. Although they might borrow quite an amount, it would be but a small recompense for the hard labor they had performed, which had enriched the Egyptians. (1SP 172.1)

Moses plead with the Lord, and said, "But behold, they will not believe me, nor hearken unto my voice; for they will say, The Lord hath not appeared unto thee." The Lord then assured him by the miracle of the rod's becoming a serpent, and the hand's turning leprous, that by such signs and wonderful works would he cause the Egyptians and Pharaoh to fear, so that they would not dare to harm him. By these signs he assured Moses that he would convince the king and his people that a greater than himself was manifesting his power before them. And yet, after they should perform many miracles before Pharaoh in the sight of the people, they would not let Israel go. Moses wished to be excused from the laborious task. He plead a lack of ready speech as an excuse; that is, he had been so long from the Egyptians, that he had not as clear knowledge and ready use of their language as when he was among them. (1SP 172.2)

The Lord reproved Moses for his fearfulness, as though the God who chose him to perform his great work was unable to qualify him for it, or as though God had made a mistake in his selection of the man: "And the Lord said unto him, Who hath made man's mouth? or who maketh the dumb, or deaf, or the seeing, or the blind? Have not I, the Lord?" What an appeal! What a rebuke to the distrustful! (1SP 173.1)

"Now, therefore, go, and I will be with thy mouth, and teach thee what thou shalt say. And he said, O my Lord, send, I pray thee, by the hand of him whom thou wilt send." He entreated the Lord to select a more proper person. The backwardness of Moses at first proceeded from humility, a modest diffidence. But after God promised to remove his difficulties, and be with his mouth, and teach him what to say, and to give him success finally, in his mission, then for him to still manifest reluctance was displeasing to

Chapter 15 - Moses (1SP 173.2)

God. His unwillingness to execute the mission God had preserved his life to fill, and had qualified him to perform, after the assurance that God would be with him, showed unbelief and criminal despondency, and distrust of God himself. The Lord rebuked him for this distrust. The deliverance of Israel out of Egypt, in the manner God proposed to do the work, looked hopeless to him of the mission's ever being successful. (1SP 173.2)

Moses excelled in wisdom in conducting affairs. Aaron, Moses' elder brother, had been in daily use of the language of the Egyptians, and understood it perfectly. He was eloquent. (1SP 174.1)

"And the anger of the Lord was kindled against Moses; and he said, Is not Aaron the Levite thy brother? I know that he can speak well. And also, behold, he cometh forth to meet thee; and when he seeth thee, he will be glad in his heart. And thou shalt speak unto him, and put words in his mouth: and I will be with thy mouth, and with his mouth, and will teach you what ye shall do. And he shall be thy spokesman unto the people: and he shall be, even he shall be to thee instead of a mouth, and thou shalt be to him instead of God. And thou shalt take this rod in thine hand, wherewith thou shalt do signs." (1SP 174.2)

Moses consented to perform the mission. He first visited his father-in-law, and obtained his consent for himself and his family to return into Egypt. He did not dare to tell Jethro his message to Pharaoh, lest he should be unwilling to let his wife and children accompany him on such a dangerous mission. The Lord strengthened him, and removed his fears by saying to him, "Return into Egypt; for all the men are dead which sought thy life." (1SP 174.3)

"And the Lord said unto Moses, When thou goest to return into Egypt, see that thou do all those wonders before Pharaoh, which I have put in thine hand; but I will harden his heart, that he shall not let the people go." That is, the display of almighty power before Pharaoh, being rejected by him, would make him harder and more firm in his rebellion. His hardness of heart would increase by a continual resistance of the power of God. But he would overrule the hardness of Pharaoh's heart, so that his refusing to let Israel go, would magnify his name before the Egyptians, and before his people also. (1SP 174.4)

The Lord directed Moses to say unto Pharaoh, "Thus saith the Lord, Israel is my son, even my first-born. And I say unto thee, Let my son go, that he may serve me. And if thou refuse to let him go, behold, I will slay thy son, even thy first-born." The Lord called Israel his first-born because he had singled them out from all the people to be the depositaries of his law, the obedience of which would preserve them pure amidst idolatrous nations. He conferred upon them special privileges, such as were generally conferred upon the first-born son. (1SP 175.1)

As Moses journeyed to Egypt, the angel of the Lord met him, and assumed a threatening posture, as though he would slay him. He was fearful of his life. He had yielded to the refusal of his wife to have their son circumcised, and, in compliance with her wishes, had neglected to obey God. His wife, fearful that her husband might be slain, overcame her feelings of undue affection for her son, and performed the act herself. After this, the angel let Moses go. In his mission to Pharaoh, he was to be placed in a perilous position, where his life would be exposed to the will of the king, if God did not by his power, through the presence of his angels, preserve him. While Moses was living in neglect of one of God's positive commands, his life would not be secure; for God's angels could not protect him while in disobedience. Therefore the angel met him in the way, and threatened his life. He did not explain to Moses why he assumed that threatening aspect. Moses knew that there was a cause. He was going to Egypt according to God's express command, therefore the journey was right. He at once remembered that he had not obeyed God in performing the ordinance of circumcision upon his youngest son, and had yielded to his wife's entreaties to postpone the ceremony. After he had obeyed the command of God, he was free to go before Pharaoh, and there was nothing in the way to hinder the ministration of angels in connection with his work. (1SP 175.2)

In the time of trouble, just previous to the coming of Christ, the lives of the righteous will be preserved through the ministration of holy angels. Those who come up to that trying time neglecting to obey God's commands, will have no security of their lives. Angels cannot protect them from the wrath of their enemies while they are living in neglect of any known duty, or

Chapter 15 - Moses

express command of Jehovah. (1SP 176.1)

The Lord had informed Moses that Aaron, his brother three years older than himself, would come forth to meet him, and when he should see him, would be glad. They had been separated for many years. Angels of God had instructed Moses in regard to the work he should perform. Angels were also sent to teach Aaron to go forth and meet Moses, for the Lord had chosen him to be with Moses; and when he should meet his brother, to listen to his words; for God had given Moses words to speak to him in regard to the part he should act in connection with the deliverance of Israel. "And the Lord said to Aaron, Go into the wilderness to meet Moses. And he went, and met him in the mount of God, and kissed him. And Moses told Aaron all the words of the Lord who had sent him, and all the signs which he had commanded him. And Moses and Aaron went and gathered together all the elders of the children of Israel. And Aaron spake all the words which the Lord had spoken unto Moses, and did the signs in the sight of the people. And the people believed. And when they heard that the Lord had visited the children of Israel, and that he had looked upon their affliction, then they bowed their heads and worshiped." (1SP 176.2)

The Hebrews expected to be delivered from their bondage without any particular trial of their faith, or suffering on their part. They were many of them ready to leave Egypt, but not all. The habits of some had become so much like the Egyptians that they preferred to remain with them. "And afterward Moses and Aaron went in, and told Pharaoh, Thus saith the Lord God of Israel, Let my people go, that they may hold a feast unto me in the wilderness. And Pharaoh said, Who is the Lord, that I should obey his voice to let Israel go? I know not the Lord, neither will I let Israel go. And they said, The God of the Hebrews hath met with us: let us go, we pray thee, three days' journey into the desert, and sacrifice unto the Lord our God; lest he fall upon us with pestilence, or with the sword." The request of Moses and Aaron was very modest. They asked to go only three days' journey. But Pharaoh haughtily refused this, and professed to be entirely ignorant of the God of Israel. But the Lord purposed to let Pharaoh know that his voice is to be obeyed; that he is above all, and will compel proud rulers to bow to his authority. "And the king of Egypt said unto them, Wherefore do ye, Moses and Aaron, let the people from their works? Get you unto your burdens. And Pharaoh said, Behold, the people of the land now are many, and ye make them rest from their burdens. And Pharaoh commanded the same day the taskmasters of the people, and their officers, saying, Ye shall no more give the people straw to make brick, as heretofore; let them go and gather straw for themselves. And the tale of the bricks, which they did make heretofore, ye shall lay upon them; ye shall not diminish aught thereof; for they be idle; therefore they cry, saying, Let us go and sacrifice to our God." (1SP 177.1)

Pharaoh's heart was becoming more unfeeling toward the children of Israel. He greatly increased their labor. The taskmasters placed over the Hebrews were Egyptians. They had officers under them who had the oversight of the work, and directed the people. These officers were Hebrews, and they were responsible for the work of the people under them. And when the unjust requirement was given them, to make them gather for their brick the scattered straw and stubble found in the fields, the people could not perform their usual amount of labor. "So the people were scattered abroad throughout all the land of Egypt, to gather stubble instead of straw. And the taskmasters hasted them, saying, Fulfill your works, your daily tasks, as when there was straw. And the officers of the children of Israel, which Pharaoh's taskmasters had set over them, were beaten, and demanded, Wherefore have ye not fulfilled your task in making brick both yesterday and today, as heretofore?" (1SP 178.1)

Because the full amount of labor was not accomplished, the Egyptian taskmasters called the officers to account, and cruelly punished them because they did not compel the people to perform their usual amount of labor. These officers thought that their oppression came from their taskmasters, and not from the king himself. Therefore they went with their case to the king, and told him their grievances, and the cruel treatment of their taskmasters. Pharaoh's heart was hardened against their distress, and he derided them, and mocked at all their complaints. He was filled with hatred against them. (1SP 179.1)

"Then the officers of the children of Israel came and cried unto Pharaoh, saying, Wherefore dealest thou thus with thy servants? There is no straw given unto thy servants, and they say to us,

Chapter 15 - Moses (1SP 179.2)

Make brick; and, behold, thy servants are beaten; but the fault is in thine own people. But he said, Ye are idle, ye are idle; therefore ye say, Let us go and do sacrifice to the Lord. Go, therefore, now, and work; for there shall no straw be given you, yet shall ye deliver the tale of bricks. And the officers of the children of Israel did see that they were in evil case, after it was said, Ye shall not minish aught from your bricks of your daily task. And they met Moses and Aaron, who stood in the way, as they came forth from Pharaoh; and they said unto them, The Lord look upon you, and judge; because ye have made our savor to be abhorred in the eyes of Pharaoh, and in the eyes of his servants, to put a sword in their hand to slay us. And Moses returned unto the Lord, and said, Lord, wherefore hast thou so evil entreated this people? Why is it that thou hast sent me? For since I came to Pharaoh to speak in thy name, he hath done evil to this people; neither hast thou delivered thy people at all." (1SP 179.2)

As the children of Israel charged all their suffering upon Moses, he was greatly distressed, and felt almost like murmuring because the Lord delayed to deliver his people. They were not yet prepared to be delivered. They had but little faith, and were unwilling to patiently suffer and perseveringly endure their afflictions, until God should work for them a glorious deliverance. (1SP 180.1)

"Then the Lord said unto Moses, Now shalt thou see what I will do to Pharaoh; for with a strong hand shall he let them go, and with a strong hand shall he drive them out of his land. And God spake unto Moses, and said unto him, I am the Lord; and I appeared unto Abraham, unto Isaac, and unto Jacob, by the name of God Almighty; but by my name Jehovah was I not known to them. And I have also established my covenant with them, to give them the land of Canaan, the land of their pilgrimage, wherein they were strangers. And I have also heard the groaning of the children of Israel, whom the Egyptians keep in bondage; and I have remembered my covenant." (1SP 180.2)

Many years had the children of Israel been in servitude to the Egyptians. Only a few families went down into Egypt, but they had become a large multitude. And being surrounded with idolatry, many of them had lost the knowledge of the true God, and had forgotten his law. And they united with the Egyptians in their worship of the sun, moon, and stars, also of beasts and images, the work of men's hands. Everything around the children of Israel was calculated to make them forget the living God. Yet there were those among the Hebrews who preserved the knowledge of the true God, the maker of the heavens and of the earth. They were grieved to see their children daily witnessing, and even engaging in, the abominations of the idolatrous people around them, and bowing down to Egyptian deities, made of wood and stone, and offering sacrifice to these senseless objects. The faithful were grieved, and in their distress they cried unto the Lord for deliverance from the Egyptian yoke; that he would bring them out of Egypt, where they might be rid of idolatry, and the corrupting influences which surrounded them. (1SP 180.3)

But many of the Hebrews were content to remain in bondage rather than to go to a new country and meet with the difficulties attending such a journey. Therefore the Lord did not deliver them by the first display of his signs and wonders before Pharaoh. He overruled events to more fully develop the tyrannical spirit of Pharaoh, and that he might manifest his great power to the Egyptians, and also before his people to make them anxious to leave Egypt, and choose the service of God. The task of Moses would have been much easier had not many of the Hebrews become corrupted, and been unwilling to leave Egypt. (1SP 181.1)

Chapter 16
The Plagues on Egypt

The Lord said unto Moses, "Wherefore, say unto the children of Israel, I am the Lord, and I will bring you out from under the burdens of the Egyptians, and I will rid you out of their bondage, and I will redeem you with a stretched-out arm, and with great judgments. And I will take you to me for a people, and I will be to you a God; and ye shall know that I am the Lord your God, which bringeth you out from under the burdens of the Egyptians. And I will bring you in unto the land, concerning the which I did swear to give it to Abraham, to Isaac, and to Jacob; and I will give it to you for an heritage; I am the Lord. And Moses spake so unto the children of Israel; but they hearkened not unto Moses for anguish of spirit, and for cruel bondage. And the Lord spake unto Moses, saying, Go in, speak unto Pharaoh king of Egypt, that he let the children of Israel go out of his land." (1SP 182.1)

Moses was somewhat discouraged. In his despondency he inquired of the Lord, If the children of Israel, thine own circumcised people, will not hearken unto me, how then shall Pharaoh, who is uncircumcised and an idolater, hear me? "And the Lord said unto Moses, See, I have made thee a God to Pharaoh; and Aaron thy brother shall be thy prophet. Thou shalt speak all that I command thee; and Aaron thy brother shall speak unto Pharaoh, that he send the children of Israel out of his land. And I will harden Pharaoh's heart, and multiply my signs and my wonders in the land of Egypt. But Pharaoh shall not hearken unto you, that I may lay my hand upon Egypt, and bring forth mine armies, and my people the children of Israel, out of the land of Egypt, by great judgments. And the Egyptians shall know that I am the Lord, when I stretch forth mine hand upon Egypt, and bring out the children of Israel from among them. And Moses and Aaron did as the Lord commanded them, so did they." (1SP 182.2)

The Lord told Moses that the signs and wonders which he should show before Pharaoh would harden his heart, because he would not receive them, and God would multiply his signs. Every punishment which the king rejected would bring the next chastisement more close and severe, until the proud heart of the king would be humbled, and he should acknowledge the Maker of the heavens and the earth as the living and all-powerful God. (1SP 183.1)

The Lord brought up his people from their long servitude in a signal manner, giving the Egyptians an opportunity to exhibit the feeble wisdom of their mighty men, and array the power of their gods in opposition to the God of Heaven. The Lord showed them by his servant Moses that the Maker of the heavens and the earth is the living and all-powerful God, above all gods; that his strength is mightier than the strongest–that Omnipotence could bring forth his people with a high hand and with an outstretched arm. The signs and miracles performed in the presence of Pharaoh were not given for his benefit alone, but for the advantage of God's people, to give them more clear and exalted views of God, and that all Israel should fear him, and be willing and anxious to leave Egypt, and choose the service of the true and merciful God. Had it not been for these wonderful manifestations, many would have been satisfied to remain in Egypt rather than to journey through the wilderness. (1SP 183.2)

"And Moses and Aaron went in unto Pharaoh, and they did so as the Lord had commanded; and Aaron cast down his rod before Pharaoh, and before his servants, and it became a serpent. Then Pharaoh also called the wise men and the sorcerers. Now the magicians of Egypt, they also did in like manner with their enchantments; for they cast down every man his rod, and they became serpents; but Aaron's rod swallowed up their rods. And he hardened Pharaoh's heart, that he hearkened not unto them, as the Lord had said." (1SP 184.1)

Chapter 16 - The Plagues on Egypt (1SP 184.2)

The magicians seemed to perform several things with their enchantments similar to those things which God wrought by the hand of Moses and Aaron. They did not really cause their rods to become serpents, but by magic, aided by the great deceiver, made them to appear like serpents, to counterfeit the work of God. Satan assisted his servants to resist the work of the Most High, in order to deceive the people, and encourage them in their rebellion. Pharaoh would grasp at the least evidence he could obtain to justify himself in resisting the work of God performed by Moses and Aaron. He told these servants of God that his magicians could do all these wonders. The difference between the work of God and that of the magicians was, one was of God, the other of Satan. One was true, the other false. (1SP 184.2)

Pharaoh declared that Moses and Aaron were impostors, and could accomplish no more than his magicians. Said Moses and Aaron to Pharaoh, That Jehovah whom thou pretendest not to know, will convince thee that he is more powerful than all gods. They informed him that God would yet perform greater wonders, which would leave him without excuse, and which would be perpetual monuments of his providence and power in behalf of Israel. (1SP 184.3)

"And the Lord said unto Moses, Pharaoh's heart is hardened, he refuseth to let the people go. Get thee unto Pharaoh in the morning; lo, he goeth out unto the water; and thou shalt stand by the river's brink against he come; and the rod which was turned to a serpent shalt thou take in thine hand. And thou shalt say unto him, The Lord God of the Hebrews hath sent me unto thee, saying, Let my people go, that they may serve me in the wilderness; and, behold, hitherto thou wouldest not hear. Thus saith the Lord, In this thou shalt know that I am the Lord; behold, I will smite with the rod that is in mine hand upon the waters which are in the river, and they shall be turned to blood. And the fish that is in the river shall die, and the river shall stink; and the Egyptians shall loathe to drink of the water of the river." (1SP 185.1)

Pharaoh would not listen to Moses and Aaron, but despised their words; yet he had no power to harm them. "And Moses and Aaron did so, as the Lord commanded; and he lifted up the rod, and smote the waters that were in the river, in the sight of Pharaoh, and in the sight of his servants; and all the waters that were in the river were turned to blood." For seven days the plague upon the waters continued. Yet the king humbled not himself, but hardened his heart. Moses and Aaron were commanded, first, before bringing the plagues, to faithfully relate to Pharaoh the nature of each plague which was to come, and the effect of the plague, that he might have the privilege of saving himself from it if he chose, by letting the children of Israel go to sacrifice unto God. But if the king should refuse to obey the command of God, then would he still visit him with judgments. (1SP 185.2)

"And the Lord spake unto Moses, Go unto Pharaoh, and say unto him, Thus saith the Lord, Let my people go, that they may serve me. And if thou refuse to let them go, behold, I will smite all thy borders with frogs." (1SP 186.1)

"And Aaron stretched out his hand over the waters of Egypt; and the frogs came up, and covered the land of Egypt. And the magicians did so with their enchantments, and brought up frogs upon the land of Egypt. Then Pharaoh called for Moses and Aaron, and said, Entreat the Lord, that he may take away the frogs from me, and from my people; and I will let the people go, that they may do sacrifice unto the Lord. And Moses said unto Pharaoh, Glory over me. When shall I entreat for thee, and for thy servants, and for thy people, to destroy the frogs from thee and thy houses, and that they may remain in the river only? And he said, Tomorrow. And he said, Be it according to thy word; that thou mayest know that there [is] none like unto the Lord our God." (1SP 186.2)

Although the magicians appeared to produce frogs like Moses and Aaron, they could not remove them. When Pharaoh saw that the magicians could not stay the plague, or remove the frogs, he was somewhat humbled, and would have Moses and Aaron entreat the Lord for him, to remove the plague of the frogs. He was beginning to know something about that God whom he professed to be wholly ignorant of. Moses and Aaron had told the Pharaoh that they did not produce the frogs by magic, or by any power they possessed; that God, the living God, had caused them to come by his power, and that he alone could remove them. Previous to this, Pharaoh had exulted over Moses and Aaron, because the magicians could cause the same things to appear with their enchantments. And when he asked Moses to entreat the Lord for him, he reminded him of his former haughty boasting and glorying because of the works performed by his magicians; and he asked Pharaoh where was now his glorying over him, and where was the power of those magicians to remove the plague. **(1SP 186.3)**

The Lord listened to the entreaties of Moses, and stayed the plague of the frogs. When the king was relieved of his immediate distress, he again stubbornly refused to let Israel go. Moses and Aaron, at the commandment of the Lord, caused the dust of the land to become lice throughout all the land of Egypt. Pharaoh called the magicians to stand before him to do the same with their enchantments, but they could not. Moses and Aaron, the servants of God, at his command, produced the plague of the lice. The magicians, the servants of Satan, at his command, tried to produce the same with their enchantments, but could not. The work of God was shown to be superior to the power of Satan; for the magicians with their enchantments could perform but a few things. When the magicians saw that they could not produce the lice, they said unto Pharaoh, "This is the finger of God. And Pharaoh's heart was hardened, and he hearkened not unto them; as the Lord had said." **(1SP 187.1)**

The Lord again commanded Moses and Aaron to say unto Pharaoh, "Let my people go, that they may serve me. Else, if thou wilt not let my people go, behold, I will send swarms of flies upon thee, and upon thy servants, and upon thy people, and into thy houses; and the houses of the Egyptians shall be full of swarms of flies, and also the ground whereon they are. And I will sever in that day the land of Goshen, in which my people dwell, that no swarms of flies shall be there; to the end thou mayest know that I am the Lord in the midst of the earth. And I will put a division between my people and thy people. Tomorrow shall this sign be. And the Lord did so; and there came a grievous swarm of flies into the house of Pharaoh, and into his servants' houses, and into all the land of Egypt; the land was corrupted by reason of the swarm of flies. And Pharaoh called for Moses and for Aaron, and said, Go ye, sacrifice to your God in the land. And Moses said, It is not meet so to do; for we shall sacrifice the abomination of the Egyptians to the Lord our God. Lo, shall we sacrifice the abomination of the Egyptians before their eyes, and will they not stone us? We will go three day's journey into the wilderness, and sacrifice to the Lord our God, as he shall command us." **(1SP 188.1)**

The Egyptians worshiped certain beasts, and they regarded it an unpardonable offense to have one of these beasts slain. And if one of their objects of worship were slain, even accidentally, the person's life alone could answer for the offense. Moses shows Pharaoh the impossibility of their sacrificing to God in the land of Egypt, in the sight of the Egyptians; for they might select for their offering some one of the beasts which they considered sacred. **(1SP 188.2)**

Moses again proposed to go three days' journey into the wilderness. The king consented, while under the chastening hand of God. "And Pharaoh said, I will let you go, that ye may sacrifice to the Lord your God in the wilderness; only ye shall not go very far away. Entreat for me. And Moses said, Behold, I go out from thee, and I will entreat the Lord that the swarms of flies may depart from Pharaoh, from his servants, and from his people, tomorrow; but let not Pharaoh deal deceitfully any more in not letting the people go to sacrifice to the Lord. And Moses went out from Pharaoh and entreated the Lord. And the Lord did according to the word of Moses; and he removed the swarms of flies from Pharaoh, from his servants, and from his people; there remained not one. And Pharaoh hardened his heart at this time also, neither would he let the people go." **(1SP 189.1)**

And the Lord commanded Moses and Aaron to go again before Pharaoh and tell him, "Thus saith the Lord God of the Hebrews, Let my people go, that they may serve me." And if he should refuse to let them go, and should hold them still, the plague should be upon their cattle. "And the Lord shall sever between the cattle of Israel, and the cattle of Egypt; and there shall nothing die of all that is the children of Israel's." And all the cattle died that were visited with the plague, but not one of the cattle of the Hebrews died. And Pharaoh sent messengers to inquire if any of the cattle of the Israelites were dead. The messenger returned to the king with the word that not one of them had died, neither were they afflicted at all with the plague. Yet his heart was hardened, and he refused to let Israel go. **(1SP 189.2)**

Then Moses and Aaron, according to the command of God, "took ashes of the furnace,

Chapter 16 - The Plagues on Egypt (1SP 190.1)

and stood before Pharaoh; and Moses sprinkled it up toward heaven; and it became a boil breaking forth with blains upon man, and upon beast. And the magicians could not stand before Moses because of the boil; for the boil was upon the magicians, and upon all the Egyptians. And the Lord hardened the heart of Pharaoh, and he hearkened not unto them, as the Lord had spoken unto Moses." (1SP 190.1)

The magicians, with all their magic and supposed power, could not, by any of their enchantments, shield themselves from the grievous plague of the boils. They could no longer stand before Moses and Aaron, because of this grievous affliction. The Egyptians were thus permitted to see how useless it would be for them to put their trust in the boasted power of the magicians, when they could not save even their own bodies from the plagues. (1SP 190.2)

"And the Lord said unto Moses; Rise up early in the morning, and stand before Pharaoh, and say unto him, Thus saith the Lord God of the Hebrews, Let my people go, that they may serve me. For I will at this time send all my plagues upon thine heart, and upon thy servants, and upon thy people; that thou mayest know that there is none like me in all the earth. For now I will stretch out my hand, that I may smite thee and thy people with pestilence; and thou shalt be cut off from the earth. And in very deed for this cause have I raised thee up, for to show in thee my power; and that my name may be declared throughout all the earth. As yet exaltest thou thyself against my people, that thou wilt not let them go? Behold, tomorrow about this time I will cause it to rain a very grievous hail, such as hath not been in Egypt since the foundation thereof even until now. Send, therefore, now, and gather thy cattle, and all that thou hast in the field, for upon every man and beast which shall be found in the field, and shall not be brought home, the hail shall come down upon them, and they shall die. He that feared the word of the Lord among the servants of Pharaoh made his servants and his cattle flee into the houses; and he that regarded not the word of the Lord left his servants and his cattle in the field. And the Lord said unto Moses, Stretch forth thine hand toward heaven, that there may be hail in all the land of Egypt, upon man, and upon beast, and upon every herb of the field, throughout the land of Egypt. And Moses stretched forth his rod toward heaven, and the Lord sent thunder and hail, and the fire ran along upon the ground; and the Lord rained hail upon the land of Egypt." (1SP 190.3)

Those who regarded the word of the Lord gathered their cattle into barns and houses, while those whose hearts were hardened, like Pharaoh's, left their cattle in the field. Here was an opportunity to test the exalted pride of the Egyptians, and to show the number whose hearts were really affected by the wonderful dealings of God with his people, whom they had despised and cruelly entreated. "So there was hail, and fire mingled with the hail, very grievous, such as there was none like it in all the land of Egypt since it became a nation. And the hail smote throughout all the land of Egypt all that was in the field, both man and beast. And the hail smote every herb of the field, and brake every tree of the field. Only in the land of Goshen, where the children of Israel were, was there no hail. And Pharaoh sent, and called for Moses and Aaron, and said unto them, I have sinned this time; the Lord is righteous, and I and my people are wicked. Entreat the Lord (for it is enough) that there be no more mighty thunderings and hail, and I will let you go, and ye shall stay no longer. And Moses said unto him, As soon as I am gone out of the city, I will spread abroad my hands unto the Lord; and the thunder shall cease, neither shall there be any more hail; that thou mayest know how that the earth is the Lord's. But as for thee and thy servants, I know that ye will not yet fear the Lord God. And the flax and the barley was smitten; for the barley was in the ear, and the flax was bolled. But the wheat and the rye were not smitten; for they were not grown up." (1SP 191.1)

After the plague was stayed, the king refused to let Israel go. Rebellion produces rebellion. The king had become so hardened with his continual opposition to the will of God, that his whole being rose in rebellion to the awful exhibitions of his divine power. (1SP 192.1)

Moses and Aaron were commanded to again go in unto Pharaoh, and request him to let Israel go. The Lord tells them that he has suffered the king to resist them, and has borne with his continual rebellion, that he might show his great signs and wonders before him, and before the children of Israel, "that thou mayest tell in the ears of thy son, and of thy son's son, what things I have wrought in Egypt, and my signs which I have done among them, that ye may know how that I am the Lord." (1SP 192.2)

Chapter 16 - The Plagues on Egypt (1SP 195.1)

Here the Lord was manifesting his power to confirm the faith of his people Israel in him as being the only true and living God. He would give them unmistakable evidences of the difference he placed between the Egyptians and his people. His wonderful works in their deliverance should cause all nations to know that although they had been bound down by hard labor, and had been despised, yet he had chosen them as his peculiar people, and that he would work for their deliverance in a wonderful manner. (1SP 193.1)

Moses and Aaron obeyed the command of God, and related to the king the nature of the grievous plague which God was about to send upon him; that if he would not let Israel go, he would bring locusts into the coasts of Egypt, which would cover the face of the earth, and would eat the residue of that which escaped the hail. The king was permitted to choose–to humble himself before God, and let Israel go, or refuse and suffer the effects of the plague. (1SP 193.2)

"And Pharaoh's servants said unto him, How long shall this man be a snare unto us? Let the men go, that they may serve the Lord their God. Knowest thou not yet that Egypt is destroyed?" The king's rulers or counselors were called his servants, because they were under Pharaoh. They entreated the king to let Israel go. They related to him that they had sustained great loss by the death of their cattle, and that Egypt was nearly ruined by lightning. And the hail mingled with fire had broken down their forests, and had destroyed their fruit, and nearly all their grain; that everything was in a ruinous condition, and that they were losing all that they had gained through the labor of the Hebrews. The king sent for Moses and Aaron, and he said unto them, "Go, serve the Lord your God; but who are they that shall go? And Moses said, We will go with our young and with our old, with our sons and with our daughters, with our flocks and with our herds will we go; for we must hold a feast unto the Lord. And he said unto them, Let the Lord be so with you, as I will let you go, and your little ones. Look to it, for evil is before you. Not so; go now ye that are men, and serve the Lord, for that ye did desire. And they were driven out from Pharaoh's presence." (1SP 193.3)

The king shows his contempt of God's command by his answer to Moses and Aaron. Let your God require this of you if he will, for you to take your little ones; I will not let you go. Your little children are not needed in your journey. Does your God think I will do this thing, and let you go with your wives and little children into the wilderness upon so dangerous an expedition to them? I will not do this; but only you that are men shall go to serve the Lord. This hard-hearted, oppressive king would now pretend to the Hebrews that he had a special interest in their welfare, and a tender care for their little ones. He had tried to destroy the Israelites with hard labor; but now, to serve his own purpose, he professes to have a very special care for them, and plainly declares to Moses and Aaron that God, who would require such a thing as for them to go with their families into the wilderness, should not be obeyed; for he would only lead them out to destroy them, and their bodies would certainly lie in the wilderness. (1SP 194.1)

"And the Lord said unto Moses, Stretch out thine hand over the land of Egypt for the locusts, that they may come up upon the land of Egypt, and eat every herb of the land, even all that the hail hath left. And Moses stretched forth his rod over the land of Egypt, and the Lord brought an east wind upon the land all that day, and all that night; and when it was morning, the east wind brought the locusts. And the locusts went up over all the land of Egypt, and rested in all the coasts of Egypt; very grievous were they; before them there were no such locusts as they, neither after them shall be such. For they covered the face of the whole earth, so that the land was darkened; and they did eat every herb of the land, and all the fruit of the trees which the hail had left; and there remained not any green thing in the trees, or in the herbs of the field, through all the land of Egypt. Then Pharaoh called for Moses and Aaron in haste; and he said, I have sinned against the Lord your God, and against you. Now, therefore, forgive, I pray thee, my sin only this once, and entreat the Lord your God, that he may take away from me this death only." The Egyptians were afraid that after the locusts had eaten everything in the field, they would even attack the people of Egypt and devour them. (1SP 195.1)

"And he went out from Pharaoh, and entreated the Lord. And the Lord turned a mighty strong west wind, which took away the locusts, and cast them into the Red Sea; there remained not one locust in all the coasts of

Chapter 16 - The Plagues on Egypt (1SP 195.2)

Egypt. But the Lord hardened Pharaoh's heart, so that he would not let the children of Israel go." Notwithstanding his humility while death threatened him, and his promise to let Israel go, after he was relieved from the plague, he hardened his heart, and refused to let them go. (1SP 195.2)

"And the Lord said unto Moses, Stretch out thine hand toward heaven, that there may be darkness over the land of Egypt, even darkness which may be felt. And Moses stretched forth his hand toward heaven; and there was a thick darkness in all the land of Egypt three days. They saw not one another, neither rose any from his place for three days; but all the children of Israel had light in their dwellings. And Pharaoh called unto Moses, and said, Go ye, serve the Lord; only let your flocks and your herds be stayed. Let your little ones also go with you. And Moses said, Thou must give us also sacrifices and burnt-offerings, that we may sacrifice unto the Lord our God. Our cattle also shall go with us; there shall not an hoof be left behind; for thereof must we take to serve the Lord our God; and we know not with what we must serve the Lord, until we come thither. But the Lord hardened Pharaoh's heart, and he would not let them go. And Pharaoh said unto him, Get thee from me, take heed to thyself, see my face no more; for in that day thou seest my face, thou shalt die. And Moses said, Thou hast spoken well; I will see thy face again no more." (1SP 196.1)

Pharaoh hardened his heart against the Lord, and he ventured, notwithstanding all the signs and mighty wonders he had witnessed, to threaten that if Moses and Aaron appeared before him again, they should die. If the king had not become hardened in his rebellion against God, he would have been humbled under a sense of the power of the living God who could save or destroy. He would have known that He who could do such miracles, and multiply his signs and wonders, would preserve the lives of his chosen servants, even if he should have to slay the king of Egypt. (1SP 196.2)

As Moses had witnessed the wonderful works of God, his faith had grown strong, and his confidence had become established, while God had been fitting him and qualifying him, by manifestations of his power, to stand at the head of the armies of Israel, and, as a shepherd of his people, to lead them from Egypt. He was elevated above fear by his firm trust in God, which led him to say to the king, "Our cattle shall go with us; there shall not an hoof be left behind." This firm courage in the presence of the king, annoyed his haughty pride, and he uttered the threat of killing the servants of God. He did not realize in his blindness that he was not only contending against Moses and Aaron, but against the mighty Jehovah, the maker of the heavens and of the earth. Moses had obtained the favor of the people. He was regarded as a very wonderful man, and the king would not dare to harm him. (1SP 197.1)

"And the Lord said unto Moses, Yet will I bring one plague more upon Pharaoh, and upon Egypt; afterward he will let you go hence. When he shall let you go, he shall thrust you out hence altogether. Speak now in the ears of the people, and let every man borrow of his neighbor, and every woman of her neighbor, jewels of silver, and jewels of gold." (1SP 197.2)

Notwithstanding Moses had been forbidden to come again into the presence of Pharaoh, for in the day he should see his face, he should die; yet he had one more message from God for the rebellious king, and he firmly walked into his presence, and stood fearlessly before him, to declare to him the word of the Lord. (1SP 197.3)

"And Moses said, Thus saith the Lord, About midnight will I go out into the midst of Egypt; and all the first-born in the land of Egypt shall die, from the first-born of Pharaoh that sitteth upon his throne, even unto the first-born of the maid-servant that is behind the mill, and all the first-born of beasts. And there shall be a great cry throughout all the land of Egypt, such as there was none like it, nor shall be like it any more. But against any of the children of Israel shall not a dog move his tongue, against man or beast; that ye may know how that the Lord doth put a difference between the Egyptians and Israel. And all these thy servants shall come down unto me, and bow down themselves unto me, saying, Get thee out, and all the people that follow thee; and after that I will go out. And he went out from Pharaoh in a great anger." (1SP 198.1)

As Moses told the king of the plague which would come upon them, more dreadful than any that had yet visited Egypt, which would cause all his great counselors to bow down before him and entreat the Israelites to leave Egypt, the king was exceedingly angry. He was enraged because he could not intimidate Moses, and make him tremble before his kingly authority. But Moses leaned for support upon a mightier arm than that of any earthly monarch. (1SP 198.2)

Chapter 17
The Passover

The Lord then gave Moses special directions to give to the children of Israel, in regard to what they must do to preserve themselves and their families from the fearful plague that he was about to send upon Egypt. Moses was also to give them instructions in regard to their leaving Egypt. He related to them the command of God to slay a lamb without blemish, and take the blood of the lamb and strike it upon the door-posts, and also upon the upper door-posts, of their houses. And while this token should be without for a sign, and they should be eating the lamb, roasted whole, with bitter herbs, within, the angel of God would be passing through the land of Egypt doing his dreadful work, slaying the first-born of man and the first-born of beast. "And thus shall ye eat it; with your loins girded, your shoes on your feet, and your staff in your hand; and ye shall eat it in haste; it is the Lord's passover. For I will pass through the land of Egypt this night, and will smite all the first-born in the land of Egypt, both man and beast; and against all the gods of Egypt I will execute judgment: I am the Lord. And the blood shall be to you for a token upon the houses where ye are; and when I see the blood, I will pass over you, and the plague shall not be upon you to destroy you, when I smite the land of Egypt. And this day shall be unto you for a memorial; and ye shall keep it a feast to the Lord throughout your generations; ye shall keep it a feast by an ordinance for ever." (1SP 199.1)

Here was a work required of the children of Israel, which they must perform on their part, to prove them, and to show their faith by their works in the great deliverance God had been bringing about for them. In order to escape the great judgment of God which he was to bring upon the Egyptians, the token of blood must be seen upon their houses. And they were required to separate themselves and their children from the Egyptians, and gather them into their own houses; for if any of the Israelites were found in the houses of the Egyptians, they would fall by the hand of the destroying angel. They were also directed to keep the feast of the passover for an ordinance, that when their children should inquire what such service meant, they should relate to them their wonderful preservation in Egypt: That when the destroying angel went forth in the night to slay the first-born of man, and the first-born of beast, he passed over their houses, and not one of the Hebrews that had the token of blood upon their door-posts was slain. And the people bowed their heads and worshiped, grateful for this remarkable memorial given to preserve to their children the remembrance of God's care for his people. There were quite a number of the Egyptians who were led to acknowledge, by the manifestations of the signs and wonders shown in Egypt, that the God of the Hebrews was the only true God. They entreated to be permitted to come to the houses of the Israelites with their families upon that fearful night when the angel of God should slay the first-born of the Egyptians. They were convinced that their gods whom they had worshiped were without knowledge, and had no power to save or to destroy. And they pledged themselves to henceforth choose the God of Israel as their God. They decided to leave Egypt, and go with the children of Israel to worship their God. The Israelites welcomed the believing Egyptians to their houses. (1SP 200.1)

The passover pointed backward to the deliverance of the children of Israel, and was also typical, pointing forward to Christ, the Lamb of God, slain for the redemption of fallen man. The blood sprinkled upon the door-posts prefigured the atoning blood of Christ, and also the continual dependence of sinful man upon the merits of that blood for safety from the power of Satan, and for final redemption. Christ ate the passover supper with his disciples just before his crucifixion, and the same night, instituted the ordinance of the Lord's supper, to be observed in commemoration of his death. The passover had been observed to commemorate the deliverance of the children of Israel from Egypt. It had been both commemorative and typical. The type had reached the antitype when Christ, the Lamb of God without blemish, died upon the cross. He left an ordinance to commemorate the events of his crucifixion. (1SP 201.1)

Christ ate the passover supper with his disciples, then arose from the table, and said unto them, "With desire have I desired to eat this passover with you before I suffer." He then performed the humiliating office of washing the feet of his disciples. Christ gave his disciples the ordinance of washing feet for them to practice, which would teach them lessons of humility. He connected this ordinance with the supper. He designed that this should be a season of self-examination, that his followers might have an opportunity to become acquainted with the true feelings of their own hearts toward God and one another. If pride existed in their hearts, how soon would it be discovered to the honestly-erring ones, as they should engage in this humble duty. If selfishness or hatred to one another existed, it would be more readily discovered as they engaged in this humble work. This ordinance was designed to result in mutual confessions to one another, and to increase feelings of forbearance, forgiveness of each other's errors, and true love, preparatory to engaging in the solemn ordinance of commemorating the sufferings and death of Christ. He loved his disciples well enough to die for them. He exhorted them to love one another, as he had loved them. (1SP 201.2)

The example of washing the feet of his disciples was given for the benefit of all who should believe in him. He required them to follow his example. This humble ordinance was not only designed to test their humility and faithfulness, but to keep fresh in their remembrance that the redemption of his people was purchased upon conditions of humility and continual obedience upon their part. "So after he had washed their feet, and had taken his garments, and was set down again, he said unto them, Know ye what I have done to you? Ye call me Master and Lord, and ye say well; for so I am. If I then, your Lord and Master, have washed your feet, ye also ought to wash one another's feet. For I have given you an example, that ye should do as I have done to you. Verily, verily, I say unto you, The servant is not greater than his lord; neither he that is sent greater than he that sent him. If ye know these things, happy are ye if ye do them." (1SP 202.1)

Jesus then took his place again at the table, whereon were placed bread and unfermented wine, which arrangements had been made according to Christ's directions. He appeared very sorrowful. "And he took bread, and gave thanks, and brake it, and gave unto them, saying, This is my body, which is given for you. This do in remembrance of me. Likewise, also, the cup after supper, saying, This cup is the New Testament in my blood, which is shed for you." "Verily I say unto you, I will drink no more of the fruit of the vine until that day that I drink it new in the kingdom of God." (1SP 202.2)

Here our Saviour instituted the Lord's supper, to be often celebrated, to keep fresh in the memory of his followers the solemn scenes of his betrayal and crucifixion for the sins of the world. He would have his followers realize their continual dependence upon his blood for salvation. The broken bread was a symbol of Christ's broken body, given for the salvation of the world. The wine was a symbol of his blood, shed for the cleansing of the sins of all those who should come unto him for pardon, and receive him as their Saviour. (1SP 203.1)

The salvation of men depends upon a continual application to their hearts of the cleansing blood of Christ. Therefore, the Lord's supper was not to be observed only occasionally or yearly, but more frequently than the annual passover. This solemn ordinance commemorates a far greater event than the deliverance of the children of Israel from Egypt. That deliverance was typical of the great atonement which Christ made by the sacrifice of his own life for the final deliverance of his people. (1SP 203.2)

Chapter 18
Israel Leaves Egypt

The children of Israel had followed the directions given them of God; and while the angel of death was passing from house to house among the Egyptians, they were all ready for their journey, and waiting for the rebellious king and his great men to bid them go. "And it came to pass, that at midnight the Lord smote all the first-born in the land of Egypt, from the first-born of Pharaoh that sat on his throne, unto the first-born of the captive that was in the dungeon, and all the first-born of cattle. And Pharaoh rose up in the night, he, and all his servants, and all the Egyptians; and there was a great cry in Egypt; for there was not a house where there was not one dead. And he called for Moses and Aaron by night, and said, Rise up, and get you forth from among my people, both ye and the children of Israel; and go, serve the Lord, as ye have said. Also take your flocks and your herds, as ye have said, and be gone; and bless me also. And the Egyptians were urgent upon the people, that they might send them out of the land in haste; for they said, We be all dead men. And the people took their dough before it was leavened, their kneading-troughs being bound up in their clothes upon their shoulders. And the children of Israel did according to the word of Moses; and they borrowed of the Egyptians jewels of silver, and jewels of gold, and raiment. And the Lord gave the people favor in the sight of the Egyptians, so that they lent unto them such things as they required; and they spoiled the Egyptians." (1SP 204.1)

The Lord revealed this to Abraham about four hundred years before it was fulfilled: "And he said unto Abram, Know of a surety that thy seed shall be a stranger in a land that is not theirs, and shall serve them; and they shall afflict them four hundred years. And also that nation whom they shall serve, will I judge; and afterward shall they come out with great substance." (1SP 205.1)

"And a mixed multitude went up also with them; and flocks, and herds, even very much cattle." The children of Israel went out of Egypt with their possessions, which did not belong to Pharaoh, for they had never sold them to him. Jacob and his sons took their flocks and cattle with them into Egypt. The children of Israel had become exceedingly numerous, and their flocks and herds had greatly increased. God had judged the Egyptians by sending the plagues upon them, and made them hasten his people out of Egypt, with all that they possessed. (1SP 205.2)

"And it came to pass, when Pharaoh had let the people go, that God led them not through the way of the land of the Philistines, although that was near; for God said, Lest peradventure the people repent when they see war, and they return to Egypt. But God led the people about, through the way of the wilderness of the Red Sea. And the children of Israel went up harnessed out of the land of Egypt. And Moses took the bones of Joseph with him; for he had straitly sworn the children of Israel, saying, God will surely visit you; and ye shall carry up my bones away hence with you. And they took their journey from Succoth, and encamped in Etham, in the edge of the wilderness. And the Lord went before them by day in a pillar of a cloud, to lead them the way; and by night in a pillar of fire, to give them light; to go by day and night. He took not away the pillar of the cloud by day, nor the pillar of fire by night, from before the people." (1SP 205.3)

The Lord knew that the Philistines would oppose their passing through their land. They would say of them, They have stolen away from their masters in Egypt, and would make war with them. Thus God, by bringing them by the way of the sea, revealed himself a compassionate God, as well as a God of judgment. The Lord informed Moses that Pharaoh would pursue them, and he directed him just where to encamp before the sea. He told Moses that he would be honored before Pharaoh and all his host. After the Hebrews had been gone from Egypt some days, the Egyptians told Pharaoh that they had fled, and would never return to serve him again. And they mourned because they had permitted them to leave Egypt. It was a very great loss for them to be deprived of their services; and they regretted that they had consented to let them go. Notwithstanding all they had suffered from the judgments of God, they were so hardened by their continual rebellion that they decided to pursue the children of Israel, and bring them back by force into Egypt. The king took a very large army and six hundred chariots, and pursued after them, and overtook them while encamped by the sea. (1SP 206.1)

"And when Pharaoh drew nigh, the children of Israel lifted up their eyes, and, behold, the Egyptians marched after them; and they were sore afraid; and the children of Israel cried out unto the Lord. And they said unto Moses, Because there were no graves in Egypt, hast thou taken us away to die in the wilderness? Wherefore hast thou dealt thus with us, to carry us forth out of Egypt? Is not this the word that we did tell thee in Egypt, saying, Let us alone, that we may serve the Egyptians? for it had been better for us to serve the Egyptians, than that we should die in the wilderness. And Moses said unto the people, Fear ye not; stand still, and see the salvation of the Lord, which he will show to you today; for the Egyptians whom ye have seen today, ye shall see them again no more forever. The Lord shall fight for you, and ye shall hold your peace." (1SP 206.2)

How soon the Israelites distrusted God! They had witnessed all his judgments upon Egypt to compel the king to let Israel go; but when their confidence in God was tested, they murmured, notwithstanding they had seen such evidences of his power in their wonderful deliverance. Instead of trusting in God in their necessity, they murmured at faithful Moses, reminding him of their words of unbelief which they uttered in Egypt. They accused him of being the cause of all their distress. He encouraged them to trust in God, and withhold their expressions of unbelief, and they should see what the Lord would do for them. Moses earnestly cried to the Lord to deliver his chosen people. (1SP 207.1)

"And the Lord said unto Moses, Wherefore criest thou unto me? Speak unto the children of Israel, that they go forward. But lift thou up thy rod, and stretch out thine hand over the sea, and divide it; and the children of Israel shall go on dry ground through the midst of the sea." God would have Moses understand that he would work for his people–that their necessity would be his opportunity. When they should go as far as they could, he must bid them still go forward; that he should use the rod God had given him to divide the waters. (1SP 207.2)

"And I, behold, I will harden the hearts of the Egyptians, and they shall follow them; and I will get me honor upon Pharaoh, and upon all his host, upon his chariots, and upon his horsemen. And the Egyptians shall know that I am the Lord, when I have gotten me honor upon Pharaoh, upon his chariots, and upon his horsemen. And the angel of God, which went before the camp of Israel, removed and went behind them, and the pillar of the cloud went from before their face, and stood behind them. And it came between the camp of the Egyptians and the camp of Israel; and it was a cloud and darkness to them, but it gave light by night to these. So that the one came not near the other all the night." (1SP 208.1)

The Egyptians could not see the Hebrews; for the cloud of thick darkness was before them, which cloud was all light to the Israelites. Thus did God display his power to prove his people, whether they would trust in him after giving them such tokens of his care and love for them, and to rebuke their unbelief and murmuring. "And Moses stretched out his hand over the sea; and the Lord caused the sea to go back by a strong east wind all that night, and made the sea dry land, and the waters were divided. And the children of Israel went into the midst of the sea upon the dry ground; and the waters were a wall unto them on their right hand and on their left." The waters rose up and stood, like congealed walls on either side, while Israel walked in the midst of the sea on dry ground. (1SP 208.2)

The Egyptian host was triumphing through that night that the children of Israel were again in their power. They thought there was no possibility of their escape; for before them stretched the Red Sea, and their large armies were close behind them. In the morning, as they came up to the sea, lo, there was a dry path, the waters were divided, and stood like a wall upon either side, and the children of Israel were half way through the sea, walking on dry land. They waited awhile to decide what course they had better pursue. They were disappointed and

Chapter 18 - Israel Leaves Egypt (1SP 209.1)

enraged, that, as the Hebrews were almost in their power, and they were sure of them, an unexpected way was opened for them in the sea. They decided to follow them. "And the Egyptians pursued, and went in after them, to the midst of the sea, even all Pharaoh's horses, his chariots, and his horsemen. And it came to pass, that in the morning watch the Lord looked unto the host of the Egyptians through the pillar of fire and of the cloud, and troubled the host of the Egyptians, and took off their chariot wheels, that they drave them heavily; so that the Egyptians said, Let us flee from the face of Israel; for the Lord fighteth for them against the Egyptians." (1SP 209.1)

The Egyptians dared to venture in the path God had prepared for his people, and angels of God went through their host and removed their chariot wheels. They were plagued. Their progress was very slow, and they began to be troubled. They remembered the judgments that the God of the Hebrews had brought upon them in Egypt, to compel them to let Israel go, and they thought that God might deliver them all into the hands of the Israelites. They decided that God was fighting for the Israelites, and they were terribly afraid, and were turning about to flee from them, when "the Lord said unto Moses, Stretch out thine hand over the sea, that the waters may come again upon the Egyptians, upon their chariots, and upon their horsemen. And Moses stretched forth his hand over the sea, and the sea returned to his strength when the morning appeared; and the Egyptians fled against it; and the Lord overthrew the Egyptians in the midst of the sea. And the waters returned, and covered the chariots, and the horsemen, and all the host of Pharaoh that came into the sea after them; there remained not so much as one of them. But the children of Israel walked upon dry land in the midst of the sea; and the waters were a wall unto them on their right hand, and on their left. Thus the Lord saved Israel that day out of the hand of the Egyptians; and Israel saw the Egyptians dead upon the sea shore. And Israel saw that great work which the Lord did upon the Egyptians; and the people feared the Lord, and believed the Lord, and his servant Moses." (1SP 209.2)

As the Hebrews witnessed the marvelous work of God in the destruction of the Egyptians, they united in an inspired song of lofty eloquence and grateful praise. Miriam, the sister of Moses, a prophetess, led the women in music. (1SP 210.1)

"Then sang Moses and the children of Israel this song unto the Lord, and spake, saying, I will sing unto the Lord, for he hath triumphed gloriously. The horse and his rider hath he thrown into the sea. The Lord is my strength and song, and he is become my salvation. He is my God, and I will prepare him an habitation; my father's God, and I will exalt him. The Lord is a man of war; the Lord is his name. Pharaoh's chariots and his host hath he cast into the sea; his chosen captains also are drowned in the Red Sea. The depths have covered them; they sank into the bottom as a stone. Thy right hand, O Lord, is become glorious in power. Thy right hand, O Lord, hath dashed in pieces the enemy. And in the greatness of thine excellency thou hast overthrown them that rose up against thee. Thou sentest forth thy wrath, which consumed them as stubble. And with the blast of thy nostrils the waters were gathered together, the floods stood upright as an heap, and the depths were congealed in the heart of the sea. The enemy said, I will pursue, I will overtake, I will divide the spoil. My lust shall be satisfied upon them; I will draw my sword, my hand shall destroy them. Thou didst blow with thy wind, the sea covered them. They sank as lead in the mighty waters. (1SP 210.2)

"Who is like unto thee, O Lord, among the gods? Who is like thee, glorious in holiness, fearful in praises, doing wonders? Thou stretchedst out thy right hand, the earth swallowed them. Thou in thy mercy hast led forth the people which thou hast redeemed; thou hast guided them in thy strength unto thy holy habitation. The people shall hear, and be afraid. Sorrow shall take hold on the inhabitants of Palestina. Then the dukes of Edom shall be amazed; the mighty men of Moab, trembling shall take hold upon them; all the inhabitants of Canaan shall melt away. Fear and dread shall fall upon them; by the greatness of thine arm they shall be as still as a stone; till thy people pass over, O Lord, till the people pass over, which thou hast purchased. Thou shalt bring them in, and plant them in the mountain of thine inheritance, in the place, O Lord, which thou hast made for thee to dwell in; in the sanctuary, O Lord, which thy hands have established. (1SP 211.1)

"The Lord shall reign forever and ever. For

the horse of Pharaoh went in with his chariots and with his horsemen into the sea, and the Lord brought again the waters of the sea upon them; but the children of Israel went on dry land in the midst of the sea." (1SP 212.1)

Pharaoh, who would not acknowledge God and bow to his authority, delighted to show his power as ruler over those whom he could control. Moses declared to Pharaoh, after he required the people to make brick without straw, that God, whom he pretended not to know, would compel him to yield to his claims, and acknowledge his authority, as supreme ruler. (1SP 212.2)

The time had come when God would answer the prayers of his oppressed people, and would bring them from Egypt with such mighty displays of his power that the Egyptians would be compelled to acknowledge that the God of the Hebrews, whom they had despised, was above all gods. He would now punish them for their idolatry, and for their proud boasting of the mercies bestowed upon them by their senseless gods. God would glorify his own name, that other nations might hear of his power and tremble at his mighty acts, and that his people, by witnessing his miraculous works, should fully turn from their idolatry to render to him pure worship. (1SP 212.3)

God commanded Moses to say unto Pharaoh, "For this cause have I raised thee up, for to show in thee my power." This does not mean that God had given him an existence for that purpose; but his providence had so overruled events that such a rebellious tyrant as Pharaoh should be upon the throne of Egypt at the time God would deliver the Hebrews. For this purpose his life had been preserved, though he had justly forfeited the mercy of God by his crimes. God saw fit to spare his life, to manifest, through his stubbornness, his wonders in the land of Egypt. He would cause Pharaoh's rebellion against him to be the occasion to multiply evidences of his power for the good of his people, and that his name might be magnified before the Egyptians, and brought to the knowledge of those who should afterward live upon the earth. The disposing of events is of his providence. He could have placed a more merciful king upon the throne of Egypt, who would not have dared to persist in his rebellion with the display of God's mighty power manifested before him as it was before Pharaoh. But then the purposes of God would not have been accomplished. His people would have been deceived in regard to the sinfulness of the idolatry of the Egyptians, and would not have experienced in themselves the hard-hearted cruelty which the idolatrous Egyptians could practice. God would manifest before them that he hates idolatry, and that he will punish cruelty and oppression wherever it exists. (1SP 212.4)

Although many of the Israelites had become corrupted by idolatry, yet the faithful stood firm. They had not concealed their faith, but openly acknowledged before the Egyptians that they served the only true and living God. They rehearsed the evidences of God's existence and power from creation down. The Egyptians had an opportunity of becoming acquainted with the faith of the Hebrews, and their God. They had tried to subvert the faithful worshipers of the true God, and were annoyed because they had not succeeded, either by threats, the promise of rewards, or by cruel treatment. (1SP 213.1)

The two last kings who had occupied the throne of Egypt had been tyrannical, and had cruelly entreated the Hebrews. The elders of Israel had endeavored to encourage the sinking faith of the Israelites, by referring to the promise made to Abraham, and the prophetic words of Joseph just before he died, foretelling their deliverance from Egypt. Some would listen and believe. Others looked at their own sad condition, and would not hope. The Egyptians had learned the expectations of the children of Israel, and derided their hopes of deliverance, and spoke scornfully of the power of their God. They pointed them to their own situation as a people, as merely a nation of slaves, and tauntingly said to them, If your God is so just and merciful, and possesses power above the Egyptian gods, why does he not make you a free people? Why not manifest his greatness and power, and exalt you? The Egyptians then called the attention of the Israelites to their own people who worshiped gods of their own choosing, which the Israelites termed false gods. They exultingly said that their gods had prospered them, and had given them food, and raiment, and great riches; and that their gods had also given the Israelites into their hands to serve them, and that they had power to oppress them, and destroy their lives, so that they should be no people. They derided the idea that the Hebrews would ever be delivered from slavery. (1SP 214.1)

Chapter 18 - Israel Leaves Egypt (1SP 215.1)

Pharaoh boasted that he would like to see their God deliver them from his hands. These words destroyed the hopes of many of the children of Israel. It appeared to them very much as the king and his counselors had said. They knew that they were treated as slaves, and that they must endure just that degree of oppression their taskmasters and rulers might put upon them. Their male children had been hunted and slain. Their own lives were a burden; and they were believing in, and worshiping, the God of Heaven. Then they contrasted their condition with that of the Egyptians. They did not believe at all in a living God, who had power to save or to destroy. Some of them worshiped idols, images made of wood and stone, while others chose to worship the sun, moon, and stars; yet they were prospered, and wealthy. And some of the Hebrews thought that if God was above all gods, he would not thus leave them as slaves to an idolatrous nation. (1SP 215.1)

The faithful servants of God understood that it was because of their unfaithfulness to God as a people, and their disposition to intermarry with other nations, and thus being led into idolatry, that the Lord suffered them to go into Egypt. And they firmly declared to their brethren that God would soon bring them up from Egypt, and break their oppressive yoke. (1SP 215.2)

In the deliverance of Israel from Egypt, God plainly showed his distinguished mercy to his people, before all the Egyptians. God saw fit to execute his judgments upon Pharaoh, that he might know by sad experience, since he would not otherwise be convinced, that his power was superior to all others. That his name might be declared throughout all the earth, he would give exemplary and demonstrative proof to all nations of his divine power and justice. It was the design of God that these exhibitions of power should strengthen the faith of his people, and that their posterity should steadfastly worship Him alone who had wrought such merciful wonders in their behalf. (1SP 215.3)

The miracle of the rod's becoming a serpent, and the river's being turned to blood, did not move the hard heart of Pharaoh, only to increase his hatred of the Israelites. The work of the magicians led him to believe that these miracles were performed by magic; but he had abundant evidence that this was not the case when the plague of frogs was removed. God could have caused them to disappear and return to dust in a moment; but he did not do this, lest, after they should be removed, the king and the Egyptians should say that it was the result of magic, like the work of the magicians. They died, and then they gathered them together into heaps. Their bodies they could see before them, and they corrupted the atmosphere. Here the king, and all Egypt, had evidences which their vain philosophy could not dispose of, that this work was not magic, but a judgment from the God of Heaven. (1SP 216.1)

The magicians could not produce the lice. The Lord would not suffer them to make it even appear to their own sight, or to that of the Egyptians, that they could produce the plague of the lice. He would remove all excuse of unbelief from Pharaoh. He compelled even the magicians themselves to say, "This is the finger of God." (1SP 216.2)

Next came the plague of the swarms of flies. They were not such flies as harmlessly annoy us in some seasons of the year; but the flies brought upon Egypt were large and venomous. Their sting was very painful upon man and beast. God separated his people from the Egyptians, and suffered no flies to appear throughout their coasts. (1SP 216.3)

The Lord then sent the plague of the murrain upon their cattle, and at the same time preserved the cattle of the Hebrews, that not one of them died. Next came the plague of the boil upon man and beast, and the magicians could not protect themselves from it. The Lord then sent upon Egypt the plague of the hail mingled with fire, with lightnings and thunder. The time of each plague was given before it came, that it might not be said to have happened by chance. The Lord demonstrated to the Egyptians that the whole earth was under the command of the God of the Hebrews–that thunder, hail, and storm, obey his voice. Pharaoh, the proud king who once inquired, "Who is the Lord that I should obey his voice?" humbled himself and said, "I have sinned. The Lord is righteous, and I and my people are wicked." He begged of Moses to be his intercessor with God, that the terrific thunder and lightning might cease. (1SP 217.1)

The Lord next sent the dreadful plague of the locusts. The king chose to receive the plagues rather than to submit to God. Without remorse, he sees his whole kingdom under the miracle of these dreadful judgments. The Lord then sent darkness upon Egypt. The people were not

Chapter 18 - Israel Leaves Egypt (1SP 219.1)

merely deprived of light, but the atmosphere was very oppressive, so that breathing was difficult; yet the Hebrews had a pure atmosphere, and light, in their dwellings. One more dreadful plague God brought upon Egypt, more severe than any before it. It was the king and his idolatrous priests who opposed to the last the request of Moses. The people desired that the Hebrews should be permitted to leave Egypt. Moses related to Pharaoh, and to the people of Egypt, also to the Israelites, the nature and effect of the last plague. On that night, so terrible to the Egyptians, and so glorious to the people of God, was the solemn ordinance of the passover instituted. (1SP 217.2)

It was very hard for the Egyptian king and a proud and idolatrous people to yield to the requirements of the God of Heaven. Very slow was the king of Egypt to yield. While under most grievous affliction, he would yield a little; but when the affliction was removed, he would take back all he had granted. Thus, plague after plague was brought upon Egypt, and he yielded no more than he was compelled to by the dreadful visitations of God's wrath. The king even persisted in his rebellion after Egypt had been ruined. Moses and Aaron related to Pharaoh the nature and effect of each plague which should follow his refusal to let Israel go. Every time, he saw these plagues come exactly as he was told they would come; yet he would not yield. First, he would only grant them permission to sacrifice to God in the land of Egypt; then, after Egypt had suffered by God's wrath, he granted that the men alone should go. After Egypt had been nearly destroyed by the plague of the locusts, then he granted that their children and their wives might go also; but would not let their cattle go. Moses then told the king that the angel of God would slay their first-born. (1SP 218.1)

Every plague had come a little closer and more severe, and this was to be more dreadful than any before it. But the proud king was exceedingly angry, and humbled not himself. And when the Egyptians saw the great preparations being made among the Israelites for that dreadful night, they ridiculed the token of blood upon their door-posts. But when the Egyptians, from the king upon his throne down to the lowliest servant, were afflicted, and their first-born were slain, then there was wailing throughout all Egypt. Then Pharaoh remembered his proud boast, "Who is the Lord, that I should obey his voice to let Israel go? I know not the Lord, neither will I let Israel go." He humbled himself, and went with his counselors and his rulers to Goshen in haste, and bowed before Moses and Aaron, and bade them go and serve their God. Their flocks and herds should go also, as they had requested. They implored them to be gone, fearing if they continued longer, they would be all as dead men. Pharaoh also entreated Moses to bless him, thinking at the time that a blessing from the servant of God would protect him from the further effects of the dreadful plague. (1SP 219.1)

The Israelites left Egypt in haste, yet in order. They were divided into several bodies, and each division had its leader. The obstinacy of Pharaoh was such that, after they had buried their dead, and had seen that the dreadful judgments of God had ceased, he repented of having given Moses permission to depart. The Egyptians regretted that they had been so foolish as to think that the death of their first-born was the result of the power of God. They asked in bitterness of one another, "Why have we done this, and let Israel go from serving us?" Pharaoh prepared a well-equipped army, composed of the priests of their idol gods, and of the rulers, and of all the great men of his kingdom. They thought if their priests accompanied them, they would be more sure of success. The most mighty of Egypt were selected, that they might intimidate the Israelites with the grand display of their power and greatness. They thought that when the news should reach other nations, that they were compelled to yield to the power of the God of Israel, whom they had despised, they would be looked upon with derision. But if they should go with great pomp and bring Israel back with force, they would redeem their glory, and would also have the services of the children of Israel again. They overtook the Hebrews at the Red Sea. This place was appointed for the last display of the power of God before the infatuated Egyptians. In the morning, they came up to the Red Sea and saw the Hebrew host walking upon a dry path prepared for them in the sea, while high walls of water stood upon either side, congealed by the power of God. This exhibition of God's power only increased their feelings of rebellion; and they had so long resisted such manifestations, that they were hardened; and in their blindness, rushed into the path that God had miraculously prepared for his people. Then were fulfilled the

Chapter 18 - Israel Leaves Egypt **(1SP 219.2)**

words which the Lord spake to Moses, "And against all the gods of Egypt, I will execute judgment. I am the Lord." The judgment of God was manifested in the utter destruction of the Egyptian host. **(1SP 219.2)**

Chapter 19
Their Journeyings

The children of Israel traveled in the wilderness, and, for three days, could find no good water to drink. They were suffering with thirst, "And the people murmured against Moses, saying, "What shall we drink? And he cried unto the Lord; and the Lord shewed him a tree, which when he had cast into the waters, the waters were made sweet. There he made for them a statute and an ordinance, and there he proved them, and said, If thou wilt diligently hearken to the voice of the Lord thy God, and wilt do that which is right in his sight, and wilt give ear to his commandments, and keep all his statutes, I will put none of these diseases upon thee, which I have brought upon the Egyptians; for I am the Lord that healeth thee." The children of Israel seemed to possess an evil heart of unbelief. They were unwilling to endure hardships in the wilderness. When they met with difficulties in the way, they would regard them as impossibilities. Their confidence in God would fail, and they could see nothing before them but death. "And the whole congregation of the children of Israel murmured against Moses and Aaron in the wilderness. And the children of Israel said unto them, Would to God we had died by the hand of the Lord in the land of Egypt, when we sat by the flesh-pots, and when we did eat bread to the full! for ye have brought us forth into this wilderness to kill this whole assembly with hunger." (1SP 221.1)

They had not really suffered the pangs of hunger. They had food for the present, but they feared for the future. They could not see how the host of Israel was to subsist, in their long travels through the wilderness, upon the simple food they then had, and in their unbelief they saw their children famishing. The Lord was willing that they should be brought short in their food, and that they should meet with difficulties, that their hearts should turn to him who had hitherto helped them, that they might believe in him. He was ready to be to them a present help. If, in their want, they would call upon him, he would manifest to them tokens of his love and continual care. But they seemed to be unwilling to trust the Lord any further than they could witness before their eyes the continual evidences of his power. If they had possessed true faith and a firm confidence in God, inconveniences and obstacles, or even real suffering, would have been cheerfully borne, after the Lord had wrought in such a wonderful manner for their deliverance from servitude. Moreover, the Lord promised them if they would obey his commandments, no disease should rest upon them; for he says, "I am the Lord that healeth thee." (1SP 221.2)

After this sure promise from God, it was criminal unbelief in them to anticipate that themselves and children might die with hunger. They had suffered greatly in Egypt by being overtaxed in labor. Their children had been put to death, and in answer to their prayers of anguish, God had mercifully delivered them. He promised to be their God, to take them to himself as a people, and to lead them to a large and good land. But they were ready to faint at any suffering they should have to endure in the way to that land. They had endured much in the service of the Egyptians, but now could not endure suffering in the service of God. They were ready to give up to gloomy doubts, and sink in discouragement, when they were tried. They murmured against God's devoted servant Moses, and charged him with all their trials, and expressed a wicked wish that they had remained in Egypt, where they could sit by the flesh-pots, and eat bread to the full. (1SP 222.1)

The unbelief and murmurings of the children of Israel illustrate the people of God now upon the earth. Many look back to them, and marvel at their unbelief and continual murmurings, after the Lord had done so much for them, in giving them repeated evidences of his love and care for them. They think that they should not have proved thus ungrateful. But some who thus think, murmur and repine at

Chapter 19 - Their Journeyings (1SP 223.1)

things of less consequence. They do not know themselves. God frequently proves them, and tries their faith in small things; and they do not endure the trial any better than did ancient Israel. (1SP 223.1)

Many have their present wants supplied, yet they will not trust the Lord for the future. They manifest unbelief, and sink into despondency and gloom, at anticipated want. Some are in continual trouble lest they shall come to want, and their children suffer. When difficulties arise, or when they are brought into strait places--when their faith and their love to God are tested--they shrink from the trial, and murmur at the process by which God has chosen to purify them. Their love does not prove pure and perfect, to bear all things. The faith of the people of the God of Heaven should be strong, active, and enduring--the substance of things hoped for. Then the language of such will be, Bless the Lord, O my soul, and all that is within me, bless his holy name; for he hath dealt bountifully with me. Self-denial is considered by some to be real suffering. Depraved appetites are indulged. And a restraint upon the unhealthy appetite would lead even many professed Christians to now start back, as though actual starvation would be the consequence of a plain diet. And, like the children of Israel, they would prefer slavery, diseased bodies, and even death, rather than to be deprived of the flesh-pots. Bread and water is all that is promised to the remnant in the time of trouble. (1SP 223.2)

"And when the dew that lay was gone up, behold, upon the face of the wilderness there lay a small round thing, as small as the hoar-frost, on the ground. And when the children of Israel saw it, they said one to another, It is manna; for they wist not what it was. And Moses said unto them, This is the bread which the Lord hath given you to eat. This is the thing which the Lord hath commanded, Gather of it every man, according to his eating, an omer for every man according to the number of your persons; take ye every man for them which are in his tents." (1SP 224.1)

"And the children of Israel did so, and gathered, some more, some less. And when they did mete it with an omer, he that gathered much had nothing over, and he that gathered little had no lack. They gathered every man according to his eating. And Moses said, Let no man leave of it till the morning. Notwithstanding, they hearkened not unto Moses; but some of them left of it until the morning, and it bred worms and stank. And Moses was wroth with them. And they gathered it every morning, every man according to his eating, and when the sun waxed hot, it melted." (1SP 224.2)

"And it came to pass, that on the sixth day they gathered twice as much bread, two omers for one man. And all the rulers of the congregation came and told Moses. And he said unto them, This is that which the Lord hath said, Tomorrow is the rest of the holy Sabbath unto the Lord. Bake that which ye will bake today, and seethe that ye will seethe; and that which remaineth over, lay up for you, to be kept until the morning. And they laid it up till the morning, as Moses bade; and it did not stink, neither was there any worm therein. And Moses said, Eat that today; for today is a Sabbath unto the Lord. Today ye shall not find it in the field. Six days ye shall gather it; but on the seventh day, which is the Sabbath, in it there shall be none." (1SP 225.1)

The Lord is no less particular now in regard to his Sabbath, than when he gave the foregoing special directions to the children of Israel. He required them to bake that which they would bake, and seethe (that is, boil) that which they would seethe, on the sixth day, preparatory to the rest of the Sabbath. Those who neglect to prepare for the Sabbath on the sixth day, and who cook food upon the Sabbath, violate the fourth commandment, and are transgressors of God's law. All who are really anxious to observe the Sabbath according to the commandment, will not cook any food upon the Sabbath. They will, in the fear of that God who gave his law from Sinai, deny themselves, and eat food prepared upon the sixth day, even if it is not so palatable. God forbade the children of Israel's baking and boiling upon the Sabbath. That prohibition should be regarded by every Sabbath-keeper, as a solemn injunction from Jehovah to them. The Lord would guard his people from indulging in gluttony upon the Sabbath, which he has set apart for sacred meditation and worship. (1SP 225.2)

The Sabbath of the Lord is a day of rest from labor; and the diet upon that day should be more simple, and partaken of in less quantities, than upon the six laboring days, because we do not have that exercise upon the Sabbath that we have upon the other days of the week. Many have erred in not practicing self-denial upon the Sabbath. By partaking of full meals, as on the six laboring days, their minds are beclouded; they are stupid, and often drowsy; some suffer with headache. Such have no truly-devotional feelings upon the Sabbath, and the blessing resting upon the Sabbath does not prove a blessing to them. The sick and suffering require care and attention upon the Sabbath, as well as upon the other six days of the week; and it may be necessary for their comfort to prepare warm food and drinks upon the Sabbath. In such instances, it is no violation of the fourth commandment to make them as comfortable as possible. The great Lawgiver is a God of compassion, as well as of justice. (1SP 226.1)

God manifested his great care and love for his people in sending them bread from heaven. "Man did eat angels' food;" that is, food provided for them by the angels. The three-fold miracle of the manna–a double quantity on the sixth day, and none upon the seventh, and its keeping fresh through the Sabbath, while upon other days it would become unfit for use–was designed to impress them with the sacredness of the Sabbath. After they were abundantly supplied with food, they were ashamed of their unbelief and murmurings, and promised to trust the Lord for the future; but they soon forgot their promise, and failed at the first trial of their faith. They journeyed from the wilderness of Sin, and pitched in Rephidim, and there was no water for the people to drink. "Wherefore, the people did chide with Moses, and said, Give us water that we may drink. And Moses said unto them, Why chide ye with me? Wherefore do ye tempt the Lord? And the people thirsted there for water; and the people murmured against Moses, and said, Wherefore is this that thou hast brought us up out of Egypt, to kill us and our children and our cattle with thirst? And Moses cried unto the Lord, saying, What shall I do unto this people? They be almost ready to stone me. And the Lord said unto Moses, Go on before the people, and take with thee of the elders of Israel; and thy rod, wherewith thou smotest the river, take in thine hand, and go. Behold, I will stand before thee there upon the rock in Horeb, and thou shalt smite the rock, and there shall come water out of it, that the people may drink. And Moses did so in the sight of the elders of Israel. And he called the name of the place Massah, and Meribah, because of the chiding of the children of Israel, and because they tempted the Lord, saying, Is the Lord among us, or not?" (1SP 226.2)

God directed the children of Israel to encamp in that place, where there was no water, to prove them, to see if they would look to him in their distress, or murmur as they had previously done. In view of what God had done for them in their wonderful deliverance, they should have believed in him in their distress. They should have known that he would not permit them to perish with thirst, whom he had promised to take unto himself as his people. But instead of entreating the Lord in humility to provide for their necessity, they murmured against Moses, and demanded of him, water. God had been continually manifesting his power in a wonderful manner before them, to make them understand that all the benefits which they received came from him; that he could give them, or remove them, according to his own will. At times they had a full sense of this, and humbled themselves greatly before the Lord; but when thirsty, or when hungry, they charged it all upon Moses, as though they had left Egypt to please him. Moses was grieved with their cruel murmurings. He inquired of the Lord what he should do; for the people were ready to stone him. The Lord bade him go smite the rock with the rod of God. The cloud of his glory rested directly before the rock. "He clave the rocks in the wilderness, and gave them drink as out of the great depths. He brought streams also out of the rock, and caused waters to run down like rivers." Moses smote the rock, but it was Christ who stood by him and caused the water to flow from the flinty rock. The people tempted the Lord in their thirst, and said, If God has brought us out here, why does he not give us water, as well as bread. That if showed criminal unbelief, and made Moses afraid that God would punish them for their wicked murmurings. The Lord tested the faith of his people, but they did not endure the trial. They murmured for food, and for water, and complained of Moses. Because of their unbelief, God suffered their enemies to make war with them, that he might manifest to his people from whence cometh their strength. (1SP 227.1)

"Then came Amalek, and fought with Israel in Rephidim. And Moses said unto Joshua, Choose us out men, and go out, fight with Amalek. Tomorrow I will stand on the top of the hill with the rod of God in mine hand. So Joshua did as Moses had said to him, and fought with

Chapter 19 - Their Journeyings (1SP 229.1)

Amalek. And Moses, Aaron, and Hur, went up to the top of the hill. And it came to pass, when Moses held up his hand, that Israel prevailed; and when he let down his hand, Amalek prevailed. But Moses' hands were heavy; and they took a stone, and put it under him, and he sat thereon; and Aaron and Hur stayed up his hands, the one on the one side, and the other on the other side; and his hands were steady until the going down of the sun." (1SP 229.1)

Moses held up his hands toward Heaven, with the rod of God in his right hand, entreating help from God. Then Israel prevailed, and drove back their enemies. When Moses let down his hands, it was seen that Israel soon lost all they had gained, and were being overcome by their enemies. Moses again held up his hands toward Heaven, and Israel prevailed, and the enemy was driven back. (1SP 229.2)

This act of Moses, reaching up his hands toward God, was to teach Israel that while they made God their trust, and laid hold upon his strength, and exalted his throne, he would fight for them, and subdue their enemies. But when they should let go their hold upon his strength, and should trust to their own power, they would be even weaker than their enemies, who had not the knowledge of God, and their enemies would prevail over them. Then "Joshua discomfited Amalek and his people with the edge of the sword. And the Lord said unto Moses, Write this for a memorial in a book, and rehearse it in the ears of Joshua; for I will utterly put out the remembrance of Amalek from under heaven. And Moses built an altar, and called the name of it Jehovah-nissi; for he said, Because the Lord hath sworn that the Lord will have war with Amalek from generation to generation." If the children of Israel had not murmured against the Lord, he would not have suffered their enemies to make war with them. (1SP 229.3)

Before Moses had left Egypt, he sent back his wife and children to his father-in-law. And after Jethro heard of the wonderful deliverance of the Israelites from Egypt, he visited Moses in the wilderness, and brought his wife and children to him. "And Moses went out to meet his father-in-law, and did obeisance, and kissed him; and they asked each other of their welfare; and they came into the tent. And Moses told his father-in-law all that the Lord had done unto Pharaoh, and to the Egyptians, for Israel's sake, and all the travail that had come upon them by the way, and how the Lord delivered them. And Jethro rejoiced for all the goodness which the Lord had done to Israel, whom he had delivered out of the hand of the Egyptians. And Jethro said, Blessed be the Lord, who hath delivered you out of the hand of the Egyptians, and out of the hand of Pharaoh, who hath delivered the people from under the hand of the Egyptians. Now I know that the Lord is greater than all gods; for in the thing wherein they dealt proudly, he was above them. And Jethro, Moses' father-in-law, took a burnt-offering and sacrifices for God. And Aaron came, and all the elders of Israel, to eat bread with Moses' father-in-law before God." (1SP 230.1)

Jethro's discerning eye soon saw that the burdens upon Moses were very great, as the people brought all their matters of difficulty to him, and he instructed them in regard to the statutes and law of God. He said to Moses, "Hearken now unto my voice, I will give thee counsel, and God shall be with thee. Be thou for the people to God-ward, that thou mayest bring the causes unto God. And thou shalt teach them ordinances and laws, and shalt show them the way wherein they must walk, and the work that they must do. Moreover, thou shalt provide out of all the people, able men, such as fear God, men of truth, hating covetousness; and place such over them, to be rulers of thousands, and rulers of hundreds, rulers of fifties, and rulers of tens. And let them judge the people at all seasons. And it shall be that every great matter they shall bring unto thee; but every small matter they shall judge. So shall it be easier for thyself, and they shall bear the burden with thee. If thou shalt do this thing, and God command thee so, then thou shalt be able to endure, and all this people shall also go to their place in peace. So Moses hearkened to the voice of his father-in-law, and did all that he had said. And Moses chose able men out of all Israel, and made them heads over the people, rulers of thousands, rulers of hundreds, rulers of fifties, and rulers of tens. And they judged the people at all seasons. The hard causes they brought unto Moses, but every small matter they judged themselves. And Moses let his father-in-law depart; and he went his way into his own land." (1SP 231.1)

Moses was not above being instructed by his father-in-law. God had exalted him greatly and wrought wonders by his hand. Yet Moses did not reason that God had chosen him to instruct others, and had accomplished wonderful things by his hand, and he therefore needed not to be instructed. He gladly listened to the suggestions of his father-in-law, and adopted his plan as a wise arrangement. (1SP 232.1)

*****

Chapter 20
The Law of God

After the children of Israel left Rephidim, they came to the "desert of Sinai, and had pitched in the wilderness; and there Israel camped before the mount. And Moses went up unto God, and the Lord called unto him out of the mountain, saying, Thus shalt thou say to the house of Jacob, and tell the children of Israel: Ye have seen what I did unto the Egyptians, and how I bare you on eagles' wings, and brought you unto myself. Now, therefore, if ye will obey my voice indeed, and keep my covenant, then ye shall be a peculiar treasure unto me above all people; for all the earth is mine. And ye shall be unto me a kingdom of priests, and an holy nation. These are the words which thou shalt speak unto the children of Israel. And Moses came and called for the elders of the people, and laid before their faces all these words which the Lord commanded him. And all the people answered together, and said, All that the Lord hath spoken we will do. And Moses returned the words of the people unto the Lord." (1SP 232.2)

The people here entered into a solemn covenant with God, and accepted him as their ruler, by which they became the peculiar subjects of his divine authority. "And the Lord said unto Moses, Lo, I come unto thee in a thick cloud, that the people may hear when I speak with thee, and believe thee forever." When the Hebrews had met with difficulties in the way, they were disposed to murmur against Moses and Aaron, and accuse them of leading the host of Israel from Egypt to destroy them. God would honor Moses before them, that they might be led to confide in his instructions, and know that he had put his Spirit upon him. (1SP 233.1)

The Lord then gave Moses express directions in regard to preparing the people for him to approach nigh to them, that they might hear his law spoken, not by angels, but by himself. "And the Lord said unto Moses, go unto the people, and sanctify them today and tomorrow, and let them wash their clothes, and be ready against the third day; for the third day the Lord will come down in the sight of all the people upon Mount Sinai." The people were required to refrain from worldly labor and care, and to possess devotional thoughts. God required them also to wash their clothes. He is no less particular now than he was then. He is a God of order, and requires his people now upon the earth to observe habits of strict cleanliness. And those who worship God with uncleanly garments and persons, do not come before him in an acceptable manner. He is not pleased with their lack of reverence for him, and he will not accept the service of filthy worshipers, for they insult their Maker. The Creator of the heavens and of the earth considered cleanliness of so much importance that he said, "And let them wash their clothes." (1SP 233.2)

"And thou shalt set bounds unto the people round about, saying, Take heed to yourselves, that ye go not up into the mount, or touch the border of it. Whosoever toucheth the mount shall be surely put to death. There shall not a hand touch it, but he shall surely be stoned, or shot through; whether it be beast or man, it shall not live. When the trumpet soundeth long, they shall come up to the mount." This command was designed to impress the minds of this rebellious people with a profound veneration for God, the author and authority of their laws. (1SP 234.1)

"And it came to pass on the third day in the morning, that there were thunders and lightnings, and a thick cloud upon the mount, and the voice of the trumpet exceeding loud; so that all the people that was in the camp trembled." The angelic host that attended the divine Majesty summoned the people by a sound resembling that of a trumpet, which waxed louder and louder until the whole earth trembled. (1SP 234.2)

"And Moses brought forth the people out of the camp to meet with God; and they stood at the nether part of the mount. And Mount Sinai was altogether on a smoke, because the Lord descended upon it in fire; and the smoke thereof ascended as the smoke of a furnace, and the whole mount quaked greatly." The divine Majesty descended in a cloud with a glorious retinue of angels, who appeared as flames of fire. (1SP 234.3)

"And when the voice of the trumpet sounded long, and waxed louder and louder, Moses spake, and God answered him by a voice. And the Lord came down upon Mount Sinai, on the top of the mount; and the Lord called Moses up to the top of the mount; and Moses went up. And the Lord said unto Moses, Go down, charge the people, lest they break through unto the Lord to gaze, and many of them perish. And let the priests also, which come near to the Lord, sanctify themselves, lest the Lord break forth upon them." Thus the Lord, in awful grandeur, speaks his law from Sinai, that the people may believe. He then accompanies the giving of his law with sublime exhibitions of his authority, that they may know that he is the only true and living God. Moses was not permitted to enter within the cloud of glory, but only draw nigh and enter the thick darkness which surrounded it. And he stood between the people and the Lord. (1SP 235.1)

After the Lord had given them such evidences of his power, he tells them who he is: "I am the Lord thy God, which have brought thee out of the land of Egypt, out of the house of bondage." The same God who exalted his power among the Egyptians, now speaks his law: (1SP 235.2)

"Thou shalt have no other gods before me. (1SP 235.3)

"Thou shalt not make unto thee any graven image, or any likeness of any thing that is in heaven above, or that is in the earth beneath, or that is in the water under the earth. Thou shalt not bow down thyself to them, nor serve them; for I the Lord thy God am a jealous God, visiting the iniquity of the fathers upon the children unto the third and fourth generation of them that hate me; and showing mercy unto thousands of them that love me and keep my commandments. (1SP 235.4)

"Thou shalt not take the name of the Lord thy God in vain; for the Lord will not hold him guiltless that taketh his name in vain. (1SP 236.1)

"Remember the Sabbath day, to keep it holy. Six days shalt thou labor, and do all thy work; but the seventh day is the Sabbath of the Lord thy God: in it thou shalt not do any work, thou, nor thy son, nor thy daughter, thy man-servant, nor thy maid-servant, nor thy cattle, nor thy stranger that is within thy gates; for in six days the Lord made heaven and earth, the sea, and all that in them is, and rested the Sabbath day; wherefore the Lord blessed the Sabbath day, and hallowed it. (1SP 236.2)

"Honor thy father and thy mother, that thy days may be long upon the land which the Lord thy God giveth thee. (1SP 236.3)

"Thou shalt not kill. (1SP 236.4)

"Thou shalt not commit adultery. (1SP 236.5)

"Thou shalt not steal. (1SP 236.6)

"Thou shalt not bear false witness against thy neighbor. (1SP 236.7)

"Thou shalt not covet thy neighbor's house, thou shalt not covet thy neighbor's wife, nor his man-servant, nor his maid-servant, nor his ox, nor his ass, nor any thing that is thy neighbor's." (1SP 236.8)

The first and second commandments spoken by Jehovah are precepts against idolatry; for idolatry, if practiced, would lead men to great lengths in sin and rebellion, and result in the offering of human sacrifices. God would guard against the least approach to such abominations. The first four commandments were given to show men their duty to God. The fourth is the connecting link between the great God and man. The Sabbath, especially, was given for the benefit of man, and for the honor of God. These last six precepts show the duty of man to his fellow-man. (1SP 236.9)

The Sabbath was to be a sign between God and his people forever. In this manner was it to be a sign–all who should observe the Sabbath, signified by such observance that they were worshipers of the living God, the creator of the heavens and the earth. The Sabbath was to be a sign between God and his people as long as he should have a people upon the earth to serve him. (1SP 237.1)

"And all the people saw the thunderings, and the lightnings, and the noise of the trumpet, and the mountain smoking; and when the people saw it, they removed, and stood afar off. And they said unto Moses, Speak thou with us, and

Chapter 20 - The Law of God (1SP 237.2)

we will hear; but let not God speak with us, lest we die. And Moses said unto the people, Fear not; for God is come to prove you, and that his fear may be before your faces, that ye sin not. And the people stood afar off; and Moses drew near unto the thick darkness where God was. And the Lord said unto Moses, Thus thou shalt say unto the children of Israel, Ye have seen that I have talked with you from Heaven." The majestic presence of God at Sinai, and the commotions in the earth occasioned by his presence, the fearful thunderings and lightnings which accompanied this visitation of God, so impressed the minds of the people with fear and reverence to his sacred majesty, that they instinctively drew back from the awful presence of God, lest they should not be able to endure his terrible glory. (1SP 237.2)

Again, God would guard the children of Israel from idolatry. He said unto them, "Ye shall not make with me gods of silver, neither shall ye make unto you gods of gold." They were in danger of imitating the example of the Egyptians, and making to themselves images to represent God. (1SP 237.3)

The Lord said to Moses, "Behold, I send an Angel before thee, to keep thee in the way, and to bring thee into the place which I have prepared. Beware of him, and obey his voice, provoke him not; for he will not pardon your transgressions; for my name is in him. But if thou shalt indeed obey his voice, and do all that I speak, then I will be an enemy unto thine enemies, and an adversary unto thine adversaries; for mine angel shall go before thee, and bring thee in unto the Amorites, and the Hittites, and the Perizzites, and the Canaanites, the Hivites, and the Jebusites; and I will cut them off." The angel who went before Israel was the Lord Jesus Christ. "Thou shalt not bow down to their gods, nor serve them, nor do after their works; but thou shalt utterly overthrow them, and quite break down their images. And ye shall serve the Lord your God, and he shall bless thy bread, and thy water; and I will take sickness away from the midst of thee." (1SP 238.1)

God would have his people understand that he alone should be the object of their worship; and when they should overcome the idolatrous nations around them, they should not preserve any of the images of their worship, but utterly destroy them. Many of these heathen deities were very costly, and of beautiful workmanship, which might tempt those who had witnessed idol worship, so common in Egypt, to even regard these senseless objects with some degree of reverence. The Lord would have his people know that it was because of the idolatry of these nations, which had led them to every degree of wickedness, that he would use the Israelites as his instruments to punish them, and destroy their gods. (1SP 238.2)

"I will send my fear before thee, and will destroy all the people to whom thou shalt come, and I will make all thine enemies turn their backs unto thee. And I will send hornets before thee, which shall drive out the Hivite, the Canaanite, and the Hittite, from before thee. I will not drive them out from before thee in one year, lest the land become desolate, and the beast of the field multiply against thee. By little and little I will drive them out from before thee, until thou be increased, and inherit the land. And I will set thy bounds from the Red Sea even unto the Sea of the Philistines, and from the desert unto the river; for I will deliver the inhabitants of the land into your hand, and thou shalt drive them out before thee. Thou shalt make no covenant with them, nor with their gods. They shall not dwell in thy land, lest they make thee sin against me; for if thou serve their gods, it will surely be a snare unto thee." (1SP 239.1)

These promises of God to his people were on condition of their obedience. If they would serve the Lord fully, he would do great things for them. After Moses had received the judgments from the Lord, and had written them for the people, also the promises, on condition of obedience, the Lord said unto him, "Come up unto the Lord, thou, and Aaron, Nadab and Abihu, and seventy of the elders of Israel; and worship ye afar off. And Moses alone shall come near the Lord; but they shall not come nigh; neither shall the people go up with him. And Moses came and told the people all the words of the Lord, and all the judgments; and all the people answered with one voice, and said, All the words which the Lord hath said will we do." (1SP 239.2)

Moses had written, not the ten commandments, but the judgments which God would have them observe, and the promises on condition that they would obey him. He read this to the people, and they pledged themselves to obey all the words which the Lord had said. Moses then wrote their solemn pledge in a book, and offered sacrifice unto God for the people.

"And he took the book of the covenant, and read in the audience of the people; and they said, All that the Lord hath said will we do, and be obedient. And Moses took the blood, and sprinkled it on the people, and said, Behold the blood of the covenant, which the Lord hath made with you concerning all these words." The people repeated their solemn pledge to the Lord to do all that he had said, and to be obedient. (1SP 240.1)

Moses obeyed the command of God, and took with him Aaron, Nadab and Abihu, with seventy of the most influential elders in Israel, who had assisted him in his work, and placed them at such distance that they might behold the majesty of the divine presence, while the people should worship at the foot of the mount. "And they saw the God of Israel; and there was under his feet as it were a paved work of a sapphire stone, and as it were the body of heaven in his clearness. And upon the nobles of the children of Israel he laid not his hand; also, they saw God, and did eat and drink." (1SP 240.2)

They did not behold the person of God, but only the inexpressible glory which surrounded him. Previous to this, had they looked upon such sacred glory, they could not have lived, for they were unprepared for it. But the exhibitions of God's power had filled them with fear, which wrought in them repentance for their past transgressions. They loved and reverenced God, and had been purifying themselves, and contemplating his great glory, purity and mercy, until they could approach nearer Him who had been the subject of all their meditations. God had enshrouded his glory with a thick cloud, so that the people could not behold it. The office of the elders whom Moses took with him, was to aid him in leading the host of Israel to the promised land. This work was of such magnitude that God condescended to put his Spirit upon them. He honored them with a nearer view of the glory which surrounded his exalted majesty, that they might with wisdom act their part in the work assigned them of guiding his people, with his fear and glory continually before them. (1SP 240.3)

"And the Lord said unto Moses, Come up to me into the mount, and be there; and I will give thee tables of stone, and a law, and commandments which I have written; that thou mayest teach them. And Moses rose up, and his minister Joshua; and Moses went up into the mount of God. And he said unto the elders, Tarry ye here for us, until we come again unto you; and, behold, Aaron and Hur are with you; if any man have any matters to do, let him come unto them. And Moses went up into the mount, and a cloud covered the mount. And the glory of the Lord abode upon Mount Sinai, and the cloud covered it six days; and the seventh day he called unto Moses out of the midst of the cloud. And the sight of the glory of the Lord was like devouring fire on the top of the mount, in the eyes of the children of Israel. And Moses went into the midst of the cloud, and gat him up into the mount; and Moses was in the mount forty days and forty nights." (1SP 241.1)

Even Moses could not go up at once into the mount; for he could not immediately approach so nigh unto God, and endure the exhibitions of his glory. Six days he was preparing to meet with God. His common thoughts and feelings must be put away. During six days he was devoting his thoughts to God, and sanctifying himself by meditation and prayer, before he could be prepared to converse with God. (1SP 242.1)

After the Lord had given Moses directions in regard to the sanctuary, he again gave him special instructions in regard to his Sabbath. And then he handed down from the cloud with his own divine hands the tables of stone to Moses, whereon he had engraven with his own finger the ten commandments. (1SP 242.2)

But while Moses was receiving special instructions from God, the children of Israel were corrupting themselves at the foot of the mount. "And when the people saw that Moses delayed to come down out of the mount, the people gathered themselves together unto Aaron, and said unto him, Up, make us gods, which shall go before us; for as for this Moses, the man that brought us up out of the land of Egypt, we wot not what is become of him. And Aaron said unto them, Break off the golden ear-rings which are in the ears of your wives, of your sons, and of your daughters, and bring them unto me. And all the people brake off the golden ear-rings which were in their ears, and brought them unto Aaron. And he received them at their hand, and fashioned it with a graving tool, after he had made it a molten calf. And they said, These be thy gods, O Israel, which brought thee up out of the land of Egypt. And when Aaron saw it, he built an altar before it; and Aaron made proclamation, and said, Tomorrow is a feast to

Chapter 20 - The Law of God (1SP 242.3)

the Lord. And they rose up early on the morrow, and offered burnt-offerings, and brought peace-offerings; and the people sat down to eat and to drink, and rose up to play." (1SP 242.3)

It was the mixed multitude that came from Egypt with the Israelites who were the principal movers in this dreadful departure from God. They were called a mixed multitude, because the Hebrews had intermarried with the Egyptians. (1SP 243.1)

The children of Israel had seen Moses ascend up into the mount, and enter into the cloud, while the top of the mountain was all in flames. They waited for his return every day; and as he did not come from the mount as soon as they expected he would, they became impatient. Especially were the believing Egyptians, who left Egypt with the Hebrew host, impatient and rebellious. (1SP 243.2)

A large company assembled around the tent of Aaron, and told him that Moses would never return–that the cloud which had hitherto led them now rested upon the mount, and would no longer direct their route through the wilderness. They desired something which they could look upon to resemble God. The gods of the Egyptians were in their minds, and Satan was improving this opportunity, in the absence of their appointed leader, to tempt them to imitate the Egyptians in their idolatry. They suggested that if Moses should never return to them, they could go back into Egypt, and find favor with the Egyptians, by bearing this image before them, acknowledging it as their god. (1SP 243.3)

Aaron remonstrated against their plans, until he thought the people were determined to carry out their purpose, and then ceased his reasoning with them. The clamors of the people made Aaron afraid of his life. And instead of standing up nobly for the honor of God, and trusting his life in his hands who had wrought wonders for his people, he lost his courage, his trust in God, and cowardly yielded to the wishes of an impatient people; and this, too, in direct opposition to the commands of God. He made an idol, and built an altar whereon they offered sacrifice to this idol. And Aaron submitted to hear the people proclaim, "These be thy gods, O Israel, which have brought thee up out of the land of Egypt." What an insult to Jehovah! They had recently listened to the proclamation of the law of God from Sinai, amid the most sublime demonstrations of divine power, and when their faith was tested, by Moses' being from them for a few weeks, they engaged in idolatry, which had been so recently specified, and expressly forbidden, by Jehovah. By so doing they transgressed the first and second commandments. God's anger was kindled against them. (1SP 244.1)

"And the Lord said unto Moses, Go, get thee down; for thy people, which thou broughtest out of the land of Egypt, have corrupted themselves. They have turned aside quickly out of the way which I commanded them. They have made them a molten calf, and have worshiped it, and have sacrificed thereunto, and said, These be thy gods, O Israel, which have brought thee up out of the land of Egypt. And the Lord said unto Moses, I have seen this people, and, behold, it is a stiff-necked people. Now, therefore, let me alone, that my wrath may wax hot against them, and that I may consume them; and I will make of thee a great nation." (1SP 244.2)

God saw that the children of Israel, especially the mixed multitude, were continually disposed to rebel, and, by their works, provoke him to destroy them. He knew that they would murmur against Moses, when in difficulty, and grieve him by their continual rebellion. He proposed to Moses to consume them, and make of him a great nation. Here the Lord proved Moses. He knew that it was a laborious and soul-trying work to lead that rebellious people through to the promised land. He would test the perseverance, faithfulness and love of Moses, for such an erring and ungrateful people. But Moses would not consent to have Israel destroyed. He showed by his intercessions with God that he valued the prosperity of God's chosen people more highly than a great name, or to be called the father of a greater nation than was Israel. (1SP 245.1)

"And Moses besought the Lord his God, and said, Lord, why doth thy wrath wax hot against thy people which thou hast brought forth out of the land of Egypt, with great power, and with a mighty hand? Wherefore should the Egyptians speak and say, For mischief did he bring them out, to slay them in the mountains, and to consume them from the face of the earth? Turn from thy fierce wrath, and repent of this evil against thy people. Remember Abraham, Isaac, and Israel, thy servants, to whom thou swarest by thine own self, and saidst unto them, I will multiply your seed as the stars of heaven, and all this land that I have spoken of will I give unto your seed, and they shall inherit it forever." (1SP 245.2)

The thought that the heathen nations, and especially the Egyptians, would triumph over Israel, and reproach God, was overwhelming to Moses. He could not let Israel go, notwithstanding all their rebellion, and their repeated murmurings against him. How could he give up a people for whom so much had been done, and who had in so wonderful a manner been brought out of Egypt. The news of their deliverance had been spread among all nations, and all people were anxiously watching to see what God would do for them. And Moses remembered well the words of the Egyptians, that he was leading them into the wilderness that they might perish, and he receive their possessions. And now if God should destroy his people, and exalt him to be a greater nation than Israel, would not the heathen triumph, and deride the God of the Hebrews, and say that he was not able to lead them to the land he had promised them? As Moses interceded for Israel before God, his timidity was lost in his deep interest and love for that people for whom he had, in the hands of God, been the means of doing so much. He presented before God his promise made to Abraham, Isaac, and Jacob. He prayed to God with firm faith and determined purpose. The Lord listened to his pleadings, and regarded his unselfish prayer, and promised Moses that he would spare Israel. (1SP 246.1)

Nobly did Moses stand the test, and show that his interest in Israel was not to obtain a great name, nor to exalt himself. The burden of God's people was upon him. God had proved him, and was pleased with his faithfulness, his simplicity of heart, and integrity before him, and he committed to him, as to a faithful shepherd, the great charge of leading his people through to the promised land. (1SP 246.2)

"And Moses turned, and went down from the mount, and the two tables of the testimony were in his hand. The tables were written on both their sides; on the one side and on the other were they written. And the tables were the work of God, and the writing was the writing of God, graven upon the tables. And when Joshua heard the noise of the people as they shouted, he said unto Moses, There is a noise of war in the camp. And he said, It is not the voice of them that shout for mastery, neither is it the voice of them that cry for being overcome; but the noise of them that sing do I hear. And it came to pass, as soon as he came nigh unto the camp, that he saw the calf, and the dancing. And Moses' anger waxed hot, and he cast the tables out of his hands, and brake them beneath the mount. And he took the calf which they had made, and burnt it in the fire, and ground it to powder, and strewed it upon the water, and made the children of Israel drink of it." (1SP 247.1)

As Moses beheld the children of Israel shouting and dancing in an excited manner, in imitation of the idolatrous feasts and idol-worshipers of Egypt, so unlike the reverential worship of God, he was overwhelmed. He had just come from the presence of God's glory, and although he had been warned of God that the people had corrupted themselves, had made an idol, and had sacrificed to it; yet he was in a measure unprepared for the dreadful exhibition which he witnessed of the degradation of Israel. He threw down the tables of stone, in utter discouragement and wrath because of Israel's great sin before God. (1SP 247.2)

The act of Moses in burning the calf and grinding it to powder, and making them drink of it, was to show them the utter worthlessness of the God which they had been worshipping–that their God had no power at all. Men could burn it in the fire, grind it to powder and drink it, without receiving any injury therefrom. He asked them how, then, they could expect such a God to save them, or to do them any good, or any evil. Then he rehearsed to them the exhibitions which they had witnessed of the unlimited power, glory, and majesty, of the living God. (1SP 248.1)

"And it came to pass, when ye heard the voice out of the midst of the darkness (for the mountain did burn with fire), that ye came near unto me, even all the heads of your tribes, and your elders. And ye said, Behold, the Lord our God hath shewed us his glory, and his greatness, and we have heard his voice out of the midst of the fire. We have seen this day that God doth talk with man, and he liveth. Now, therefore, why should we die? for this great fire will consume us. If we hear the voice of the Lord our God any more, then we shall die. For who is there of all flesh that hath heard the voice of the living God speaking out of the midst of the fire, as we have, and lived? Go thou near, and hear all that the

Chapter 20 - The Law of God (1SP 248.2)

Lord our God shall say; and speak thou unto us all that the Lord our God shall speak unto thee; and we will hear it, and do it. And the Lord heard the voice of your words, when ye spake unto me. And the Lord said unto me, I have heard the voice of the words of this people, which they have spoken unto thee. They have well said all that they have spoken. Oh, that there were such an heart in them, that they would fear me, and keep all my commandments always, that it might be well with them, and with their children forever!" (1SP 248.2)

Moses then presented before them their disgraceful conduct in worshiping a calf, the work of man, in the place of offering sincere devotion to the living God. He pointed them to the broken tables of stone, which represented to them that thus had they broken the covenant which they had so recently made with God. God did not reprove Moses for breaking the tables of stone, but was very angry with Aaron because of his sin; and he would have destroyed him, had it not been for the special intercessions of Moses in his behalf. Moses inquired of Aaron, "What did this people unto thee, that thou hast brought so great a sin upon them?" (1SP 249.1)

Aaron endeavored to excuse his sin, and related to Moses the clamors of the people–that if he had not complied with their wishes, they would have killed him. "And Aaron said, Let not the anger of my Lord wax hot. Thou knowest the people, that they are set on mischief. For they said unto me, Make us gods, which shall go before us; for as for this Moses, the man that brought us up out of the land of Egypt, we wot not what is become of him. And I said unto them, Whosoever hath any gold, let them break it off. So they gave it me; then I cast it into the fire, and there came out this calf." He would have Moses think that a miracle had been performed–that the gold was cast into the fire, and by some miraculous power it was changed to a calf. This was to lessen his guilt in the eyes of Moses, and cause it to appear that he had a plausible excuse for permitting the people to sacrifice to it, and to proclaim, "These be thy gods, O Israel, which brought thee up out of the land of Egypt." (1SP 249.2)

Moses rebuked Aaron, and informed him that his conduct was highly censurable; for he had been blessed above the people, and had been admitted into close converse with God. That he should commit so great a sin, even to save his life, was a matter of astonishment to faithful Moses. He saw that the people were naked; that is, were stripped of their ornaments; for Aaron had made them naked to their shame, among their enemies. He had deprived them of their ornaments, and put them to a shameful use. They had not merely lost their ornaments, but they were divested of their defense against Satan; for they had lost their piety and consecration to God, and had forfeited his protection. He had, in his displeasure, removed his sustaining hand, and they were left exposed to the contempt and power of their enemies. Their enemies were well acquainted with the wonderful works performed by the hand of Moses in Egypt. And they knew that Moses had brought them from Egypt, in obedience to the command of the God of the Hebrews, to rid them of idolatry, and to secure to himself their undivided affections and their sacred worship. (1SP 250.1)

The children of Israel had broken their allegiance to God; and, if he should see fit, he would punish them as they deserved. "Then Moses stood in the gate of the camp, and said, Who is on the Lord's side? let him come unto me. And all the sons of Levi gathered themselves together unto him. And he said unto them, Thus saith the Lord God of Israel, Put every man his sword by his side, and go in and out from gate to gate throughout the camp, and slay every man his brother, and every man his companion, and every man his neighbor. And the children of Levi did according to the word of Moses; and there fell of the people that day about three thousand men. For Moses had said, Consecrate yourselves today to the Lord, even every man upon his son, and upon his brother; that he may bestow upon you a blessing this day." (1SP 250.2)

Moses requested all who had been free from this great sin of idolatry, to come and stand by him at his right hand; also, those who had joined the rebellious in worshiping this idol, but who had repented of their sin in so quickly departing from God, to stand at his left hand. There was quite a large company, mostly of the mixed multitude, who instigated the making of the calf, who were stubborn in their rebellion, and would not stand with Moses, either at his right hand or at his left. (1SP 251.1)

Moses then commanded those at his right hand to take their swords, and go forth and slay the rebellious, who wished to go back into Egypt. None were to execute the judgment of God on the transgressors only those who had taken no part in the idolatry. He commanded them to spare neither brother, companion, nor neighbor. Those who engaged in this work of slaying, however painful, were now to realize that they were executing upon their brethren a solemn punishment from God; and for executing this painful work, contrary to their own feelings, God would bestow upon them his blessing. By performing this act, they showed their true feelings relative to the high crime of idolatry, and consecrated themselves more fully to the sacred worship of the only true God. The terror of the Lord was upon the people, and they were afraid that they would all be destroyed. As Moses saw their distress, he promised, according to their earnest request, to plead with the Lord to pardon their great sin. (1SP 251.2)

"And it came to pass on the morrow, that Moses said unto the people, ye have sinned a great sin; and now I will go up unto the Lord; peradventure I shall make an atonement for your sin. And Moses returned unto the Lord, and said, Oh! this people have sinned a great sin, and have made them gods of gold. Yet now, if thou wilt forgive their sin–; and if not, blot me, I pray thee, out of thy book which thou has written. And the Lord said unto Moses, Whosoever hath sinned against me, him will I blot out of my book. Therefore, now go, lead the people unto the place of which I have spoken unto thee. Behold, mine Angel shall go before thee; nevertheless, in the day when I visit, I will visit their sin upon them. And the Lord plagued the people, because they made the calf, which Aaron made." (1SP 252.1)

Moses manifested his great love for the people in his entreaty to the Lord to forgive their sin, or blot his name out of the book which he had written. His intercessions here illustrate Christ's love and mediation for the sinful race. The Lord refused to let Moses suffer for the sins of his backsliding people. He declared to him that those who had sinned against him he would blot out of his book which he had written; for the righteous should not suffer for the guilt of the sinner. The book here referred to is the book of records in Heaven, where every name is recorded, and their acts, their sins, and obedience, are faithfully written. When any one commits sins which are too grievous for the Lord to pardon, their names are erased from the book, and they are devoted to destruction. Although Moses realized the dreadful fate of those whose names should be dropped from the book of God, yet he plainly declared before God that if the names of his erring Israel should be blotted out, and be no more remembered by him for good, he wished his name to be blotted out with theirs; for he could never endure to see the fullness of his wrath come upon the people for whom he had wrought such wonders. (1SP 252.2)

"And the Lord said unto Moses, Depart, and go up hence, thou and the people which thou hast brought up out of the land of Egypt, unto the land which I swear unto Abraham, to Isaac, and to Jacob, saying, Unto thy seed will I give it. And I will send an Angel before thee; and I will drive out the Canaanite, the Amorite, and the Hittite, and the Perizzite, the Hivite, and the Jebusite; unto a land flowing with milk and honey; for I will not go up in the midst of thee; for thou art a stiff-necked people; lest I consume thee in the way. And when the people heard these evil tidings, they mourned; and no man did put on him his ornaments. For the Lord had said unto Moses, Say unto the children of Israel, Ye are a stiff-necked people. I will come up into the midst of thee in a moment, and consume thee; therefore, now, put off thy ornaments from thee, that I may know what to do unto thee. And the children of Israel stripped themselves of their ornaments by the mount of Horeb. And Moses took the tabernacle, and pitched it without the camp, afar off from the camp, and called it the tabernacle of the congregation. And it came to pass that every one which sought the Lord, went out unto the tabernacle of the congregation, which was without the camp." (1SP 253.1)

The tabernacle here mentioned was a temporary tent arranged for the worship of God. The tabernacle, the pattern of which God gave to Moses, had not yet been built. (1SP 254.1)

All who sincerely repented of their sins, made supplication unto God in the tabernacle, confessing their sins with great humility, and then returned again to their tents. Then Moses went into the tabernacle. The people watched with the deepest interest to see if God would accept his intercessions in their behalf; and if he condescended to meet with Moses, then they might hope that they might not be utterly consumed. When the cloudy pillar descended and stood at the door of the tabernacle, then all the people wept for joy, and rose up and worshiped, every man in his tent door. They bowed themselves upon their faces to the earth

Chapter 20 - The Law of God (1SP 254.2)

in humility. As the pillar of cloud, a token of God's presence, continued to rest at the door of the tabernacle, they knew that Moses was pleading in their behalf before God. "And the Lord spake unto Moses face to face, as a man speaketh unto his friend." (1SP 254.2)

"And Moses said unto the Lord, See, thou sayest unto me, Bring up this people; and thou hast not let me know whom thou wilt send with me. Yet thou hast said, I know thee by name, and thou hast also found grace in my sight. Now, therefore, I pray thee, If I have found grace in thy sight, show me now thy way, that I may know thee, that I may find grace in thy sight; and consider that this nation is thy people." Moses was very urgent that the Lord should show him just the course which he would have him pursue toward Israel. He wished to have God mark out his course, that his instructions to Israel might be with such wisdom that the people would receive his teachings, and their course be approved of God, and that he would again consider them as his people. (1SP 254.3)

The Lord answered Moses' anxious inquiry, and said, "My presence shall go with thee, and I will give thee rest. And he said unto him, If thy presence go not with me, carry us not up hence. For wherein shall it be known here that I and thy people have found grace in thy sight? Is it not in that thou goest with us? So shall we be separated, I and thy people, from all the people that are upon the face of the earth." He plead with God to know how it should be known that he and his people had found grace in his sight, if he did not let the token of his presence rest upon the tabernacle as formerly. Moses was not willing to cease his entreaties with God until he should obtain the assurance that the token of his presence would still rest upon the tabernacle as it had done, and that he would continue to direct their journeyings by a pillar of cloud by day, and a pillar of fire by night. Then could Moses the more easily perform his laborious task of leading the people; for this token would be continually reminding them of the living God, and would also be an assurance to them of his divine presence. Then he could the more easily influence the people to right actions, as he could point them to the evidence of the nearness of God to them. (1SP 255.1)

The Lord granted the earnest entreaty of his servant. "And the Lord said unto Moses, I will do this thing also that thou hast spoken; for thou has found grace in my sight, and I know thee by name. And he said, I beseech thee, show me thy glory. And he said, I will make all my goodness pass before thee, and I will proclaim the name of the Lord before thee; and will be gracious to whom I will be gracious, and will show mercy on whom I will show mercy. And he said, Thou canst not see my face; for there shall no man see me, and live. And the Lord said, Behold, there is a place by me, and thou shalt stand upon a rock, and it shall come to pass, while my glory passeth by, that I will put thee in a cleft of the rock, and will cover thee with my hand while I pass by; and I will take away mine hand, and thou shalt see my back parts; but my face shall not be seen." (1SP 255.2)

Never before had fallen man been thus favored of God. As he laid upon Moses the great work of leading his people through to the promised land, he condescended to manifest to him his glory as he never had to any others upon the earth. (1SP 256.1)

"And the Lord said unto Moses, Hew thee two tables of stone like unto the first; and I will write upon these tables the words that were in the first tables which thou brakest. And be ready in the morning, and come up in the morning unto Mount Sinai, and present thyself there to me in the top of the mount. And no man shall come up with thee, neither let any man be seen throughout all the mount; neither let the flocks nor herds feed before that mount." (1SP 256.2)

The Lord forbade any man's being seen throughout the mount, because of their recent transgression, lest his glory should consume them. This will give all to understand how God regards the transgression of his commandments. If the people could not look upon his glory, which appeared upon Sinai the second time, as he again wrote his law, how will the wicked, who have trampled upon the authority of God, bear his burning glory as they meet the great Lawgiver over his broken law? (1SP 256.3)

"And he hewed two tables of stone, like unto the first; and Moses rose up early in the morning, and went up unto Mount Sinai, as the Lord had commanded him, and took in his hand the two tables of stone. And the Lord descended in the cloud, and stood with him there, and proclaimed the name of the Lord. And the Lord passed by before him and proclaimed, The Lord, the Lord God, merciful and gracious, long-suffering, and abundant in goodness and truth, keeping mercy for thousands, forgiving iniquity and transgression and sin, and that will by no means clear the guilty; visiting the iniquity of the fathers upon the children, and upon the children's children, unto the third and to the fourth generation." (1SP 257.1)

God did not mean in this threatening that the children should be compelled to suffer for their parents' sins, but that the example of the parents would be imitated by the children. If the children of wicked parents should serve God and do righteousness, he would reward their right-doing. But the effects of a sinful life are often inherited by the children. They follow in the footsteps of their parents. Sinful example has its influence from father to son, to the third and fourth generations. If parents indulge in depraved appetites, they will, in almost every case, see the same acted over in their children. The children will develop characters similar to those of their parents; and unless they are renewed by grace, and overcome, they are truly unfortunate. If parents are continually rebellious, and inclined to disobey God, their children will generally imitate their example. Godly parents, who instruct their children by precept and example in the ways of righteousness, will generally see their children following in their footsteps. The example of God-fearing parents will be imitated by their children, and their children's children will imitate the right example their parents have set before them; and thus the influence is seen from generation to generation. (1SP 257.2)

As the Lord impressed upon the heart of Moses a clear sense of his goodness, his mercy and compassion, he was filled with transports of joy, which led him to worship God with profound reverence. He entreated that the Lord would pardon the iniquity of his people, and take them for his inheritance. Then God graciously promised Moses that he would make a covenant before all Israel to do great things for his people; and that he would evidence to all nations his special care and love for them. (1SP 258.1)

God then charged Moses to make no covenant with the inhabitants of the land whither they should go, lest they should be insnared thereby. But they should destroy their idol altars, break their images, and cut down their groves, which were dedicated to their idols, and where the people assembled to hold their idolatrous feasts, given in honor of their idol gods. He then said to them, "Thou shalt worship no other god; for the Lord, whose name is Jealous, is a jealous God." God claims supreme worship as his due. He gave special directions in regard to his Sabbath: "Six days thou shalt work, but on the seventh day thou shalt rest. In earing time and in harvest thou shalt rest." The Lord knew that Satan was continually at work to lead his people to transgress the law of God, and he condescended to be very definite in his directions to his erring people, that they might not err, and transgress his commandments, for want of knowledge. He knew that in the busiest season of the year, when their fruits and grains were to be secured, they would be tempted to transgress the Sabbath, and labor on sacred time. He would have them understand that their blessings would be increased or diminished according to their integrity of soul, or unfaithfulness in his service. (1SP 258.2)

God is no less particular now in regard to his Sabbath than when he made this requirement of the children of Israel. His eye is upon all his people, and over all the works of their hands. He will not pass by unnoticed those who crowd upon his Sabbath, and employ time for their own use which belongs to him. Some professed Sabbath-keepers will intrude upon the Sabbath in doing those things which should have been done previous to the Sabbath. Such may think they gain a little time; but instead of being advantaged by robbing God of holy time, which he has reserved to himself, they will lose. The Lord will afflict them for their transgression of the fourth commandment; and that time they thought to gain by intruding upon the Sabbath, will prove a curse to them. God's prospering hand withdrawn, will cause a decrease in all their possessions, instead of an increase. God will surely punish the transgressor. Although he may bear with him for a while, his punishment may come suddenly. Such do not always realize that judgments are from God. He is a jealous God, and requires heart service and perfect obedience to all his commandments. (1SP 259.1)

"And it came to pass, when Moses came down from Mount Sinai (with the two tables of testimony in Moses' hand, when he came down from the mount), that Moses wist not that the skin of his face shone while he talked with Him. And when Aaron and all the children of Israel saw Moses, behold, the skin of his face shone,

Chapter 20 - The Law of God (1SP 260.1)

and they were afraid to come nigh him. And Moses called unto them; and Aaron and all the rulers of the congregation returned unto him, and Moses talked with them. And afterward all the children of Israel came nigh; and he gave them in commandment all that the Lord had spoken with him in Mount Sinai. And till Moses had done speaking with them, he put a vail on his face. But when Moses went in before the Lord, to speak with him, he took the vail off, until he came out. And he came out and spake unto the children of Israel that which he was commanded. And the children of Israel saw the face of Moses, that the skin of Moses' face shone; and Moses put the vail upon his face again, until he went in to speak with him." (1SP 260.1)

Those who trample upon God's authority, and show open contempt to the law given in such grandeur at Sinai, virtually despise the Lawgiver, the great Jehovah. The children of Israel who transgressed the first and second commandments, were charged not to be seen anywhere near the mount, where God was to descend in glory to write the law a second time upon tables of stone, lest they should be consumed with the burning glory of his presence. And if they could not even look upon the face of Moses for the glory of his countenance, because he had been communing with God, how much less can the transgressors of God's law look upon the Son of God when he shall appear in the clouds of heaven in the glory of his Father, surrounded by all the angelic host, to execute judgment upon all who have disregarded the commandments of God, and have trodden under foot his blood! (1SP 260.2)

The law of God existed before man was created. The angels were governed by it. Satan fell because he transgressed the principles of God's government. After Adam and Eve were created, God made known to them his law. It was not then written, but was rehearsed to them by Jehovah. (1SP 261.1)

The Sabbath of the fourth commandment was instituted in Eden. After God had made the world, and created man upon the earth, he made the Sabbath for man. After Adam's sin and fall, nothing was taken from the law of God. The principles of the ten commandments existed before the fall, and were of a character suited to the condition of a holy order of beings. After the fall, the principles of those precepts were not changed, but additional precepts were given to meet man in his fallen state. (1SP 261.2)

A system was then established requiring the sacrificing of beasts, to keep before fallen man that which the serpent made Eve disbelieve, that the penalty of disobedience is death. The transgression of God's law made it necessary for Christ to die a sacrifice, and thus make a way possible for man to escape the penalty, and yet the honor of God's law be preserved. The system of sacrifices was to teach man humility, in view of his fallen condition, and lead him to repentance, and to trust in God alone, through the promised Redeemer, for pardon for past transgression of his law. If the law of God had not been transgressed, there never would have been death, and there would have been no need of additional precepts to suit man's fallen condition. (1SP 261.3)

Adam taught his descendants the law of God, which law was handed down to the faithful through successive generations. The continual transgression of God's law called for a flood of waters upon the earth. The law was preserved by Noah and his family, who for right-doing were saved in the ark by a miracle of God. Noah taught his descendants the ten commandments. The Lord preserved a people for himself from Adam down, in whose hearts was his law. He says of Abraham, He "obeyed my voice, and kept my charge, my commandments, my statutes, and my laws." (1SP 262.1)

The Lord appeared unto Abraham, and said unto him, "I am the Almighty God. Walk before me, and be thou perfect. And I will make a covenant between me and thee, and will multiply thee exceedingly." "And I will establish my covenant between me and thee, and thy seed after thee, in their generations, for an everlasting covenant, to be a God unto thee, and to thy seed after thee." (1SP 262.2)

He then required of Abraham and his seed, circumcision, which was a circle cut in the flesh, as a token that God had cut them out and separated them from all nations as his peculiar treasure. By this sign they solemnly pledged themselves that they would not intermarry with other nations; for by so doing they would lose their reverence for God and his holy law, and would become like the idolatrous nations around them. (1SP 262.3)

By the act of circumcision they solemnly agreed to fulfill on their part the conditions of the covenant made with Abraham, to be separate from all nations, and to be perfect. If the descendants of Abraham had kept separate from other nations, they would not have been seduced into idolatry. By keeping separate from other nations, a great temptation to engage in their sinful practices, and rebel against God, would be removed from them. They lost in a great measure their peculiar, holy character, by mingling with the nations around them. To punish them, the Lord brought a famine upon their land, which compelled them to go down into Egypt to preserve their lives. But God did not forsake them while they were in Egypt, because of his covenant with Abraham. He suffered them to be oppressed by the Egyptians, that they might turn to him in their distress, choose his righteous and merciful government, and obey his requirements. (1SP 262.4)

There were but a few families that first went down into Egypt. These increased to a great multitude. Some were careful to instruct their children in the law of God; but many of the Israelites had witnessed so much idolatry that they had confused ideas of God's law. Those who feared God, cried to him in anguish of spirit to break their yoke of grievous bondage and bring them from the land of their captivity, that they might be free to serve him. God heard their cries, and raised up Moses as his instrument to accomplish the deliverance of his people. After they had left Egypt, and the waters of the Red Sea had been divided before them, the Lord proved them to see if they would trust in him who had taken them, a nation from another nation, by signs, temptations, and wonders. But they failed to endure the trial. They murmured against God because of difficulties in the way, and wished to return again to Egypt. To leave them without excuse, the Lord himself condescended to come down upon Sinai, enshrouded in glory, and surrounded by his angels, and in a most sublime and awful manner made known his law of ten commandments. He did not trust them to be taught by any one, not even his angels, but spoke his law with an audible voice in the hearing of all the people. He did not, even then, trust them to the short memory of a people who were prone to forget his requirements, but wrote them with his own holy finger upon tables of stone. He would remove from them all possibility of mingling with his holy precepts any tradition, or of confusing his requirements with the practices of men. (1SP 263.1)

He then came still closer to his people, who were so readily led astray, and would not leave them with merely the ten precepts of the decalogue. He commanded Moses to write, as he should bid him, judgments and laws, giving minute directions in regard to what he required them to perform, and thereby guarded the ten precepts which he had engraved upon the tables of stone. These specific directions and requirements were given to draw erring man to the obedience of the moral law, which he is so prone to transgress. (1SP 264.1)

If man had kept the law of God, as given to Adam after his fall, preserved in the ark by Noah, and observed by Abraham, there would have been no necessity for the ordinance of circumcision. And if the descendants of Abraham had kept the covenant, of which circumcision was a token or pledge, they would never have gone into idolatry, nor been suffered to go down into Egypt; and there would have been no necessity of God's proclaiming his law from Sinai, and engraving it upon tables of stone, and guarding it by definite directions in the judgments and statutes given to Moses. (1SP 264.2)

Moses wrote these judgments and statutes from the mouth of God while he was with him in the mount. If the people of God had obeyed the principles of the ten commandments, there would have been no need of the specific directions given to Moses, which he wrote in a book, relative to their duty to God and to one another. The definite directions which the Lord gave to Moses in regard to the duty of his people to one another, and to the stranger, are the principles of the ten commandments simplified and given in a definite manner, that they need not err. (1SP 265.1)

The Lord said of the children of Israel, "Because they had not executed my judgments, but had despised my statutes, and had polluted my Sabbaths, and their eyes were after their fathers' idols, wherefore I gave them also statutes that were not good, and judgments whereby they should not live." Because of continual disobedience, the Lord annexed penalties to the transgression of his law, which were not good for the transgressor, or whereby he should not live in his rebellion. (1SP 265.2)

By transgressing the law which God had

Chapter 20 - The Law of God (1SP 265.3)

given in such majesty, and amid glory which was unapproachable, the people showed open contempt of the great Lawgiver, and death was the penalty. (1SP 265.3)

"Moreover also, I gave them my sabbaths, to be a sign between me and them, that they might know that I am the Lord that sanctify them. But the house of Israel rebelled against me in the wilderness: they walked not in my statutes, and they despised my judgments, which if a man do, he shall even live in them; and my sabbaths they greatly polluted. Then I said, I would pour out my fury upon them in the wilderness, to consume them." (1SP 265.4)

The statutes and judgments given of God were good for the obedient. "They should live in them." But they were not good for the transgressor; for in the civil law given to Moses, punishment was to be inflicted on the transgressor, that others should be restrained by fear. (1SP 266.1)

Moses charged the children of Israel to obey God. He said unto them, "Now therefore hearken, O Israel, unto the statutes and unto the judgments, which I teach you, for to do them, that ye may live, and go in and possess the land which the Lord God of your fathers giveth you." (1SP 266.2)

The Lord instructed Moses definitely in regard to the ceremonial sacrifices, which were to cease at the death of Christ. The system of sacrifices foreshadowed the offering of Christ as a Lamb without blemish. (1SP 266.3)

The Lord first established the system of sacrificial offerings with Adam after his fall, which he taught to his descendants. This system was corrupted before the flood, and by those who separated themselves from the faithful followers of God and engaged in the building of the tower of Babel. They sacrificed to gods of their own [making] instead of the God of Heaven. They did not offer sacrifices because they had faith in the Redeemer to come, but because they thought they should please their gods by offering a great many beasts upon polluted idol altars. Their superstition led them to great extravagances. They taught the people that the more valuable the sacrifice, the greater pleasure would it give their idol gods, and the greater would be the prosperity and riches of their nation. Hence, human beings were often sacrificed to these senseless idols. Those nations had laws and regulations to control the actions of the people, which were cruel in the extreme. Their laws were made by those whose hearts were not softened by grace; and while they would pass over the most debasing crimes, a small offense would call forth the most cruel punishment from those in authority. (1SP 266.4)

Moses had this in view when he said to Israel, "Behold, I have taught you statutes and judgments, even as the Lord my God commanded me, that ye should do so in the land whither ye go to possess it. Keep, therefore, and do them; for this is your wisdom and your understanding in the sight of the nations which shall hear all these statutes, and say, Surely this great nation is a wise and understanding people. For what nation is there so great, who hath God so nigh unto them, as the Lord our God is in all things that we call upon him for? And what nation is there so great, that hath statutes and judgments so righteous as all this law, which I set before you this day?" (1SP 267.1)

God was a wise and compassionate lawgiver, judging all cases righteously, and without partiality. While the Israelites were in Egyptian bondage, they were surrounded with idolatry. The Egyptians had received traditions in regard to sacrificing. They did not acknowledge the existence of the God of Heaven. They sacrificed to their idol gods. With great pomp and ceremony they performed their idol worship. They erected altars to the honor of their gods, and they required even their own children to pass through the fire. After they had erected their altars, they required their children to leap over the altars through the fire. If they could do this without being burned, the idol priests and the people received it as an evidence that their God accepted their offerings, and favored especially the person who passed through the fiery ordeal. He was loaded with benefits, and was ever afterward greatly esteemed by all the people. He was never allowed to be punished, however aggravating might be his crimes. If another person who leaped through the fire was so unfortunate as to be burned, then his fate was fixed; for they thought that their gods were angry, and would be appeased with nothing short of the unhappy victim's life, and he was offered up as a sacrifice upon their idol altars. (1SP 267.2)

Even some of the children of Israel had so far degraded themselves as to practice these abominations, and God caused the fire to kindle upon their children, whom they made to pass through the fire. They did not go to all the lengths of the heathen nations; but God deprived them of their children by causing the fire to consume them in the act of passing through it. (1SP 268.1)

Because the people of God had confused ideas of the ceremonial sacrificial offerings, and had heathen traditions confounded with their ceremonial worship, God condescended to give them definite directions, that they might understand the true import of those sacrifices which were to last only till the Lamb of God should be slain, who was the great antitype of all their sacrificial offerings. (1SP 268.2)

Chapter 21
The Sanctuary

The tabernacle was made according to the commandment of God. The Lord raised up men, and qualified them with more than natural abilities to perform the most ingenious work. Neither Moses nor those workmen were left to plan the form and workmanship of the building. God himself devised the plan, and gave it to Moses, with particular directions as to its size and form, and the materials to be used, and specified every article of furniture which was to be in it. He presented before Moses a miniature model of the heavenly sanctuary, and commanded him to make all things according to the pattern showed him in the mount. Moses wrote all the directions in a book, and read them to the most influential of the people. (1SP 269.1)

Then the Lord required the people to bring a free-will offering, to make him a sanctuary, that he might dwell among them. "And all the congregation of the children of Israel departed from the presence of Moses. And they came, every one whose heart stirred him up, and every one whom his spirit made willing, and they brought the Lord's offering to the work of the tabernacle of the congregation, and for all his service, and for the holy garments. And they came, both men and women, as many as were willing-hearted, and brought bracelets, and ear-rings, and rings, and tablets, all jewels of gold; and every man that offered, offered an offering of gold unto the Lord." (1SP 269.2)

Great and expensive preparations were necessary. Precious and costly materials must be collected. But the Lord accepted only the free-will offerings. Devotion to the work of God and sacrifice from the heart were first required in preparing a place for God. And while the building of the sanctuary was going on, and the people were bringing their offerings unto Moses, and he was presenting them to the workmen, all the wise men who wrought in the work examined the gifts, and decided that the people had brought enough, and even more than they could use. And Moses proclaimed throughout the camp, saying, "Let neither man nor woman make any more work for the offering of the sanctuary. So the people were restrained from bringing." (1SP 269.3)

The repeated murmurings of the Israelites, and the visitations of God's wrath because of their transgressions, are recorded in sacred history for the benefit of God's people who should afterward live upon the earth; but more especially to prove a warning to those who should live near the close of time. Also their acts of devotion, their energy, and liberality, in bringing their free-will offerings to Moses, are recorded for the benefit of the people of God. Their example in preparing material for the tabernacle so cheerfully, is an example for all who truly love the worship of God. Those who prize the blessing of God's sacred presence, when preparing a building that he may meet with them, should manifest greater interest and zeal in the sacred work in proportion as they value their heavenly blessings higher than their earthly comforts. They should realize that they are preparing a house for God. (1SP 270.1)

Many will expend much to erect comfortable and tasty buildings for themselves; but when they would prepare a place that they may receive the presence of the high and exalted One, they manifest a wonderful indifference, and have no particular interest as to the convenience, arrangement, and workmanship. Their offerings are not given cheerfully from the heart, but are bestowed grudgingly; and they are continually studying in what manner the sacred building can be made to cost the least, and answer the purpose as a house of worship. Some manifest more interest in building their barns, wherein to keep their cattle, than they do in building a place for the worship of God. Such value sacred privileges just in that proportion which their works show. And their prosperity and spiritual strength will be just according to their works.

God will not cause his blessing to rest upon those who have so little estimate of the value of divine things. Unwilling and stinted offerings are not accepted of God. Those who manifest that earnestness to bring to the Lord acceptable offerings, of the very best they have, willingly, as the children of Israel brought their presents to Moses, will be blessed in that proportion that they have estimated the value of divine things. (1SP 270.2)

It is of some consequence that a building prepared expressly for God to meet with his people, should be arranged with care–made comfortable, neat, and convenient; for it is to be dedicated to God, and presented to him, and he is to be entreated to abide in that house, and make it sacred by his holy presence. Enough should be willingly given to the Lord, to liberally accomplish the work, and then the workmen be able to say, Bring no more offerings. A house built for God never should be left in debt, for God would be dishonored. He is acquainted with every heart, and he will reward every one who freely gives back to him, when he requires, that which he has given them. If they withhold that which belongs to God, he will afflict them in their families, and cause decrease in their possessions, just according to their disposition to rob him. (1SP 271.1)

After the building of the tabernacle was completed, Moses examined all the work, and compared it with the pattern, and directions he had received of God, and he saw that every part of it agreed with the pattern; and he blessed the people. God gave a pattern of the ark to Moses, with special directions how to make it. The ark was made to contain the tables of stone, on which God engraved, with his own finger, the ten commandments. It was in form like a chest, and was overlaid and inlaid with pure gold. It was ornamented with crowns of gold round about the top. The cover of this sacred chest was the mercy-seat, made of solid gold. On each end of the mercy-seat was fixed a cherub of pure, solid gold. Their faces were turned toward each other, and were looking reverentially downward toward the mercy-seat, which represents all the heavenly angels looking with interest and reverence to the law of God deposited in the ark in the heavenly sanctuary. These cherubs had wings. One wing of each angel was stretched forth on high, while the other wing of each angel covered their forms. The ark of the earthly sanctuary was the pattern of the true ark in Heaven. There, beside the heavenly ark, stand living angels, at either end of the ark, each with one wing overshadowing the mercy-seat, and stretching forth on high, while the other wings are folded over their forms in token of reverence and humility. (1SP 272.1)

In the earthly ark Moses was required to place the tables of stone. These were called the tables of the testimony; and the ark was called the ark of the testimony, because they contained God's testimony in the ten commandments. The tabernacle was composed of two apartments, separated by a curtain, or vail. (1SP 273.1)

All the furniture of the tabernacle was made of solid gold, or plated with gold. The curtains of the tabernacle were of a variety of colors, most beautifully arranged, and in these curtains were wrought, with threads of gold and silver, cherubims, which were to represent the angelic host, who are connected with the work of the heavenly sanctuary, and who are ministering angels to the saints upon the earth. (1SP 273.2)

Within the second vail was placed the ark of the testimony, and the beautiful and rich curtain was drawn before the sacred ark. This curtain did not reach to the top of the building. The glory of God, which was above the mercy-seat, could be seen from both apartments, but in a much less degree from the first apartment. Directly before the ark, but separated by the curtain, was the golden altar of incense. The fire upon this altar was kindled by the Lord himself, and was sacredly cherished by feeding it with holy incense, which filled the sanctuary with its fragrant cloud, day and night. Its fragrance extended for miles around the tabernacle. When the priest offered the incense before the Lord, he looked to the mercy-seat. Although he could not see it, he knew it was there; and as the incense arose like a cloud, the glory of the Lord descended upon the mercy-seat, and filled the most holy place, and was visible in the holy place; and the glory often so filled both apartments that the priest was unable to officiate, and was obliged to stand at the door of the tabernacle. The priest in the holy place, directing his prayer by faith to the mercy-seat, which he could not see, represents the people of God directing their prayers to Christ before the mercy-seat in the heavenly sanctuary. They cannot behold their Mediator with the natural eye, but with the eye of faith they see Christ before the mercy-seat, and direct their prayers to

Chapter 21 - The Sanctuary (1SP 273.3)

him, and with assurance claim the benefits of his mediation. (1SP 273.3)

These sacred apartments had no windows to admit light. The candlestick was made of purest gold, and was kept burning night and day, and gave light to both apartments. The light of the lamps upon the candlestick reflected upon the boards plated with gold, at the sides of the building, and upon the sacred furniture, and upon the curtains of beautiful colors with cherubims wrought with threads of gold and silver, which appearance was glorious beyond description. No language can describe the beauty and loveliness, and sacred glory, which these apartments presented. The gold in the sanctuary reflected the colors of the curtains, which appeared like the different colors of the rainbow. (1SP 274.1)

Only once a year could the high priest enter into the most holy place, after the most careful and solemn preparation. No mortal eye but that of the high priest could look upon the sacred grandeur of that apartment, because it was the especial dwelling-place of God's visible glory. The high priest always entered it with trembling, while the people waited his return with solemn silence. Their earnest desires were to God for his blessing. Before the mercy-seat, God conversed with the high priest. If he remained an unusual time in the most holy, the people were often terrified, fearing that because of their sins, or some sin of the priest, the glory of the Lord had slain him. But when the sound of the tinkling of the bells upon his garments was heard, they were greatly relieved. He then came forth and blessed the people. (1SP 274.2)

After the work of the tabernacle was finished, "a cloud covered the tent of the congregation, and the glory of the Lord filled the tabernacle. And Moses was not able to enter into the tent of the congregation, because the cloud abode thereon, and the glory of the Lord filled the tabernacle. And when the cloud was taken up from over the tabernacle, the children of Israel went onward in all their journeys. But if the cloud were not taken up, then they journeyed not till the day that it was taken up. For the cloud of the Lord was upon the tabernacle by day, and fire was on it by night, in the sight of all the house of Israel, throughout all their journeys." The tabernacle was constructed so as to be taken to pieces, and borne with them in all their journeyings. (1SP 275.1)

The Lord directed the Israelites in all their travels through the wilderness. When it was for the good of the people, and the glory of God, that they should pitch their tents in a certain place, and there abide, God signified his will to them by the pillar of cloud resting low directly over the tabernacle. And there it remained until God would have them journey again. Then the cloud of glory was lifted up high above the tabernacle, and then they journeyed again. In all their journeyings they observed perfect order. Every tribe bore a standard, with the sign of their father's house upon it, and every tribe was commanded to pitch by their own standard. And when they traveled, the different tribes marched in order, every tribe under their own standard. When they rested from their journeyings, the tabernacle was erected, and then the different tribes pitched their tents in order, in just such a position as God commanded, around the tabernacle, at a distance from it. (1SP 275.2)

When the people journeyed, the ark of the covenant was borne before them. "And the cloud of the Lord was upon them by day, when they went out of the camp. And it came to pass, when the ark set forward, that Moses said, Rise up, Lord, and let thine enemies be scattered; and let them that hate thee flee before thee. And when it rested, he said, Return, O Lord, unto the many thousands of Israel." (1SP 276.1)

*****

Chapter 22
Strange Fire

"And Nadab and Abihu, the sons of Aaron, took either of them his censer, and put fire therein, and put incense thereon, and offered strange fire before the Lord, which he commanded them not. And there went out fire from the Lord, and devoured them, and they died before the Lord. Then Moses said unto Aaron, This is it that the Lord spake, saying, I will be sanctified in them that come nigh me, and before all the people I will be glorified. And Aaron held his peace." (1SP 276.2)

The sons of Aaron did not take the sacred fire from the altar, which the Lord himself had kindled, and which he had commanded the priests to use when they offered incense before him. They took common fire, and put it in their censers, and put incense thereon. This was a transgression of God's express command, and his judgment speedily followed. Aaron's sons, who officiated in holy things, would not have thus transgressed if they had not indulged freely in the use of wine, and been partially intoxicated. They gratified the appetite, which debased their faculties, and disqualified them for their sacred office. Their intellects were beclouded, so that they did not have a realizing sense of the difference between the sacredness of the fire which God let fall from Heaven, and which was kept burning continually upon the altar, and the common fire, which he had said they should not use. If they had had the full and clear use of their reasoning powers, they would have recoiled with horror at the presumptuous transgression of God's positive commands. They had been especially favored of God in being of the number of the elders who witnessed the glory of God in the mount. They understood that the most careful self-examination and sanctification were required on their part before presenting themselves in the sanctuary, where God's presence was manifested. (1SP 277.1)

"And Moses said unto Aaron, and unto Eleazar, and unto Ithamar, his sons, Uncover not your heads, neither rend your clothes, lest ye die, and lest wrath come upon all the people; but let your brethren, the whole house of Israel, bewail the burning which the Lord hath kindled. And ye shall not go out from the door of the tabernacle of the congregation, lest ye die; for the anointing oil of the Lord is upon you. And they did according to the word of Moses." The father of the men slain, and their brothers, were forbidden to manifest any signs of grief for the ones who had been justly punished of God. When Moses reminded Aaron of the words of the Lord, that he would be sanctified in them that came nigh to him, Aaron was silent. He knew that God was just; and he murmured not. His heart was grieved at the dreadful death of his sons while in their disobedience; yet, according to God's command, he made no expression of his sorrow, lest he should share the same fate of his sons, and the congregation also be infected with the spirit of unreconciliation, and God's wrath come upon them. (1SP 277.2)

When the Israelites committed sin, and God punished them for their transgression, and the people mourned for the fate of the one punished, instead of sorrowing because God had been dishonored, the sympathizers were accounted equally guilty with the transgressor. (1SP 278.1)

The Lord teaches us, in the directions given to Aaron, reconciliation to his just punishments, even if his wrath comes very nigh. He would have his people acknowledge the justness of his corrections, that others may fear. In these last days, many are liable to be self-deceived, and they are unable to see their own wrongs. If God, through his servants, reproves and rebukes the erring, there are those who stand ready to sympathize with those who deserve reproof. They will seek to lighten the burden which God compelled his servants to lay upon them. These sympathizers think they are performing a virtuous act by sympathizing with the one at fault, whose course may have greatly injured the

Chapter 22 - Strange Fire (1SP 278.2)

cause of God. Such are deceived. They are only arraying themselves against God's servants, who have done his will, and against God himself, and are equally guilty with the transgressor. There are many erring souls who might have been saved if they had not been deceived by receiving false sympathy. **(1SP 278.2)**

"And the Lord spake unto Aaron, saying, Do not drink wine nor strong drink, thou, nor thy sons with thee, when ye go into the tabernacle of the congregation, lest ye die; it shall be a statute forever throughout your generations; and that ye may put difference between holy and unholy, and between unclean and clean." **(1SP 279.1)**

The case of Aaron's sons has been placed upon record for the benefit of God's people, and should teach those especially who are preparing for the second coming of Christ, that the indulgence of a depraved appetite destroys the fine feelings of the soul, and so affects the reasoning powers which God has given to man, that spiritual and holy things lose their sacredness. Disobedience looks pleasing, instead of exceedingly sinful. Satan rejoices to see men formed in the image of their Maker, yield themselves as slaves to a depraved appetite; for he can then successfully control the powers of the mind, and lead those who are intemperate to act in a manner to debase themselves and dishonor God, by losing the high sense of his sacred requirements. It was the indulgence of the appetite which caused the sons of Aaron to use common, instead of sacred, fire for their offerings. **(1SP 279.2)**

The sons of Aaron, departing from God's commands, represent those who transgress the fourth commandment of Jehovah, which is very plain: "Six days shalt thou labor, and do all thy work; but the seventh day is the Sabbath of the Lord thy God: in it thou shalt not do any work," &c. Nearly all the professed followers of Christ do not keep the day God has sanctified and required them to keep sacred, to rest upon it because he has rested upon it himself. They labor upon God's holy time, and honor the first day of the week by resting upon it, which is a common working day, a day upon which God did not rest, and upon which he has placed no sacred honor. **(1SP 279.3)**

A departure from the fourth commandment will not now be immediately visited with temporal death; yet God does not regard the violation of his commandments any more lightly than he did the transgression of Aaron's sons. Death is the final punishment of all who reject light, and continue in transgression. When God says, Keep holy the seventh day, he does not mean the sixth, nor the first, but the very day he has specified. If men substitute a common day for the sacred, and say that will do just as well, they insult the Maker of the heavens and of the earth, who made the Sabbath to commemorate his resting upon the seventh day, after creating the world in six days. It is dangerous business in the service of God to deviate from his institutions. Those who have to do with God, who is infinite, and who explicitly directs in regard to his own worship, should follow the exact course he has prescribed, and not feel at liberty to deviate in the least particular because they think it will answer just as well. God will teach all his creatures that he means just what he says. **(1SP 280.1)**

Chapter 23
The Quails

God continued to feed the Hebrew host with the bread rained from Heaven; but they were not satisfied. Their depraved appetites craved meat, which God in his wisdom had withheld, in a great measure, from them. "And the mixed multitude that was among them fell a lusting; and the children of Israel also wept again, and said, Who shall give us flesh to eat? We remember the fish which we did eat in Egypt freely; the cucumbers, and the melons, and the leeks, and the onions, and the garlic. But now our soul is dried away; there is nothing at all, besides this manna, before our eyes." They became weary of the food prepared for them by angels, and sent to them from Heaven. They knew it was just the food God wished them to have, and that it was healthful for them and their children. Notwithstanding their hardships in the wilderness, there was not a feeble one in all their tribes. Satan, the author of disease and misery, will approach God's people where he can have the greatest success. He has controlled the appetite in a great measure from the time of his successful experiment with Eve, in leading her to eat the forbidden fruit. He came with his temptations first to the mixed multitude, the believing Egyptians, and stirred them up to seditious murmurings. They would not be content with the healthful food which God had provided for them. Their depraved appetites craved a greater variety, especially flesh-meats. (1SP 281.1)

This murmuring soon infected nearly the whole body of the people. At first, God did not gratify their lustful appetites, but caused his judgments to come upon them, and consumed the most guilty by lightning from heaven. Yet this, instead of humbling them, seemed only to increase their murmurings. When Moses heard the people weeping in the door of their tents, and complaining throughout their families, he was displeased. He presented before the Lord the difficulties of his situation, the unsubmissive spirit of the Israelites, and the position in which God had placed him to the people, that of a nursing father, who should make the sufferings of the people his own. He inquired of the Lord how he could bear this great burden of continually witnessing the disobedience of Israel, and hearing their murmurings against his commands, and against God himself. He declared before the Lord that he would rather die than to see Israel, by their perverseness, drawing down judgments upon themselves, while the enemies of God were rejoicing in their destruction. In his distress he said, I am not able to bear all this responsibility alone, because it is too heavy for me. (1SP 282.1)

The Lord directed Moses to gather before him seventy of the elders, whom he knew to be the elders of the people. They were not only to be those advanced in years, but men of dignity, sound judgment, and experience, who were qualified to be judges, or officers. "And bring them unto the tabernacle of the congregation, that they may stand there with thee. And I will come down and talk with thee there; and I will take of the Spirit which is upon thee, and will put it upon them; and they shall bear the burden of the people with thee, that thou bear it not thyself alone. And say thou unto the people, Sanctify yourselves against tomorrow, and ye shall eat flesh; for ye have wept in the ears of the Lord, saying, Who shall give us flesh to eat? for it was well with us in Egypt; therefore the Lord will give you flesh, and ye shall eat. Ye shall not eat one day, nor two days, nor five days, neither ten days, nor twenty days; but even a whole month, until it come out at your nostrils, and it be loathsome unto you; because that ye have despised the Lord which is among you, and have wept before him, saying, Why came we forth out of Egypt? And Moses said, The people, among whom I am, are six hundred thousand footmen; and thou hast said, I will give them flesh, that they may eat a whole month. Shall the flocks and the herds be slain for them, to suffice them? or shall all the fish or the sea be gathered together for them, to

Chapter 23 - The Quails (1SP 282.2)

suffice them? And the Lord said unto Moses, Is the Lord's hand waxed short? Thou shalt see now whether my word shall come to pass unto thee or not." (1SP 282.2)

Moses himself showed a manifest distrust of the power of God, for which the Lord rebuked him. By this question of the Lord to Moses, he was made to understand that nothing was impossible with the great Ruler of the universe. He reproved Moses for his forgetfulness of his miracles. He who could divide the Red Sea, and bind the waters, so that they were like a wall on either side of Israel as they passed through on dry land, and could rain them bread from heaven, and bring them water out of the flinty rock, could provide meat to supply the host of Israel. (1SP 283.1)

"And Moses went out, and told the people the words of the Lord, and gathered the seventy men of the elders of the people, and set them round about the tabernacle. And the Lord came down in a cloud, and spake unto him, and took of the Spirit that was upon him, and gave it unto the seventy elders; and it came to pass, that when the Spirit rested upon them, they prophesied, and did not cease." This prophetic gift rested upon the judges and elders, to establish the confidence of the people in them, and to be a sign that God had chosen them to unite their authority with that of Moses, and assist him in the work of subduing the murmurings of the people during their sojourn in the wilderness, and thus ease the task upon Moses. (1SP 283.2)

"And there went forth a wind from the Lord, and brought quails from the sea, and let them fall by the camp, as it were a day's journey on this side, and as it were a day's journey on the other side, round about the camp, and as it were two cubits high upon the face of the earth. And the people stood up all that day, and all that night, and all the next day, and they gathered the quails; he that gathered least gathered ten homers; and they spread them all abroad for themselves round about the camp. And while the flesh was yet between their teeth, ere it was chewed, the wrath of the Lord was kindled against the people, and the Lord smote the people with a very great plague." (1SP 284.1)

In this instance the Lord gave the people that which was not for their best good, because they would have it. They would not submit to receive from the Lord only those things which would prove for their good. They gave themselves up to seditious murmurings against Moses, and against the Lord, because they did not receive those things which would prove an injury to them. Their depraved appetites controlled them, and God gave them flesh-meats, as they desired, and let them suffer the results of gratifying their lustful appetites. Burning fevers cut down very large numbers of the people. Those who had been the most guilty in their murmurings, were slain as soon as they tasted the meat for which they had lusted. If they had submitted to have the Lord select their food for them, and had been thankful, and satisfied with food of which they could eat freely without injury, they would not have lost the favor of God, and then been punished for their rebellious murmurings, by great numbers of them being slain. (1SP 284.2)

*****

Chapter 24
Miriam

After Moses had told the Lord that he was unable to bear the burden of the people alone, and God had directed him to choose seventy of the elders, and he had put the same Spirit upon them which was upon Moses, Aaron and Miriam were jealous because they had not been consulted in the matter. They had not felt reconciled to the act of Moses in so readily receiving the counsel of Jethro, his father-in-law. They feared that he had more influence over Moses than they had. And now, seventy elders had been chosen without their being consulted; and as they had never themselves felt the responsibility and burdens which Moses had borne for the people, they did not see any real necessity for the help of the seventy elders. "And they said, Hath the Lord indeed spoken only by Moses? hath he not spoken also by us? And the Lord heard it." (1SP 285.1)

Aaron and Miriam thought, as they had been chosen to aid Moses in the work, that they bore the burden of the work as well as Moses. And as the Lord had spoken by them, as well as by Moses, why should he complain of such heavy burdens as to need seventy of the judges and elders appointed to the work of aiding him. Moses felt his weakness. He felt the importance of the great work committed to him, as no other man had ever felt it. Aaron had shown his weakness by yielding to the people, and making a molten calf, in the absence of Moses. God had ever been Moses' counselor. (1SP 286.1)

As Miriam became jealous of Moses, she was disposed to find fault with the events of his life which God had especially overruled. She complained of Moses because he married an Ethiopian woman, instead of taking a wife from among the Hebrews. The wife of Moses was not black, but her complexion was somewhat darker than the Hebrews. She was of a timid disposition, tender-hearted, and was greatly affected upon witnessing suffering. This was the reason that Moses consented to have her return to Midian, while he was in Egypt, that she might not witness the terrific plagues which the Lord was to bring upon Egypt. After she met her husband in the wilderness, she saw that his burdens and anxieties were liable to wear away his strength, and in her distress she acquainted her father with the matter. Jethro had marked that the care of all the people was upon Moses, and therefore he counseled him to look after the religious interests of the Hebrew host, while worthy men, free from covetousness, should be selected to look after the secular concerns of the people. (1SP 286.2)

After Miriam became jealous, she imagined that Aaron and herself had been neglected, and that Moses' wife was the cause–that she had influenced the mind of her husband–that he did not consult them in important matters as much as formerly. (1SP 287.1)

The Lord heard the words of murmuring against Moses, and he was displeased; for Moses was very meek, above all the men which were upon the face of the earth. "And the Lord spake suddenly unto Moses, and unto Aaron, and unto Miriam, Come out, ye three, unto the tabernacle of the congregation. And they three came out. And the Lord came down in the pillar of the cloud, and stood in the door of the tabernacle, and called Aaron and Miriam, and they both came forth. And he said, Hear now my words: If there be a prophet among you, I the Lord will make myself known unto him in a vision, and will speak unto him in a dream. My servant Moses is not so, who is faithful in all mine house. With him will I speak mouth to mouth, even apparently, and not in dark speeches; and the similitude of the Lord shall he behold; wherefore, then, were ye not afraid to speak against my servant Moses? And the anger of the Lord was kindled against them, and he departed. And the cloud departed from off the tabernacle, and behold, Miriam became leprous, white as snow; and Aaron looked upon Miriam, and behold, she was leprous. And Aaron said unto Moses, Alas,

Chapter 24 - Miriam (1SP 287.2)

my lord, I beseech thee, lay not the sin upon us, wherein we have done foolishly, and wherein we have sinned. Let her not be as one dead." "And Moses cried unto the Lord, saying, Heal her now, O God, I beseech thee." "And Miriam was shut out of the camp seven days; and the people journeyed not till Miriam was brought in again." (1SP 287.2)

The cloud was removed from the tabernacle because the wrath of God rested upon Miriam, and it did not return until she was removed out of the camp. God had chosen Moses, and put his Spirit upon him; and by the complaints of Miriam against God's chosen servant, she not only behaved irreverently to Moses, but toward God himself, who had chosen him. Aaron was drawn into the jealous spirit of his sister Miriam. He might have prevented the evil if he had not sympathized with her, and had presented before her the sinfulness of her conduct. But instead of this, he listened to her words of complaint. The murmurings of Miriam and Aaron are left upon record as a rebuke to all who will yield to jealousy, and complain of those upon whom God lays the burden of his work. (1SP 288.1)

*****

Chapter 25
Caleb and Joshua

The Lord commanded Moses to send men to search the land of Canaan, which he would give unto the children of Israel. A ruler of each tribe was to be selected for this purpose. They went, and after forty days, returned from their search, and came before Moses and Aaron, and all the congregation of Israel, and showed them the fruit of the land. All agreed that it was a good land, and they exhibited the rich fruit which they had brought as evidence. One cluster of the grapes was so large that two men carried it between them on a staff. They also brought of the figs, and the pomegranates, which grew there in abundance. After they had spoken of the fertility of the land, all but two spoke very discouragingly of their being able to possess it. They said that the people were very strong that dwelt in the land, and the cities were surrounded with great and high walls; and, more than all this, they saw the children of the giant Anak there. They then described how the people were situated around Canaan, and the impossibility of their ever being able to possess it. (1SP 288.2)

As the people listened to this report, they gave vent to their disappointment with bitter reproaches and wailing. They did not wait, and reflect, and reason, that God, who had brought them out thus far, would certainly give them the land. But they yielded to discouragement at once. They limited the power of the Holy One, and trusted not in God, who had hitherto led them. They reproached Moses, and murmuringly said to one another, This, then, is the end of all our hopes. This is the land that we have been traveling from Egypt to obtain. Caleb and Joshua sought to obtain a hearing; but the people were so excited that they could not command themselves to listen to these two men. After they were calmed a little, Caleb ventured to speak. He said to the people, "Let us go up at once, and possess it; for we are well able to overcome it." But the men that went up with him said, "We be not able to go up against the people; for they are stronger than we." And they continued to repeat their evil report, and declared that all the men were of great stature. "And there we saw the giants, the sons of Anak, which come of the giants. And we were in our own sight as grasshoppers, and so we were in their sight. And all the congregation lifted up their voice, and cried; and the people wept that night. And all the children of Israel murmured against Moses and against Aaron; and the whole congregation said unto them, Would God that we had died in the land of Egypt! or would God we had died in this wilderness! And wherefore hath the Lord brought us unto this land, to fall by the sword, that our wives and our children should be a prey? Were it not better for us to return into Egypt? And they said one to another, Let us make a captain, and let us return into Egypt. Then Moses and Aaron fell on their faces before all the assembly of the congregation of the children of Israel." (1SP 289.1)

The Israelites not only gave vent to their complaints against Moses, but accused God himself of dealing deceitfully with them, by promising them a land which they were unable to possess. Their rebellious spirit here rose so high that, forgetful to the strong arm of Omnipotence which had brought them out of the land of Egypt, and had thus far conducted them by a series of miracles, they resolved to choose a commander to lead them back to Egypt, where they had been slaves, and had suffered so many hardships. They actually appointed them a captain, thus discarding Moses, their patient, suffering leader; and they murmured bitterly against God. (1SP 290.1)

Moses and Aaron fell upon their faces before the Lord in the presence of all the assembly of the congregation, to implore the mercy of God in favor of a rebellious people. But their distress and grief were too great for utterance. They remained upon their faces in utter silence. Caleb and Joshua rent their clothes, as an expression of the greatest sorrow. "And they

Chapter 25 - Caleb and Joshua (1SP 290.2)

spake unto all the company of the children of Israel, saying, The land, which we passed through to search it, is an exceeding good land. If the Lord delight in us, then he will bring us into this land, and give it us; a land which floweth with milk and honey. Only rebel not ye against the Lord, neither fear ye the people of the land; for they are bread for us. Their defense is departed from them, and the Lord is with us. Fear them not." (1SP 290.2)

"Their defense is departed from them." That is, the Canaanites had filled up the measure of their iniquity, and the divine protection was withdrawn from them, and they felt perfectly secure, and were unprepared for battle; and, by the covenant of God, the land is insured to us. Instead of these words having the designed effect upon the people, they increased their determined rebellion. They became in a rage, and cried out with a loud and angry cry, that Caleb and Joshua should be stoned, which would have been done, had not the Lord interposed by a most signal display of his terrible glory in the tabernacle of the congregation, before all the children of Israel. (1SP 291.1)

Moses went into the tabernacle to converse with God. "And the Lord said unto Moses, How long will this people provoke me? and how long will it be ere they believe me, for all the signs which I have showed among them? I will smite them with a pestilence, and disinherit them, and will make of thee a greater nation and mightier than they. And Moses said unto the Lord, Then the Egyptians shall hear it, (for thou broughtest up this people in thy might from among them;) and they will tell it to the inhabitants of this land; for they have heard that thou, Lord, art among this people, that thou, Lord, art seen face to face, and that thy cloud standeth over them, and that thou goest before them, by daytime in a pillar of cloud, and in a pillar of fire by night. Now, if thou shalt kill all this people as one man, then the nations which have heard the fame of thee will speak, saying, Because the Lord was not able to bring this people into the land which he sware unto them, therefore he hath slain them in the wilderness." (1SP 291.2)

Moses again refuses to have Israel destroyed, and himself made a mightier nation than was Israel. This favored servant of God manifests his love for Israel, and shows his zeal for the glory of his Maker and the honor of his people: As thou hast forgiven this people from Egypt even until now, thou hast been long-suffering and merciful hitherto toward this ungrateful people, however unworthy they may be, thy mercy is the same. He pleads, Wilt thou not, therefore, spare them this once, and add this one more instance of divine patience to the many thou hast already given? (1SP 292.1)

"And the Lord said, I have pardoned according to thy word. But as truly as I live, all the earth shall be filled with the glory of the Lord. Because all those men which have seen my glory, and my miracles, which I did in Egypt and in the wilderness, and have tempted me now these ten times, and have not hearkened to my voice; surely they shall not see the land which I sware unto their fathers, neither shall any of them that provoked me see it. But my servant Caleb, because he had another spirit with him, and hath followed me fully, him will I bring into the land whereinto he went; and his seed shall possess it." (1SP 292.2)

The Lord bade the Hebrews return, and go into the wilderness by the way of the Red Sea. They were very near the good land; but, by their wicked rebellion, they forfeited the protection of God. Had they received the report of Caleb and Joshua, and gone immediately up, God would have given them the land of Canaan. But they were unbelieving, and showed such an insolent spirit against God, that they brought upon themselves the denunciation, that they should never enter the promised land. It was in pity and mercy that God sent them back by the Red Sea, for the Amalekites and Canaanites, while they were delaying and murmuring, heard of the spies, and prepared themselves to make war with the children of Israel. (1SP 293.1)

"And the Lord spake unto Moses and unto Aaron, saying, How long shall I bear with this evil congregation, which murmur against me? I have heard the murmurings of the children of Israel, which they murmur against me." The Lord told Moses and Aaron to say to the people that he would do to them as they had spoken. They had said, "Would God that we had died in the land of Egypt! or would God we had died in this wilderness." Now God will take them at their word. He tells his servants to say to them that they should fall in the wilderness, from twenty years old and upward, because of their rebellion and murmurings against the Lord. Only Caleb and Joshua should go unto the land of Canaan. "But your little ones, which ye said should be a prey, them will I bring in, and they shall know the land which ye have despised." (**1SP 293.2**)

The Lord declared that the children of the Hebrews should wander in the wilderness forty years, reckoning from the time they left Egypt, because of the rebellion of their parents, until their parents should all die. Thus should they bear and suffer the consequence of their iniquity forty years, according to the number of days they were searching the land, a day for a year. "And ye shall know my breach of promise." They should fully realize that it was the punishment for their idolatry, and rebellious murmurings, which had obliged the Lord to change his purpose concerning them. Caleb and Joshua were promised a reward in preference to all the host of Israel, because the latter had forfeited all claim to God's favor and protection. (**1SP 294.1**)

The Lord sent fire from his presence and consumed the men who had brought the evil report, which made all the congregation murmur against Moses and against the Lord. But Caleb and Joshua lived before the Lord, and before the people, which evidenced to them that their report was correct. (**1SP 294.2**)

When the people learned from Moses the purpose of God concerning them, they mourned greatly. Early the next morning they gathered themselves before Moses, all equipped for war, and said, We be here, and will go unto the place the Lord hath promised; for we have sinned. The Lord had said that they should not possess the land, but should die in the wilderness; and if they should go up to battle, they would not prosper. Moses said, "Go not up, for the Lord is not among you; that ye be not smitten before your enemies; for the Amalekites and the Canaanites are there before you, and ye shall fall by the sword; because ye are turned away from the Lord, therefore the Lord will not be with you." But they ventured to go out against their enemies without their appointed leader, and without the ark of the covenant of the Lord; and they were met by their enemies, and smitten, and driven before them. Here the Israelites repented too late; and when God had said they should not go up to possess the land, they were as forward to go, as they had been backward before. (**1SP 294.3**)

Notwithstanding the recent murmurings of the Israelites, and the declaration from God that they should die in the wilderness, they did not walk carefully and humbly before him. (**1SP 295.1**)

The Lord had made the case of Miriam a special example of warning to the Israelites. They had seen exhibited upon her the wrath of God because of her jealousy and complaints against his chosen servant Moses. The Lord then told them that Moses was greater than a prophet, and that he had revealed himself to Moses in a more direct manner than to a prophet. Said the Lord, "With him will I speak mouth to mouth." He then inquired of them, "Wherefore then were ye not afraid to speak against my servant Moses?" And Miriam became leprous. The instructions given in this instance to Aaron and Miriam were not intended alone for their benefit, but for the good of all the congregation of Israel. (**1SP 295.2**)

Chapter 26
Korah, Dathan, and Abiram

The Lord knew that Korah was rebellious at heart, and was secretly at work against Moses in the congregation of Israel, although his rebellion had not yet developed itself. The Lord made an example of Miriam, as a warning to all who might be tempted to rebel against Moses. Korah was not satisfied with his position. He was connected with the service of the tabernacle, yet he desired to be exalted to the priesthood. God had established Moses as chief governor, and the priesthood was given to Aaron and his sons. Korah determined to compel Moses to change the order of things, whereby he should be raised to the dignity of the priesthood. To be more sure of accomplishing his purpose, he drew Dathan and Abiram, the descendants of Reuben, into his rebellion. (1SP 296.1)

They reasoned that, being descendants from the eldest sons of Jacob, the chief authority, which Moses usurped, belonged to them; and, with Korah, they were resolved to obtain the office of the priesthood. These three became very zealous in an evil work. They influenced two hundred and fifty men of renown to join them, who were also determined to have a share in the priesthood and government. God had honored the Levites to do service in the tabernacle, because they took no part in making and worshiping the golden calf, and because of their faithfulness in executing the order of God upon the idolaters. (1SP 296.2)

To the Levites was assigned the office of erecting the tabernacle, and encamping around about it, while the hosts of Israel pitched their tents at a distance from the tabernacle. And when they journeyed, the Levites took down the tabernacle, and bore it, and the ark, and the candlestick, and the other sacred articles of furniture. Because God thus honored the Levites, they became ambitious for still higher office, that they might obtain greater influence with the congregation. "And they gathered themselves together against Moses and against Aaron, and said unto them, Ye take too much upon you, seeing all the congregation are holy, every one of them, and the Lord is among them. Wherefore, then, lift ye up yourselves above the congregation of the Lord?" (1SP 296.3)

Korah, Dathan and Abiram, and two hundred and fifty princes who had joined them, first became jealous, then envious, and next rebellious. They had talked in regard to Moses' position as ruler of the people, until they imagined that it was a very enviable position, which any of them could fill as well as Moses. And they gave themselves up to discontent, until they really deceived themselves, and one another, in thinking that Moses and Aaron had placed themselves in the position which they occupied to Israel. They said that Moses and Aaron exalted themselves above the congregation of the Lord, in taking upon them the priesthood and government, and that this office should not be conferred on their house alone. They said that it was sufficient for them if they were on a level with their brethren; for they were no more holy than the people, who were equally favored with God's peculiar presence and protection. (1SP 297.1)

As Moses listened to the words of Korah, he was filled with anguish, and fell upon his face before the people. "And he spake unto Korah and unto all his company, saying, Even tomorrow the Lord will show who are his, and who is holy; and will cause him to come near unto him; even him whom he hath chosen will he cause to come near unto him. This do: Take you censers, Korah, and all his company; and put fire therein, and put incense in them before the Lord tomorrow; and it shall be that the man whom the Lord doth choose, he shall be holy. Ye take too much upon you, ye sons of Levi. And Moses said unto Korah, Hear, I pray you, ye sons of Levi: Seemeth it but a small thing unto you, that the God of Israel hath separated you from the congregation of Israel, to bring you near to himself to do the service of the tabernacle of the Lord, and to stand before the congregation to minister unto them? And he hath brought thee near to him, and all thy brethren the sons of Levi with thee; and seek ye the priesthood also? for which cause both thou and all thy company are gathered together against the Lord. And what is Aaron, that ye murmur against him?" Moses told them that Aaron had assumed no office of himself; that God had placed him in the sacred office. (1SP 297.2)

Dathan and Abiram said, "Is it a small thing that thou hast brought us up out of a land that floweth with milk and honey, to kill us in the wilderness, except thou make thyself altogether a prince over us? Moreover, thou hast not brought us into a land that floweth with milk and honey, or given us inheritance of fields and vineyards. Wilt thou put out the eyes of these men? We will not come up." (1SP 298.1)

They accused Moses of being the cause of their not entering the promised land. They said that God had not dealt with them thus. He had not said that they should die in the wilderness. They would never believe that he had thus said; but that it was Moses who had said this, not the Lord; and that it was all arranged by Moses to never bring them to the land of Canaan. They spoke of his leading them from a land that flowed with milk and honey. They forgot, in their blind rebellion, their sufferings in the land of Egypt, and the desolating plagues brought upon that land. But they now accuse Moses of bringing them from a good land, to kill them in the wilderness, that he might be made rich with their possessions. They inquired of Moses, in an insolent manner, if he thought that none of all the host of Israel were wise enough to understand his motives, and discover his imposture; or if he thought they would all submit to have him lead them about like blind men, as he pleased, sometimes toward Canaan, then back again toward the Red Sea and Egypt. These words they spoke before the congregation, and utterly refused to any longer acknowledge the authority of Moses and Aaron. (1SP 298.2)

Moses was greatly moved at these unjust accusations. He appealed to God before the people whether he had ever acted arbitrarily, and implored him to be his judge. The people in general were disaffected, and influenced by the misrepresentation of Korah. "And Moses said unto Korah, Be thou and all thy company before the Lord, thou, and they, and Aaron, tomorrow; and take every man his censer, and put incense in them, and bring ye before the Lord every man his censer, two hundred and fifty censers, thou also, and Aaron, each of you his censer. And they took every man his censer, and put fire in them, and laid incense thereon, and stood in the door of the tabernacle of the congregation with Moses and Aaron." (1SP 299.1)

Korah and his company, who aspired to the priesthood in their self-confidence, even took the censers and stood in the door of the tabernacle with Moses. Korah had cherished his envy and rebellion until he was self-deceived, and he really thought that the congregation was a very righteous people, and that Moses was a tyrannical ruler, continually dwelling upon the necessity of the congregation's being holy, when there was no need of it, for they were holy. (1SP 300.1)

These rebellious ones had flattered the people in general to believe that they were right, and that all their troubles arose from Moses, their ruler, who was continually reminding them of their sins. The people thought that if Korah could lead them, and encourage them, and dwell upon their righteous acts, instead of reminding them of their failures, they should have a very peaceful, prosperous journey, and he would without doubt lead them, not back and forward in the wilderness, but into the promised land. They said that it was Moses who had told them that they could not go into the land, and that the Lord had not thus said. (1SP 300.2)

Korah, in his exalted self-confidence, gathered all the congregation against Moses and Aaron, "unto the door of the tabernacle of the congregation. And the glory of the Lord appeared unto all the congregation. And the Lord spake unto Moses and unto Aaron, saying, Separate yourselves from among this congregation, that I may consume them in a moment. And they fell upon their faces, and said, O God, the God of the spirits of all flesh, shall one man sin, and wilt thou be wroth with all the congregation? And the Lord spake unto Moses, saying, Speak unto the congregation, saying, Get you up from about the tabernacle of Korah, Dathan, and Abiram. And Moses rose up and went unto Dathan and Abiram, and the elders of Israel followed him. And he spake unto the congregation, saying, Depart, I pray you, from the tents of these wicked men, and touch nothing

Chapter 26 - Korah, Dathan, and Abiram (1SP 300.3)

of theirs, lest ye be consumed in all their sins. So they gat up from the tabernacle of Korah, Dathan, and Abiram, on every side; and Dathan and Abiram came out, and stood in the door of their tents, and their wives, and their sons, and their little children. And Moses said, Hereby ye shall know that the Lord hath sent me to do all these works; for I have not done them of mine own mind. If these men die the common death of all men, or if they be visited after the visitation of all men, then the Lord hath not sent me. But if the Lord make a new thing, and the earth open her mouth, and swallow them up, with all that appertain unto them, and they go down quick into the pit, then ye shall understand that these men have provoked the Lord." As Moses ceased speaking, the earth opened and swallowed them up, and their tents, and all that pertained unto them. They went down alive into the pit, and the earth closed over them, and they perished from among the congregation. (1SP 300.3)

As the children of Israel heard the cry of the perishing ones, they fled at a great distance from them. They knew that they were, in a measure, guilty; for they had received the accusations against Moses and Aaron; and they were afraid that they should also perish with them. The judgment of God was not yet finished. A fire came from the cloud of glory, and consumed the two hundred and fifty men that offered incense. They were princes; that is, men generally of good judgment, and of influence in the congregation, men of renown. They were highly esteemed, and their judgment had often been sought in difficult matters. But they were affected by a wrong influence, and became envious, jealous, and rebellious. They perished not with Korah, Dathan, and Abiram, because they were not the first in rebellion. They were to see their end first, and have an opportunity of repenting of their crime. But they were not reconciled to the destruction of those wicked men; and the wrath of God came upon them, and destroyed them also. (1SP 301.1)

"And the Lord spake unto Moses, saying, Speak unto Eleazar, the son of Aaron the priest, that he take up the censers out of the burning, and scatter thou the fire yonder; for they are hallowed. The censers of these sinners against their own souls, let them make them broad plates for a covering of the altar; for they offered them before the Lord, therefore they are hallowed; and they shall be a sign unto the children of Israel."

After this exhibition of God's judgment, the people returned to their tents, but not humbled. They were terrified. They had been deeply influenced by the spirit of rebellion, and had been flattered by Korah and his company to believe that they were a very good people, and that they had been wronged and abused by Moses. They had their minds so thoroughly imbued with the spirit of those who had perished, that it was difficult to free themselves of their blind prejudice. If they should admit that Korah and his company were all wicked, and Moses righteous, then they would be compelled to receive as the word of God, that which they were unwilling to believe, that they should certainly all die in the wilderness. They were not willing to submit to this, and tried to believe that it was all imposture, and that Moses had deceived them. The men who had perished had spoken pleasant words to them, and manifested especial interest and love for them; and they thought Moses a designing man. They decided that they could not be wrong; that, after all, those men who had perished were good men, and Moses had by some means been the cause of their destruction. (1SP 302.1)

Satan can lead deceived souls to great lengths. He can pervert their judgment, their sight, and their hearing. It was so in the case of the Israelites. "But on the morrow all the congregation of the children of Israel murmured against Moses and against Aaron, saying, Ye have killed the people of the Lord." The people were disappointed in the matter's resulting as it did in favor of Moses and Aaron. The appearance of Korah and his company, all impiously exercising the priests' office with their censers, struck the people with admiration. They did not see that these men were offering a daring affront to the divine Majesty. When they were destroyed, the people were terrified; but after a short time, all came in a tumultuous manner to Moses and Aaron, and charged them with the blood of those men who had perished by the hand of God. (1SP 303.1)

"And it came to pass when the congregation was gathered against Moses and against Aaron, that they looked toward the tabernacle of the congregation; and, behold, the cloud covered it, and the glory of the Lord appeared. And Moses and Aaron came before the tabernacle of the congregation. And the Lord spake unto Moses, saying, Get you up from among this congregation, that I may consume them as in a moment. And they fell upon their faces." Notwithstanding the rebellion of Israel, and their cruel conduct to Moses, yet he manifested for them the same interest as before. He fell upon his face before the Lord, and implored him to spare the people. While Moses was praying before the Lord to pardon the sin of his people, he requested Aaron to make an atonement for their sin, while he remained before the Lord, that his prayers might ascend with the incense, and be acceptable to God, that all the congregation might not perish in their rebellion. "And Moses said unto Aaron, Take a censer, and put fire therein from off the altar, and put on incense, and go quickly unto the congregation, and make an atonement for them; for there is wrath gone out from the Lord. The plague is begun. And Aaron took as Moses commanded, and ran into the midst of the congregation; and, behold, the plague was begun among the people. And he put on incense, and made an atonement for the people. And he stood between the dead and the living; and the plague was stayed. Now they that died in the plague were fourteen thousand and seven hundred, besides them that died about the matter of Korah. And Aaron returned unto Moses unto the door of the tabernacle of the congregation, and the plague was stayed." (1SP 303.2)

Chapter 27
Aaron's Rod

God mercifully condescended to give the host of Israel another evidence, one calculated to correct their perverted judgment. He therefore required that each tribe should take a rod, and write upon the rod the name of the house of their fathers. "And thou shalt write Aaron's name upon the rod of Levi; for one rod shall be for the head of the house of their fathers. And thou shalt lay them up in the tabernacle of the congregation before the testimony, where I will meet with you. And it shall come to pass, that the man's rod whom I shall choose shall blossom. And I will make to cease from me the murmurings of the children of Israel, whereby they murmur against you." "And Moses laid up the rods before the Lord in the tabernacle of witness. And it came to pass, that on the morrow Moses went into the tabernacle of witness; and, behold, the rod of Aaron for the house of Levi was budded, and brought forth buds, and bloomed blossoms, and yielded almonds. And Moses brought out all the rods from before the Lord unto all the children of Israel; and they looked, and took every man his rod. And the Lord said unto Moses, Bring Aaron's rod again before the testimony, to be kept for a token against the rebels; and thou shalt quite take away their murmurings from me, that they die not." God here wrought a miracle which was sufficient to silence the complaints of the Israelites, and which was to be a standing testimony that God had settled the priesthood upon Aaron. All the remarkable changes in the rod occurred in one night, to convince them that God had positively distinguished between Aaron and the rest of the children of Israel. After this miracle of divine power, the authority of the priesthood was no longer called in question. This wonderful rod was preserved to be frequently shown to the people, to remind them of the past, to prevent them from murmuring, and again calling in question to whom the priesthood rightfully belonged. (1SP 305.1)

After the children of Israel were fully convinced of their wrong, in unjustly accusing Moses and Aaron as they had done, they saw their past rebellion in its true light, and they were terrified. They "spake unto Moses, saying, Behold we die, we perish; we all perish." They are at length compelled to believe the unwelcome truth that their fate is to die in the wilderness. After they believed that it was indeed the Lord who had said that they should not enter the promised land, but should die, they then acknowledged that Moses and Aaron were right, and that they had sinned against the Lord, in rebelling against their authority. They also confessed that Korah, and those who perished with him, were sinners against the Lord, and that they had justly suffered his wrath. (1SP 306.1)

The facts relative to Korah and his company, who rebelled against Moses and Aaron, and against Jehovah, are recorded for a warning to God's people, especially those who live upon the earth near the close of time. Satan has led persons to imitate the example of Korah, Dathan, and Abiram, in raising insurrection among the people of God. Those who permit themselves to rise in opposition to the plain testimony, become self-deceived. Such have really thought that those upon whom God has laid the burden of his work were exalted above the people of God, and that their counsels and reproofs were uncalled for. They have risen in opposition to the plain testimony which God would have his servants bear in rebuking the wrongs among God's people. The testimonies borne against hurtful indulgences, as tea, coffee, snuff and tobacco, have irritated a certain class, because it would destroy their idols. Many for awhile were undecided whether to make an entire sacrifice of all these hurtful things, or reject the plain testimonies borne, and yield to the clamors of appetite. They occupied an unsettled position. There was a conflict between their convictions of truth and their self-indulgences. Their state of indecision made them weak, and, with many, appetite prevailed. Their sense of sacred things was perverted by the use of these slow poisons;

Chapter 27 - Aaron's Rod (1SP 308.1)

and they at length fully decided, let the consequence be what it might, that they would not deny self. This fearful decision at once raised a wall of separation between them and those who were cleansing themselves, as God has commanded, from all filthiness of the flesh, and of the spirit, and were perfecting holiness in the fear of the Lord. The straight testimonies borne were in their way, and caused them great uneasiness; and they found relief in warring against them, and striving to make themselves and others believe that they were untrue. They said that the people were all right, but it was the reproving testimonies which made the trouble. And when the rebellious unfurl their banner, all the disaffected rally around the standard, and all the spiritually defective, the lame, the halt, and the blind, unite their influence to scatter, and to sow discord. **(1SP 306.2)**

Every advance of God's servants at the head of the work has been watched with suspicion by those who have had a spirit of insurrection, and all their actions have been misrepresented by the fault-finding, until honest souls have been drawn into the snare for want of correct knowledge. Those who lead them astray are so affected themselves by blind prejudice, and by rejecting the testimonies God has sent them, that they cannot see or hear aright. It is as difficult to undeceive some of these who have permitted themselves to be led into rebellion, as it was to convince the rebellious Israelites that they were wrong, and that Moses and Aaron were right. Even after God, in a miraculous manner, caused the earth to swallow up Korah, Dathan, and Abiram, the leaders in the rebellion, the people still would have it that Moses and Aaron were wrong, and that they had killed the people of the Lord. The Hebrews were not cured of their rebellion until fourteen thousand and seven hundred of the people who had joined the rebellious had been slain. And then, after all this, God in mercy condescended to perform a remarkable miracle upon the rod of Aaron, to settle their minds forever in regard to the priesthood. **(1SP 308.1)**

Chapter 28
The Sin of Moses

Again the congregation of Israel was brought into the wilderness, to the very place where God proved them soon after their leaving Egypt. The Lord brought them water out of the rock, which had continued to flow until just before they came again to the rock, when the Lord caused that living stream to cease, to prove his people again, to see if they would endure the trial of their faith, or would again murmur against him. (1SP 309.1)

When the Hebrews were thirsty, and could find no water, they became impatient, and did not remember the power of God which had, nearly forty years before, brought them water out of the rock. Instead of trusting in God, they complained of Moses and Aaron, and said to them, "Would God that we had died when our brethren died before the Lord!" that is, they wished that they had been of that number who had been destroyed by the plague in the rebellion of Korah, Dathan, and Abiram. (1SP 309.2)

They angrily inquired, "Why have ye brought up the congregation of the Lord into this wilderness, that we and our cattle should die there? And wherefore have ye made us to come up out of Egypt, to bring us in unto this evil place? it is no place of seed, or of figs, or of vines, or of pomegranates; neither is there any water to drink. And Moses and Aaron went from the presence of the assembly unto the door of the tabernacle of the congregation, and they fell upon their faces; and the glory of the Lord appeared unto them. And the Lord spake unto Moses, saying, Take the rod, and gather thou the assembly together, thou and Aaron thy brother, and speak ye unto the rock before their eyes; and it shall give forth his water, and thou shalt bring forth to them water out of the rock. So thou shalt give the congregation and their beasts drink. And Moses took the rod from before the Lord, as he commanded him. And Moses and Aaron gathered the congregation together before the rock; and he said unto them, Hear, now, ye rebels; must we fetch you water out of this rock? And Moses lifted up his hand, and with his rod he smote the rock twice; and the water came out abundantly; and the congregation drank, and their beasts also. And the Lord spake unto Moses and Aaron, Because ye believed me not, to sanctify me in the eyes of the children of Israel, therefore ye shall not bring this congregation into the land which I have given them." (1SP 309.3)

Here Moses sinned. He became wearied with the continual murmurings of the people against him, and at the commandment of the Lord, took the rod, and, instead of speaking to the rock, as God commanded him, he smote it with the rod twice, after saying, "Must we fetch you water out of this rock?" He here spoke unadvisedly with his lips. He did not say, God will now show you another evidence of his power, and bring you water out of this rock. He did not ascribe the power and glory to God for causing water to again flow from the flinty rock, and therefore did not magnify him before the people. For this failure on the part of Moses, God would not permit him to lead the people to the promised land. (1SP 310.1)

This necessity for the manifestation of God's power made the occasion one of great solemnity; and Moses and Aaron should have improved it to make a favorable impression upon the people. But Moses was stirred; and in impatience and anger with the people because of their murmurings, he said, "Hear, now, ye rebels; must we fetch you water out of this rock?" In thus speaking, he virtually admitted to murmuring Israel that they were correct in charging him with leading them from Egypt. God had forgiven the people greater transgressions than this error upon the part of Moses; but he could not regard a sin in a leader of his people as in those who were led. He could not excuse the sin of Moses, and permit him to enter the promised land. (1SP 310.2)

Chapter 28 - The Sin of Moses (1SP 314.1)

The Lord here gave his people unmistakable proof that he who had wrought such a wonderful deliverance for them in bringing them from Egyptian bondage, was the mighty Angel, and not Moses, who was going before them in all their travels, and of whom he had said, "Behold, I send an Angel before thee, to keep thee in the way, and to bring thee into the place which I have prepared. Beware of him, and obey his voice; provoke him not; for he will not pardon your transgressions; for my name is in him." Moses took glory to himself which belonged to God, and made it necessary for God to do that in his case which should forever satisfy rebellious Israel that it was not Moses who has led them from Egypt, but God himself. The Lord had committed to Moses the burden of leading his people, while the mighty Angel went before them in all their journeyings, and directed all their travels. Because they were so ready to forget that God was leading them by his Angel, and to ascribe to man that which God's power alone could perform, he had proved them, and tested them, to see whether they would obey him. At every trial they failed. Instead of believing in, and acknowledging, God, who had strown their path with evidences of his power, and signal tokens of his care and love, they distrusted him, and ascribed their leaving Egypt to Moses, charging him as the cause of all their disasters. Moses had borne with their stubbornness with remarkable forbearance. At one time they threatened to stone him. (1SP 311.1)

The Lord would remove this impression forever from their minds, by forbidding Moses to enter the promised land. The Lord had highly exalted Moses. He had revealed to him his great glory. He had taken him into a sacred nearness with himself upon the mount, and had condescended to talk with him as a man speaketh with a friend. He had communicated to Moses, and through him to the people, his will, his statutes and his laws. His being thus exalted and honored of God made his error of greater magnitude. Moses repented of his sin, and humbled himself greatly before God. He related to all Israel his sorrow for his sin. The result of his sin he did not conceal, but told them that for thus failing to ascribe glory to God, he could not lead them to the promised land. He then asked them, if this error upon his part was so great as to be thus corrected of God, how God would regard their repeated murmurings in charging him (Moses) with the uncommon visitations of God because of their sins. (1SP 312.1)

For this single instance, Moses had allowed the impression to be entertained that he had brought them water out of the rock, when he should have magnified the name of the Lord among his people. The Lord would now settle the matter with his people, that Moses was merely a man, following the guidance and direction of a mightier than he, even the Son of God. In this he would leave them without doubt. Where much is given, much is required. Moses had been highly favored with special views of God's majesty. The light and glory of God had been imparted to him in rich abundance. His face had reflected upon the people the glory that the Lord had let shine upon him. All will be judged according to the privileges they have had, and the light and benefits bestowed. (1SP 312.2)

The sins of good men, whose general deportment has been worthy of imitation, are peculiarly offensive to God. They cause Satan to triumph, and to taunt the angels of God with the failings of God's chosen instruments, and give the unrighteous occasion to lift themselves up against God. The Lord had himself led Moses in a special manner, and had revealed to him his glory, as to no other upon the earth. He was naturally impatient, but had taken hold firmly of the grace of God, and so humbly implored wisdom from Heaven, that he was strengthened from God, and had overcome his impatience so that he was called of God the meekest man upon the face of the whole earth. (1SP 313.1)

Aaron died at Mount Hor; for the Lord had said that he should not enter the promised land; because, with Moses, he had sinned at the time of bringing water from the rock at Meribah. Moses and the sons of Aaron buried him in the mount, that the people might not be tempted to make too great ceremony over his body, and be guilty of the sin of idolatry. (1SP 313.2)

The Canaanites made war with Israel, and took some of them prisoners; and the host of the Israelites besought the Lord to go with them to battle against the Canaanites, and deliver them into their hands, and they would utterly destroy their cities, and would be faithful in following God. He heard their prayer, and went out with their armies to battle, and the Israelites overcame their enemies, and utterly destroyed them and their cities. (1SP 314.1)

*****

Chapter 29
Fiery Serpents

As the people journeyed from Hor by the way of the Red Sea, to compass the land of Edom, they were much discouraged, and complained of the hardships of the way. "And the people spake against God, and against Moses, Wherefore have ye brought us up out of Egypt to die in the wilderness? for there is no bread, neither is there any water; and our soul loatheth this light bread. And the Lord sent fiery serpents among the people, and they bit the people; and much people of Israel died. Therefore the people came to Moses, and said, We have sinned; for we have spoken against the Lord, and against thee; pray unto the Lord, that he take away the serpents from us. And Moses prayed for the people. And the Lord said unto Moses, Make thee a fiery serpent, and set it upon a pole; and it shall come to pass, that every one that is bitten, when he looketh upon it, shall live. And Moses made a serpent of brass, and put it upon a pole; and it came to pass, that if a serpent had bitten any man, when he beheld the serpent of brass, he lived." (1SP 314.2)

The murmurings of the children of Israel were unreasonable; and the unreasonable always go to extremes. They uttered falsehoods in saying that they had no bread nor water. They had both given them by a miracle of God's mercy. To punish them for their ingratitude, and complaining against God, the Lord permitted fiery serpents to bite them. They were called fiery, because their bite produced painful inflammation and speedy death. The Israelites, up to this time, had been preserved from these serpents in the wilderness by a continual miracle; for the wilderness through which they traveled was infested with poisonous serpents. (1SP 315.1)

Moses told the people that God had hitherto preserved them, that they had not been harmed by the serpents, which was a token of his care for them. He told them it was because of their needless murmurings, complaining of the hardships in their journey, that God had permitted them to be bitten of serpents. This was to show them that God had preserved them from many and great evils, which if he had permitted to come upon them, they would have suffered that which they could call hardships. But God had prepared the way before them. There was no sickness among them. Their feet had not swollen in all their journeys, neither had their clothes waxed old. God had given them angels' food, and purest water out of the flinty rock. And with all these tokens of his love, if they complained, he would send his judgments upon them for their ingratitude, and make them to realize his past merciful care for them, of which they had been unmindful. (1SP 315.2)

The Israelites were terrified and humbled because of the serpents, and confessed their sin in murmuring. Moses was directed to erect the brazen serpent upon a pole, and if those who were bitten looked upon that, they should be healed. (1SP 316.1)

Here the Israelites were required to do something. They must look upon the brazen serpent if they would live. Many had died by the bite of the serpents. When Moses raised the serpent upon the pole, some had no faith that merely looking at that would heal them, and they died. Mothers, fathers, brothers and sisters, were all anxiously engaged in helping their suffering, dying relatives and friends, to fix their languid eyes upon the serpent. If they could only once look while fainting and dying, they revived, and were healed of all the effects of their poisonous wounds. There was no virtue in the serpent of brass to cause such a change immediately in those who looked upon it. The healing virtue received by their looking upon the serpent was derived from God alone. He chose, in his wisdom, this manner to display his power. It was the faith of the people in the provision made, which was acceptable to God. By this simple means, the people were made sensible that God

Chapter 29 - Fiery Serpents (1SP 316.2)

had permitted these serpents to afflict them because of their murmurings and lack of faith in him. If they would obey God, they had no reason to fear; for he would be their friend, and preserve them from dangers to which they were continually exposed in the wilderness. (1SP 316.2)

The Hebrews in their affliction could not save themselves from the effect of the fiery serpents. God alone could save sinful, rebellious Israel, by his infinite power; yet, in his wisdom, he did not see fit to pardon their transgressions without testing their repentance and faith. They were required, by an act of their own, to show their penitence, and faith in the provision that God had made for their recovery. They, on their part, must act. They must look, in order to live. The act of looking showed their faith in the Son of God, whom the serpent represented. The lifting up of the brazen serpent was to teach Israel a lesson. They had presented their offerings to God, and felt that in thus doing they had made ample atonement for their sins. They did not, by faith, rely upon the merits of the Redeemer to come, of which their offerings were only the type. The serpent, made of brass to resemble the fiery serpent, was to be placed in the midst of the camp, lifted upon a pole. This was to show to Israel that their offerings, of themselves, had no more saving virtue or power than the serpent of brass, which was to revive in their minds the future sacrifice of the Son of God. So, also, their offerings were to be brought with subdued wills and penitent hearts, they having faith in the meritorious offering of God's dear Son. None were compelled to look upon the brazen serpent. All could look and live, or disbelieve the simple provision God had made, refuse to look, and die. (1SP 316.3)

The requirements of God may not always be appreciated by his people, and many are unable to understand the dealings of God with them; yet it is not their part to question the purposes of God, but to yield submissive obedience; for God has a purpose in all his requirements, which we may not fully see here, but shall see hereafter. (1SP 317.1)

Israel had been preserved by a miracle of God's mercy during every day of their travels in the wilderness. The mighty Angel who went before them was the Son of God. He evened their path, so that their feet did not swell. It was the Majesty of Heaven who subdued and restrained the strong and dangerous beasts of the forest, as well as the poisonous serpents that infested the wilderness. The children of Israel did not realize the thousand dangers they were preserved from in their travels, because they were kept from them. They had hard hearts of unbelief, and were unreconciled to be guided and controlled by God. They imagined evils. They dwelt upon the dangers which threatened them, although they experienced them not. The Lord permitted the serpents to distress them, that they might realize how much they might have suffered if God had not mercifully encompassed them, and preserved them from affliction and death. The Lord had just given them a wonderful victory over their enemies, in answer to prayer. The Lord proved them, to see if they would look to him, and trust in him, if brought into strait places. But they did not stand the test; they complained of God, and of Moses' killing them with hunger. The Lord punished them, by permitting the death they had complained of to come upon them. (1SP 318.1)

The brazen serpent, lifted upon a pole, illustrates the Son of God, who was to die upon the cross. The people who are suffering from the effects of sin can find hope and salvation alone in the provision God has made. As the Israelites saved their lives by looking upon the brazen serpent, so sinners can look to Christ and live. Unlike the brazen serpent, he has virtue and power in himself to heal the suffering, repenting, believing sinner. Christ says of himself, "And as Moses lifted up the serpent in the wilderness, even so must the Son of man be lifted up; that whosoever believeth in him should not perish, but have eternal life." (1SP 318.2)

*****

Chapter 30
Balaam

The Israelites moved forward, and pitched in the plains of Moab, on this side of Jordan, by Jericho. Balak, the king of the Moabites, saw that the Israelites were a powerful people; and as they learned that they had destroyed the Amorites, and had taken possession of their land, they were exceedingly terrified. All Moab was in trouble. "And Moab said unto the elders of Midian, Now shall this company lick up all that are round about us, as the ox licketh up the grass of the field. And Balak, the son of Zippor, was king of the Moabites at that time. He sent messengers, therefore, unto Balaam, the son of Beor, to Pethor, which is by the river of the land of the children of his people, to call him, saying, Behold, there is a people come out from Egypt; behold, they cover the face of the earth, and they abide over against me. Come now, therefore, I pray thee, curse me this people; for they are too mighty for me; peradventure I shall prevail, that we may smite them, and that I may drive them out of the land; for I wot that he whom thou blessest is blessed, and he whom thou cursest is cursed." **(1SP 319.1)**

Balaam had been a prophet of God, and a good man; but he apostatized, and gave himself up to covetousness, so that he loved the wages of unrighteousness. At the time Balak sent messengers for him, he was double-minded, pursuing a course to gain and retain the favor and honor of the enemies of the Lord, for the sake of rewards that he received from them. At the same time, he was professing to be a prophet of God. Idolatrous nations believed that curses might be uttered which would affect individuals, and even whole nations. As the messengers related their errand to Balaam, he very well knew what answer to give them; but he asked them to tarry that night, and he would bring them word as the Lord should speak unto him. The presents in the hands of the men excited his covetous disposition. God came to Balaam in the night, through one of his angels, and inquired of him, What men are these with thee? "And Balaam said unto God, Balak, the son of Zippor, king of Moab, hath sent unto me, saying, Behold, there is a people come out of Egypt, which covereth the face of the earth. Come, now, curse me them; peradventure I shall be able to overcome them, and drive them out. And God said unto Balaam, Thou shalt not go with them. Thou shalt not curse the people; for they are blessed." The angel tells Balaam that the children of Israel are conducted under the banner of the God of Heaven, and that no curse from man could retard their progress. In the morning, he arose and reluctantly told the men to return to Balak, for the Lord would not suffer him to go with them. Then Balak sent other princes, more of them in number, and more honorable, or occupying a more exalted position than the former messengers; and this time Balak's call was more urgent: "Let nothing, I pray thee, hinder thee from coming unto me; for I will promote thee unto very great honor, and I will do whatsoever thou sayest unto me. Come, therefore, I pray thee, curse me this people. And Balaam answered and said unto the servants of Balak, If Balak would give me his house full of silver and gold, I cannot go beyond the word of the Lord my God, to do less or more." **(1SP 320.1)**

His fear of God's power holds the ascendency over his covetous disposition; yet his course of conduct shows that his love of honor and gain was striving hard for the mastery, and he did not subdue it. He would have gratified his covetousness, if he had dared to do it. After God had said that he should not go, he was anxious to be granted the privilege of going. He urged them to remain that night, that he might make inquiry again of God. An angel was sent to Balaam to say unto him, "If the men come to call thee, rise up, and go with them; but yet the word which I shall say unto thee, that shalt thou do." The Lord suffered Balaam to follow his own inclinations, and try, if he choose so to do, to please both God and man. **(1SP 321.1)**

Chapter 30 - Balaam (1SP 321.2)

The messengers of Balak did not call upon him in the morning to have him go with them. They were annoyed with his delay, and expected a second refusal. Balaam could have excused himself, and easily avoided going; but he thought that because the Lord the second time did not forbid his going, he would go and overtake the ambassadors of Balak. The anger of the Lord was kindled against Balaam because he went; and he sent his angel to stand in the way, and to slay him for his presumptuous folly. The beast saw the angel of the Lord, and turned aside. Balaam was beside himself with rage. The speaking of the beast was unnoticed by him as anything remarkable, for he was blinded by passion. As the angel revealed himself to Balaam, he was terrified, and left his beast and bowed in humility before the angel. He related to Balaam the word of the Lord, and said, "I went out to withstand thee, because thy way is perverse before me." It was important to Israel to overcome the Moabites, in order to overcome the inhabitants of Canaan. After the angel had impressively warned Balaam against gratifying the Moabites, he gave him permission to pursue his journey. God would glorify his name, even through the presumptuous Balaam, before the enemies of Israel. This could not be done in a more effectual manner than by showing them that a man of Balaam's covetous disposition dared not, for any promises of promotion or rewards, pronounce a curse against Israel. (1SP 321.2)

Balak met Balaam, and inquired of him why he thus delayed to come when he sent for him; and told him that he had power to promote him to honor. Balaam answered, Lo, I am come unto thee. He then told him that he had no power to say anything. The word that God should give him, that could he speak, and could go no further. Balaam ordered the sacrifices according to the religious rites. God sent his angel to meet with Balaam, to give him words of utterance, as he had done on occasions when Balaam was wholly devoted to the service of God. "And the Lord put a word in Balaam's mouth, and said, Return unto Balak, and thus thou shalt speak. And he returned unto him, and, lo, he stood by his burnt sacrifice, he, and all the princes of Moab. And he took up his parable, and said, Balak, the king of Moab, hath brought me from Aram, out of the mountains of the east, saying, Come, curse me Jacob, and come, defy Israel. How shall I curse, whom God hath not cursed? or how shall I defy, whom the Lord hath not defied? For from the top of the rocks I see him, and from the hills I behold him. Lo, the people shall dwell alone, and shall not be reckoned among the nations. Who can count the dust of Jacob, and the number of the fourth part of Israel? Let me die the death of the righteous, and let my last end be like his!" (1SP 322.1)

Balaam spoke in a solemn, prophetic style. How shall I defy, or devote to destruction, those whom God hath promised to prosper? He declared in prophetic words that Israel should remain a distinct people; that they should not be united with, swallowed up by, or lost in, any other nation; that they would become far more numerous than they then were; and he related their prosperity and strength. He saw that the end of the righteous was truly desirable, and prophetically expressed his desire that his life might end like theirs. (1SP 323.1)

Balak was disappointed and angry. He exclaims, "What hast thou done unto me? I took thee to curse mine enemies, and, behold, thou hast blessed them altogether." Balak thinks it is the grand appearance of the Israelites in their tents, which Balaam views from a high mount, that keeps him from cursing them. He thinks if he takes him to another place, where Israel will not appear to such advantage, he can obtain a curse from Balaam. Again, at Zophim, at the top of Pisgah, Balaam offered burnt-offerings, and then went by himself to commune with the angel of God. And the angel told Balaam what to say. When he returned, Balak inquired anxiously, "What hath the Lord spoken?" "And he took up his parable, and said, Rise up, Balak, and hear; hearken unto me, thou son of Zippor: God is not a man, that he should lie; neither the son of man, that he should repent. Hath he said, and shall he not do it? or hath he spoken, and shall he not make it good? Behold, I have received commandment to bless; and he hath blessed, and I cannot reverse it. He hath not beheld iniquity in Jacob, neither hath he seen perverseness in Israel. The Lord his God is with him, and the shout of a king is among them. God brought them out of Egypt; he hath, as it were, the strength of a unicorn. Surely there is no enchantment against Jacob, neither is there any divination against Israel. According to this time it shall be said of Jacob and of Israel, What hath God wrought! Behold, the people shall rise up as a great lion, and lift up himself as a young lion.

Chapter 30 - Balaam (1SP 326.2)

He shall not lie down until he eat of the prey, and drink the blood of the slain." (1SP 323.2)

Balak still flattered himself with the vain hope that God was subject to variation, like man. Balaam informs him that God will never be induced to break his word, or alter his purpose concerning Israel, and that it is in vain for him to hope to obtain a curse for his people, or to expect him to reverse the blessing he has promised to them; and no enchantment or curse uttered by a diviner could have the least influence upon that nation that has the protection of Omnipotence. (1SP 324.1)

Balaam had wished to appear to be favorable to Balak, and had permitted him to be deceived, and to think that he used superstitious ceremonies and enchantments when he besought the Lord. But as he followed the command given him of God, he grew bolder in proportion as he obeyed the divine impulse, and he laid aside his pretended conjuration, and, looking toward the encampment of the Israelites, he beholds them all encamped in perfect order, under their respective standards, at a distance from the tabernacle. Balaam was permitted to behold the glorious manifestation of God's presence, overshadowing, protecting, and guiding, the tabernacle. He was filled with admiration at the sublime scene. He opened his parable with all the dignity of a true prophet of God. His prophetic words are these: "How goodly are thy tents, O Jacob, and thy tabernacles, O Israel! As the valleys are they spread forth, as gardens by the river's side, as the trees of lign aloes which the Lord hath planted, and as cedar trees beside the waters. He shall pour the water out of his buckets, and his seed shall be in many waters, and his king shall be higher than Agag, and his kingdom shall be exalted. God brought him forth out of Egypt; he hath, as it were, the strength of a unicorn. He shall eat up the nations, his enemies, and shall break their bones, and pierce them through with his arrows. He couched, he lay down as a lion, and as a great lion. Who shall stir him up? Blessed is he that blesseth thee, and cursed is he that curseth thee. And Balak's anger was kindled against Balaam, and he smote his hands together. And Balak said unto Balaam, I called thee to curse mine enemies, and, behold, thou hast altogether blessed them these three times." (1SP 325.1)

The Moabites understood the import of the prophetic words of Balaam–that the Israelites, after conquering the Canaanites, should settle in their land, and all attempts to subdue them would be of no more avail than for a feeble beast to arouse the lion out of his den. Balaam told Balak that he would inform him what the Israelites should do to his people at a later period. The Lord unfolded the future before Balaam, and permitted events which would occur to pass before his sight, that the Moabites should understand that Israel should finally triumph. As Balaam prophetically rehearsed the future to Balak and his princes, he was struck with amazement at the future display of God's power. (1SP 326.1)

After Balaam had returned to his place, and the controlling influence of God's Spirit had left him, his covetousness, which had not been overcome, but merely held in check, prevailed. He could think of nothing but the reward and promotion to honor which he might have received of Balak, until he was willing to resort to any means to obtain that which he desired. Balaam knew that the prosperity of Israel depended upon their observance of the law of God; and that there was no way to bring a curse upon them but by seducing them to transgression. He decided to secure to himself Balak's reward and the promotion he desired, by advising the Moabites what course to pursue to bring the curse upon Israel. He counseled Balak to proclaim an idolatrous feast in honor of their idol gods, and he would persuade the Israelites to attend, that they might be delighted with the music; and then the most beautiful Midianitish women should entice the Israelites to transgress the law of God, and corrupt themselves, and also influence them to offer sacrifice to idols. This satanic counsel succeeded too well. Many of the Israelites were persuaded by Balaam, because they regarded him as a prophet of God, to join him, and mix with that idolatrous people, and engage with him in idolatry and fornication. (1SP 326.2)

"And Israel joined himself unto Baal-peor; and the anger of the Lord was kindled against Israel. And the Lord said unto Moses, Take all the heads of the people, and hang them up before the Lord against the sun, that the fierce anger of the Lord may be turned away from Israel. And Moses said unto the judges of Israel, Slay ye every one his men that were joined unto Baal-peor." Moses commanded the judges of the people to execute the punishment of God against

Chapter 30 - Balaam (1SP 327.1)

those who had transgressed, and hang the heads of the transgressors up before the Lord, to cause Israel to fear to follow their example. The Lord commanded Moses to vex the Midianites, and smite them, because they had vexed Israel with their wiles, wherewith they had beguiled them to transgress the commandments of God. (1SP 327.1)

The Lord commanded Moses to avenge the children of Israel of the Midianites; and then he should be gathered to his people. Moses commanded the men of war to prepare for battle against the Midianites. And they warred against them, as the Lord commanded, and slew all the males, but they took the women and children captives. Balaam was slain with the Midianites. "And Moses, and Eleazar the priest, and all the princes of the congregation, went forth to meet them without the camp. And Moses was wroth with the officers of the host, with the captains over thousands, and captains over hundreds, which came from the battle. And Moses said unto them, Have ye saved all the women alive? Behold, these caused the children of Israel, through the counsel of Balaam, to commit trespass against the Lord in the matter of Peor, and there was a plague among the congregation of the Lord." (1SP 327.2)

Moses commanded the men of war to destroy the women and male children. Balaam had sold the children of Israel for a reward, and he perished with the people whose favor he had obtained at the sacrifice of twenty-four thousand of the Israelites. The Lord is regarded as cruel, by many, in requiring his people to make war with other nations. They say that it is contrary to his benevolent character. But he who made the world, and formed man to dwell upon the earth, has unlimited control over all the works of his hands; and it is his right to do as he pleases, and what he pleases, with the work of his hands. Man has no right to say to his Maker, Why doest thou thus? There is no injustice in his character. He is the ruler of the world, and a large portion of his subjects have rebelled against his authority, and have trampled upon his law. He has bestowed upon them liberal blessings, and surrounded them with everything needful; yet they have bowed to images of wood and stone, silver and gold, which their own hands have made. They teach their children that these are the gods that give them life and health, and make their lands fruitful, and give them riches and honor. They scorn the God of Israel. They despise his people because their works are righteous. "The fool hath said in his heart, There is no God. They are corrupt, they have done abominable works." God has borne with them until they filled up the measure of their iniquity, and then he has brought upon them swift destruction. He has used his people as instruments of his wrath, to punish wicked nations who have vexed them, and seduced them into idolatry. (1SP 328.1)

A family picture was presented before me: A part of the children seem anxious to learn and obey the requirements of the father, while the others trample upon his authority, and seem to exult in showing contempt of his family government. They share the benefits of their father's house, and are constantly receiving of his bounty; they are wholly dependent upon him for all they receive, yet are not grateful, but conduct themselves proudly, as though all the favors they received of their indulgent parent were supplied by themselves. The father notices all the disrespectful acts of his disobedient, ungrateful children, yet he bears with them. (1SP 329.1)

At length, these rebellious children go still further, and seek to influence and lead to rebellion those members of their father's family who have hitherto been faithful. Then all the dignity and authority of the father is called into action; and he expels from his house the rebellious children, who have not only abused his love and blessings themselves, but tried to subvert the remaining few who had submitted to the wise and judicious laws of their father's household. (1SP 329.2)

For the sake of the few who are loyal, whose happiness was exposed to the seditious influence of the rebellious members of his household, he separates his undutiful children from his family, while at the same time he labors to bring the remaining faithful and loyal ones closer to himself. All would honor the wise and just course of such a parent, in punishing most severely his undutiful, rebellious children. (1SP 329.3)

God has dealt thus with his children. But man, in his blindness, will overlook the abominations of the ungodly, and pass by unnoticed the continual ingratitude and rebellion, and Heaven-daring sins of those who trample upon God's law and defy his authority. They do not stop here, but exult in subverting his people, and influencing them by their wiles to transgress, and show open contempt for, the wise requirements of Jehovah. (1SP 330.1)

Some can see only the destruction of God's enemies, which looks to them unmerciful and severe. They do not look upon the other side. But let everlasting thanks be given, that impulsive, changeable man, with all his boasted benevolence, is not the disposer and controller of events. "The tender mercies of the wicked are cruel." (1SP 330.2)

*****

Chapter 31
Death of Moses

Moses was soon to die; and he was commanded of God to gather the children of Israel together before his death, and relate to them all the journeyings of the Hebrew host since their departure from Egypt, and all the great transgressions of their fathers, which brought his judgments upon them, and compelled him to say that they should not enter the promised land. Their fathers had died in the wilderness, according to the word of the Lord. Their children had grown up, and to them the promise was to be fulfilled of possessing the land of Canaan. Many of these were small children when the law was given, and they had no remembrance of the grandeur of the event. Others were born in the wilderness; and lest they should not realize the necessity of their obeying the ten commandments, and all the laws and judgments given to Moses, he was instructed of God to recapitulate the ten commandments, and all the circumstances connected with the giving of the law. (1SP 330.3)

Moses had written in a book all the laws and judgments given him of God, and had faithfully recorded all his instructions given them by the way, and all the miracles which he had performed for them, and all the murmurings of the children of Israel. Moses had also recorded his being overcome in consequence of their murmurings. (1SP 331.1)

All the people were assembled before him, and he read the events of their past history out of the book which he had written. He read, also, the promises of God to them if they would be obedient, and the curses which would come upon them if they were disobedient. He related to the people his great sorrow because of his fault at Meribah. "And I besought the Lord at that time, saying, O Lord God, thou hast begun to show thy servant thy greatness, and thy mighty hand; for what God is there in Heaven or in earth, that can do according to thy works, and according to thy might? I pray thee, let me go over, and see the good land that is beyond Jordan, that goodly mountain, and Lebanon. But the Lord was wroth with me for your sakes, and would not hear me. And the Lord said unto me, Let it suffice thee; speak no more unto me of this matter. Get thee up into the top of Pisgah, and lift up thine eyes westward, and northward, and southward, and eastward, and behold it with thine eyes; for thou shalt not go over this Jordan. But charge Joshua, and encourage him, and strengthen him; for he shall go over before this people, and he shall cause them to inherit the land which thou shalt see." "Now, therefore, hearken, O Israel, unto the statutes and unto the judgments, which I teach you, for to do them, that ye may live, and go in and possess the land which the Lord God of your fathers giveth you. Ye shall not add unto the word which I command you, neither shall ye diminish aught from it, that ye may keep the commandments of the Lord your God which I command you." (1SP 331.2)

Moses told them that, for their rebellion, the Lord had several times purposed to destroy them; but he had interceded for them so earnestly that God had graciously spared them. He reminded them of the miracles which the Lord did unto Pharaoh and all the land of Egypt. He said to them, "But your eyes have seen all the great acts of the Lord which he did. Therefore shall ye keep all the commandments which I command you this day, that ye may be strong, and go in and possess the land, whither ye go to possess it." (1SP 332.1)

Moses especially warned the children of Israel against being seduced into idolatry. He earnestly charged them to obey the commandments of God. If they would prove obedient, and love the Lord, and serve him with their undivided affections, he would give them rain in due season, and cause their vegetation to flourish, and increase their cattle. They should also enjoy especial and exalted privileges, and should triumph over their enemies. He related to them the advantages of the land of Canaan over that of Egypt. In certain seasons of the year, the cultivated lands in Egypt had to be watered from the river by machinery which was worked by the foot. This was a laborious process. (1SP 332.2)

Moses said to them, "For the land, whither thou goest in to possess it, is not as the land of Egypt, from whence ye came out, where thou sowedst thy seed, and wateredst it with thy foot, as a garden of herbs; but the land, whither ye go to possess it, is a land of hills and valleys, and drinketh water of the rain of heaven; a land which the Lord thy God careth for. The eyes of the Lord thy God are always upon it, from the beginning of the year even unto the end of the year." (1SP 333.1)

Many of the Egyptians paid that devotion to the river which belonged alone to God. They acknowledged it as their God, because they were dependent on its waters to quench their thirst, and to use upon their lands to cause vegetation to flourish; and it liberally supplied their tables with fish. (1SP 333.2)

During the plagues on Egypt, Pharaoh was punctual in his superstitious devotion to the river, and visited it every morning; and, as he stood upon its banks, he offered praise and thanksgiving to the water, recounting the great good it accomplished, and telling the water of its great power; that without it they could not exist; for their lands were watered by it, and it supplied meat for their tables. The first plague which visited Egypt was to come upon the waters, one of the exalted gods of Pharaoh. Moses smote the water before Pharaoh and his great men, and they saw the water which they were adoring turned to blood. It was a putrid mass for seven days; and all the fish that were in it died. The people could not use the water for any purpose. (1SP 333.3)

Moses instructed the children of Israel in an earnest, impressive manner. He knew that it was his last opportunity to address them. He then finished writing in a book all the laws, judgments, and statutes, which God had given him; also, the various regulations respecting sacrificial offerings. He placed the book in the hands of men in the sacred office, and requested that, for safe keeping, it should be put in the side of the ark; for God's care was continually upon that sacred chest. This book of Moses was to be preserved, that the judges of Israel might refer to it if any case should come up to make it necessary. An erring people often understand God's requirements to suit their own case; therefore the book of Moses was preserved in a most sacred place, for future reference. (1SP 334.1)

Moses closed his last instructions to the people by a most powerful, prophetic address. It was pathetic and eloquent. By inspiration of God, he blessed separately the tribes of Israel. In his closing words, he dwelt largely upon the majesty of God, and the excellency of Israel, which would ever continue if they would obey God, and take hold of his strength. He said to them, "There is none like unto the God of Jeshurun, who rideth upon the heaven in thy help, and in his excellency on the sky. The eternal God is thy refuge, and underneath are the everlasting arms. And he shall thrust out the enemy from before thee, and shall say, Destroy them. Israel, then, shall dwell in safety alone. The fountain of Jacob shall be upon a land of corn and wine; also, his heavens shall drop down dew. Happy art thou, O Israel. Who is like unto thee, O people saved by the Lord, the shield of thy help, and who is the sword of thy excellency! And thine enemies shall be found liars unto thee; and thou shalt tread upon their high places." (1SP 334.2)

Joshua was selected of God to be Moses' successor in leading the Hebrew host to the promised land. He was most solemnly consecrated to the future important work of leading, as a faithful shepherd, the people of Israel. "And Joshua, the son of Nun, was full of the spirit of wisdom; for Moses had laid his hands upon him. And the children of Israel hearkened unto him, and did as the Lord commanded Moses." And he gave Joshua charge before all the congregation of Israel, "Be strong and of a good courage; for thou shalt bring the children of Israel unto the land which I sware unto them; and I will be with thee." He spoke to Joshua in God's stead. He also had the elders and officers of the tribes gathered before him, and he solemnly charged them to deal justly and righteously in their religious offices, and to faithfully obey all the instructions he had given them from God. He called Heaven and earth to record against them, that if they should depart from God, and transgress his commandments, he was clear; for he had faithfully instructed and

Chapter 31 - Death of Moses (1SP 335.1)

warned them. (1SP 335.1)

"And Moses went up from the plains of Moab unto the mountain of Nebo, to the top of Pisgah, that is over against Jericho; and the Lord shewed him all the land of Gilead, unto Dan, and all Naphtali, and the land of Ephraim, and Manasseh, and all the land of Judah, unto the utmost sea, and the south, and the plain of the valley of Jericho, the city of palm trees, unto Zoar. And the Lord said unto him, This is the land which I sware unto Abraham, unto Isaac, and unto Jacob, saying, I will give it unto thy seed. I have caused thee to see it with thine eyes, but thou shalt not go over thither. So Moses, the servant of the Lord, died there in the land of Moab, according to the word of the Lord. And he buried him in a valley in the land of Moab, over against Beth-peor; but no man knoweth of his sepulchre unto this day. And Moses was a hundred and twenty years old when he died; his eye was not dim, nor his natural force abated." (1SP 335.2)

Moses ascended to Pisgah, the highest prominence of the mountain which he could attain, and there his clear and undimmed eyes viewed the land, the promised home of Israel. God opened before his sight the whole land of Canaan. He there in the mount fully realized the rich blessings Israel would enjoy if they would faithfully obey the commandments of God. (1SP 336.1)

While upon the mount, Moses again confesses his sin before God, and implores pardon for his transgression. He had greatly deplored his sin which had debarred him from the promised land. It was a severe affliction to him not to be permitted to enter the earthly Canaan. Yet he humbly accepts the punishment of his transgression, and murmurs not at the decree of God; notwithstanding it was the continual murmuring of the people which had afflicted him, and was the cause of his becoming for a moment impatient, which resulted in his failing to ascribe the glory of the great miracle they witnessed to its true Author. This was the purpose of God in proving his people, that in their trials they would be induced to call upon him for deliverance; and he would answer them by revealing his greatness and power to them, that their faith and trust might be in God alone. Here was a favorable opportunity for Moses to adore and magnify the goodness and power of God, and to make a deep impression upon the people, while their hearts were softened, and their gratitude awakened, and a solemn, sacred awe pervaded the place. He could have exalted God before them, whose threatenings never fail, and whose promises are ever sure. (1SP 336.2)

Moses, alone upon the mount, reviewed his past life of vicissitudes and hardships since he turned from courtly honors and from a prospective kingdom in Egypt, refusing to be called the son of Pharaoh's daughter, choosing rather to suffer affliction with the people of God. He calls to mind his humble shepherd's life, and, while tending his flock, the wonderful sight of the flaming bush, and the Lord's there sanctifying him for the work, and intrusting to him the responsible mission of delivering Israel from their oppression. He came down from point to point in his experience. He called to mind the mighty miracles of God's power in the plagues of Egypt to make Pharaoh willing to let the people go; the Hebrews' walking through the Red Sea on dry ground, while the waters were standing as a wall on either side; the symbol of the divine presence in the pillar of cloud by day, and of fire by night; the water given them from the flinty rock; the daily bread which, during the night, fell from heaven round about their tents; the victories God had given them over their enemies; their quiet and secure rest in the midst of a vast wilderness; and the unsurpassed glory and majesty of God which he had been permitted to witness. As he reviewed these things, he was overwhelmed with a sense of the goodness and power of God. His promises were sure to Israel. When they were faithful and obedient, no good thing promised had been withheld from them. But in consequence of their continual backslidings and grievous sins, forty years were consumed in their wanderings in the wilderness. (1SP 337.1)

He had been disappointed and grieved because of the continual rebellion of Israel; yet he had not sinned against God until he became impatient with Israel, and spoke unadvisedly with his lips. Notwithstanding all his labors and burdens for rebellious Israel during their forty years' journeying, only two of those in that vast army who were above twenty years old when they left Egypt, were found so faithful that they could see the promised land. The Lord had said that they should fall in the wilderness for their transgressions. They had evil hearts of unbelief. Moses' laborious task, as he reviewed the result

Chapter 31 - Death of Moses (1SP 341.1)

of his labors, seemed almost in vain. (1SP 338.1)

Moses submitted to God's decree in regard to himself. He regretted not the burdens he had borne for an ungrateful people who had not appreciated his labors, his anxious care and love for them. He knew that his mission and work were of God's own appointing. When the Lord first made known to Moses his purposes to qualify him to lead his people from slavery, he shrank from the responsibility, and entreated the Lord to choose some one better qualified to execute this sacred work. His request was not granted. Since he had taken up the work, he had not laid it down, nor cast aside the burden. Several times the Lord proposed to release him, and destroy rebellious Israel; but Moses could not let Israel go. He chose still to bear the burden the Lord had intrusted to him. He had been so especially favored of God, and had obtained so rich an experience during his travels in the wilderness, in witnessing the manifestations of God's miracles and his excellent glory, that he concluded, in reviewing the scenes of his life, that he had made a wise decision in choosing to suffer affliction with the people of God, rather than to enjoy the pleasures of sin for a season. He regretted not his sufferings and hardships. Only one unfortunate act marred his illustrious experience. If he could atone for this one transgression, he would be reconciled to die. He was told that repentance, humiliation, and faith in the Son of God, who was to die man's sacrifice, was all that God required. This sinless and perfect offering would be fully acceptable with God, and would link finite man, though fallen, if repentant and obedient, to his own sacredness. (1SP 338.2)

As angels presented to Moses a panoramic view of the land of promise, he could take in the whole scene, and appreciate with almost divine clearness its magnificence. It was as a second Eden, abounding in fruit trees of almost every variety, and very beautiful ornamental trees and flowers. There were goodly cities, with brooks and springs of water. There were fields of wheat and barley, and vineyards, and fig trees, and pomegranates, and oil olive, and honey. The Lord had said, "Thou shalt eat bread without scarceness, thou shalt not lack anything in it." (1SP 339.1)

Moses was shown future events, especially those connected with the first advent of Jesus Christ. He was shown important, thrilling scenes in the life of Christ, and the very places where these scenes would be enacted. He saw his humble birth, and the angels proclaiming the glad tidings to the shepherds, "Behold, I bring you good tidings of great joy, which shall be to all people. For unto you is born this day, in the city of David, a Saviour, which is Christ the Lord." Moses saw that Christ had exchanged his majesty and splendor for the manger of Bethlehem. He heard the joyful voices of the shining host of Heaven break forth in that divine song, "Glory to God in the highest, and on earth peace, good will toward men." He saw the Saviour of the world humbly walking through the streets of Bethlehem, divested of kingly honors, without pomp or grandeur. He saw the manner of his rejection by the proud and corrupt Jewish nation. They despised and rejected Him who had come to give them life. Here was their only star of hope. He saw the great agony of the Son of God in the garden of Gethsemane, and the betrayal of Jesus into the hands of a mob which was infuriated by Satan. He saw the cruel mockings and scourgings instigated by his own nation, and their last crowning act of nailing him to the cross; and Moses saw that, as he had lifted up the serpent in the wilderness, so the Son of God was lifted up on the wooden cross. He saw him bleeding and dying, that whosoever should believe in him should not perish, but have eternal life. (1SP 340.1)

Grief, amazement, indignation, and horror, were depicted on the countenance of Moses, as he viewed the hypocrisy and satanic hatred manifested by the Jewish nation against their Redeemer, the mighty angel who had gone before their fathers, and wrought so wonderfully for them in all their journeyings. He heard his agonizing cry, "My God, my God, why hast thou forsaken me?" He saw him rise from the dead, and walk forth a triumphant conqueror, and ascend to his Father escorted by adoring angels. The gates of the city were opened by angels, who welcomed their divine Commander back with songs of glory and everlasting triumph. Moses' countenance changed, and shone with a holy radiance, as he viewed the glory and triumph of Christ. How small appeared all his hardships, trials, and sacrifices, when compared with those of the divine Son of God! He rejoiced that he had chosen to suffer affliction with the people of God, and in a small measure be a partaker with Christ of his sufferings. (1SP 341.1)

Chapter 31 - Death of Moses (1SP 341.2)

It was not the will of God that any one should go up with Moses to the top of Pisgah. There he stood, upon a high prominence upon Pisgah's top, in the presence of God and heavenly angels. After he had viewed Canaan to his satisfaction, he lay down, like a tired warrior, to rest. Sleep came upon him, but it was the sleep of death. Angels took his body and buried it in the valley. The Israelites could never find the place where he was buried. His secret burial was to prevent the people from sinning against the Lord by committing idolatry over his body. (1SP 341.2)

Those who had not been careful to heed his instruction during his life, would be in the greatest danger of manifesting an unsanctified grief in the event of his death, and would commit idolatry over his lifeless body if they could obtain it. God designed to hide Moses from them, where his grave would be unknown except by himself and heavenly angels. Moses had accomplished much for Israel. In all his instructions to them could be seen justice, intelligence, and purity. (1SP 341.3)

The life of Moses was marked with supreme love to God. His piety, humility and forbearance, gave him influence with the host of Israel. His zeal and faith in God were greater than those of any other man upon the earth. He had often addressed his people in words of stirring eloquence. No one knew better than he how to move the affections of the people. He conducted all matters connected with the religious interests of the people with great wisdom. (1SP 342.1)

Satan exulted that he had succeeded in causing Moses to sin against God. For this transgression, Moses came under the dominion of death. If he had continued faithful, and his life had not been marred with that one transgression, in failing to give to God the glory of bringing water from the rock, he would have entered the promised land, and would have been translated to Heaven without seeing death. Michael, or Christ, with the angels that buried Moses, came down from Heaven, after he had remained in the grave a short time, and resurrected him, and took him to Heaven. (1SP 342.2)

As Christ and the angels approached the grave, Satan and his angels appeared at the grave, and were guarding the body of Moses, lest it should be removed. As Christ and his angels drew nigh, Satan resisted their approach, but was compelled, by the glory and power of Christ and his angels, to fall back. Satan claimed the body of Moses, because of his one transgression; but Christ meekly referred him to his Father, saying, "The Lord rebuke thee." Christ told Satan that he knew Moses had humbly repented of this one wrong, that no stain rested upon his character, and that his name in the heavenly book of records stood untarnished. Then Christ resurrected the body of Moses, which Satan had claimed. (1SP 342.3)

At the transfiguration of Christ, Moses, and Elijah who had been translated, were sent to talk with Christ in regard to his sufferings, and be the bearers of God's glory to his dear Son. Moses had been greatly honored of God. He had been privileged to talk with God face to face, as a man speaketh with his friend. And God had revealed to him his excellent glory, as he had never done to any other. (1SP 343.1)

Moses was a type of Christ. He received the words from the mouth of God, and spoke them to the people. God saw fit to discipline Moses in the school of affliction and poverty, before he could be prepared to lead the armies of Israel in their travels from Egypt to the earthly Canaan. The Israel of God who are now passing on to the heavenly Canaan have a Captain who needed no earthly teaching, as did Moses, to perfect him for the work of a divine teacher and leader to guide his people into a better and heavenly country. He manifested no human weakness or imperfection; yet he died in order to obtain an entrance for us into the promised land. Moses pointed the people forward to Christ. He said, "The Lord thy God will raise up unto thee a Prophet, from the midst of thee, of thy brethren, like unto me; unto him ye shall hearken." He continues, "The Lord said unto me, They have well spoken that which they have spoken. I will raise them up a Prophet, from among their brethren, like unto thee, and will put my words in his mouth; and he shall speak unto them all that I shall command him." (1SP 343.2)

Through outward signs and ceremonies, the Lord made known to the Hebrews his purity and holiness, and his stern justice. He also multiplied evidences of his willingness to pardon the erring and sinful who manifested true repentance, and submission to his just requirements, while they presented their offerings in faith of the future perfect offering of the Son of God. When the high priest performed his service before the people, their minds were directed to the coming Saviour, of whom the Jewish priest was a striking and beautiful representation. **(1SP 344.1)**

*****

Chapter 32
Joshua

After the death of Moses, Joshua was to be the leader of Israel, to conduct them to the promised land. He had been prime minister to Moses during the greater part of the time the Israelites had wandered in the wilderness. He had seen the wonderful works of God wrought by Moses, and well understood the disposition of the people. He was one of the twelve spies who were sent out to search the promised land, and one of the two who gave a faithful account of its richness, and who encouraged the people to go up in the strength of God and possess it. He was well qualified for this important office. The Lord promised Joshua to be with him as he had been with Moses, and to make Canaan fall an easy conquest to him, provided he would be faithful to observe all his commandments. He was anxious as to how he should execute his commission in leading the people to the land of Canaan; but this encouragement removed his fears. (1SP 344.2)

Joshua commanded the children of Israel to prepare for a three-days' journey, and that all the men of war should go out to battle. "And they answered Joshua, saying, All that thou commandest us, we will do, and whithersoever thou sendest us, we will go. According as we hearkened unto Moses in all things, so will we hearken unto thee; only the Lord thy God be with thee, as he was with Moses. Whosoever he be that doth rebel against thy commandment, and will not hearken unto thy words in all that thou commandest him, he shall be put to death; only be strong and of a good courage." (1SP 345.1)

The passage of the Israelites over Jordan was to be miraculous. "And Joshua said unto the people, Sanctify yourselves; for tomorrow the Lord will do wonders among you. And Joshua spake unto the priests, saying, Take up the ark of the covenant, and pass over before the people. And they took up the ark of the covenant, and went before the people. And the Lord said unto Joshua, This day will I begin to magnify thee in the sight of all Israel, that they may know that, as I was with Moses, so I will be with thee." (1SP 345.2)

The priests were to go before the people and bear the ark containing the law of God. And as their feet were dipped in the brim of Jordan, the waters were cut off from above, and the priests passed on, bearing the ark, which was a symbol of the Divine Presence; and the Hebrew host followed. When the priests were half way over Jordan, they were commanded to stand in the bed of the river until all the host of Israel had passed over. Here, the then existing generation of the Israelites were convinced that the waters of Jordan were subject to the same power that their fathers had seen displayed at the Red Sea, forty years before. Many of these passed through the Red Sea when they were children. Now they pass over Jordan, men of war, fully equipped for battle. After all the host of Israel had passed over Jordan, Joshua commanded the priests to come up out of the river. As soon as the priests, bearing the ark of the covenant, came up out of the river, and stood on dry land, Jordan rolled on as before, and overflowed all his banks. This wonderful miracle performed for the Israelites greatly increased their faith. That this wonderful miracle might never be forgotten, the Lord directed Joshua to command that men of note, one of each tribe, take up stones from the bed of the river, the place where the priests' feet stood while the Hebrew host was passing over, and bear them upon their shoulders, and erect a monument in Gilgal, to keep in remembrance the fact that Israel passed over Jordan on dry land. After the priests had come up from Jordan, God removed his mighty hand, and the waters rushed like a mighty cataract down their own channel. (1SP 345.3)

When all the kings of the Amorites and the kings of the Canaanites heard that the Lord had stayed the waters of Jordan before the children of

Chapter 32 - Joshua (1SP 349.1)

Israel, their hearts melted with fear. The Israelites had slain two of the kings of Moab; and their miraculous passage over the swollen and impetuous Jordan, filled them with the greatest terror. Joshua then circumcised all the people which had been born in the wilderness. After this ceremony, they kept the passover in the plains of Jericho. "And the Lord said unto Joshua, This day have I rolled away the reproach of Egypt from off you." (1SP 346.1)

Heathen nations had reproached the Lord and his people because the Hebrews had not possessed the land of Canaan, which they expected to inherit soon after leaving Egypt. Their enemies had triumphed because they had so long wandered in the wilderness; and they proudly lifted themselves up against God, declaring that he was not able to lead them into the land of Canaan. They had now passed over Jordan on dry land, and their enemies could no longer reproach them. (1SP 347.1)

The manna had continued up to this time; but now as the Israelites were about to possess Canaan, and eat of the fruit of the land, they had no more need of it, and it ceased. (1SP 347.2)

As Joshua withdrew from the armies of Israel, to meditate and pray for God's special presence to attend him, he saw a man of lofty stature, clad in warlike garments, with his sword drawn in his hand. Joshua did not recognize him as one of the armies of Israel, and yet he had no appearance of being an enemy. In his zeal he accosted him, and said, "Art thou for us, or for our adversaries? And he said, Nay; but as captain of the host of the Lord am I now come. And Joshua fell on his face to the earth, and did worship, and said unto him, What saith my Lord unto his servant? And the captain of the Lord's host said unto Joshua, Loose thy shoe from off thy foot; for the place whereon thou standest is holy. And Joshua did so." (1SP 347.3)

This was no common angel. It was the Lord Jesus Christ, he who had conducted the Hebrews through the wilderness, enshrouded in the pillar of fire by night, and a pillar of cloud by day. The place was made sacred by his presence, therefore Joshua was commanded to put off his shoes. (1SP 348.1)

The burning bush seen by Moses was also a token of the Divine Presence; and as he drew nigh to behold the wonderful sight, the same voice which here speaks to Joshua, said to Moses, "Draw not nigh hither. Put off thy shoes from off thy feet; for the place whereon thou standest is holy ground." (1SP 348.2)

The glory of God hallowed the sanctuary; and for this reason the priests never entered the place sanctified by God's presence with shoes upon their feet. Particles of dust might cleave to their shoes, which would desecrate the sanctuary; therefore the priests were required to leave their shoes in the court, before entering the sanctuary. In the court, beside the door of the tabernacle, stood the brazen laver, wherein the priests washed their hands and their feet before entering the tabernacle, that all impurity might be removed, "that they die not." All who officiated in the sanctuary were required of God to make special preparations before entering where God's glory was revealed. (1SP 348.3)

In order to convey to the mind of Joshua that he was no less than Christ, the exalted one, he says, "Loose thy shoe from off thy foot." The Lord then instructed Joshua what course to pursue in order to take Jericho. All the men of war should be commanded to compass the city once each day for six days, and on the seventh day they should go around Jericho seven times. (1SP 348.4)

"And Joshua, the son of Nun, called the priests, and said unto them, Take up the ark of the covenant, and let seven priests bear seven trumpets of rams' horns before the ark of the Lord. And he said unto the people, Pass on, and compass the city, and let him that is armed pass on before the ark of the Lord. And it came to pass, when Joshua had spoken unto the people, that the seven priests bearing seven trumpets of rams' horns passed on before the Lord, and blew with the trumpets; and the ark of the covenant of the Lord followed them. And the armed men went before the priests that blew with the trumpets, and the rearward came after the ark, the priests going on, and blowing with the trumpets. And Joshua had commanded the people, saying, Ye shall not shout, nor make any noise with your voice, neither shall any word proceed out of your mouth, until the day I bid you shout; then shall ye shout. So the ark of the Lord compassed the city, going about it once; and they came into the camp, and lodged in the camp." (1SP 349.1)

The Hebrew host marched in perfect order. First went a select body of armed men, clad in

Chapter 32 - Joshua (1SP 349.2)

their warlike dress, not now to exercise their skill in arms, but only to believe and obey the directions given them. Next followed seven priests with trumpets. Then came the ark of God, glittering with gold, a halo of glory hovering over it, borne by priests in their rich and peculiar dress denoting their sacred office. The vast army of Israel followed in perfect order, each tribe under its respective standard. Thus they compassed the city with the ark of God. No sound was heard but the tread of that mighty host, and the solemn voice of the trumpets, echoed by the hills, and resounding through the city of Jericho. With wonder and alarm the watchmen of that doomed city mark every move, and report to those in authority. They cannot tell what all this display means. Some ridicule the idea of that city's being taken in this manner, while others are awed, as they behold the splendor of the ark, and the solemn and dignified appearance of the priests, and the host of Israel following, with Joshua at their head. They remember that the Red Sea, forty years before, parted before them, and that a passage had just been prepared for them through the river Jordan. They are too much terrified to sport. They are strict to keep the gates of the city closely shut, and mighty warriors to guard each gate. For six days, the armies of Israel perform their circuit around the city. On the seventh day, they compassed Jericho seven times. The people were commanded, as usual, to be silent. The voice of the trumpets alone was to be heard. The people were to observe, and when the trumpeters should make a longer blast than usual, then all were to shout with a loud voice, for God had given them the city. "And it came to pass on the seventh day, that they rose early, about the dawning of the day, and compassed the city, after the same manner, seven times; only on that day they compassed the city seven times. And it came to pass at the seventh time, when the priests blew with the trumpets, Joshua said unto the people, Shout; for the Lord hath given you the city." "So the people shouted when the priests blew with the trumpets. And it came to pass, when the people heard the sound of the trumpet, and the people shouted with a great shout, that the wall fell down flat, so that the people went up into the city, every man straight before him, and they took the city." (1SP 349.2)

God intended to show the Israelites that the conquest of Canaan was not to be ascribed to them. The captain of the Lord's host overcame Jericho. He and his angels were engaged in the conquest. Christ commanded the armies of Heaven to throw down the walls of Jericho, and prepare an entrance for Joshua and the armies of Israel. God, in this wonderful miracle, not only strengthened the faith of his people in his power to subdue their enemies, but rebuked their former unbelief. (1SP 351.1)

Jericho had defied the armies of Israel and the God of Heaven. And as they beheld the host of Israel marching around their city once each day, they were alarmed; but they looked at their strong defenses, their firm and high walls, and felt sure that they could resist any attack. But when their firm walls suddenly tottered and fell, with a stunning crash, like peals of loudest thunder, they were paralyzed with terror, and could offer no resistance. (1SP 351.2)

No stain rested upon the holy character of Joshua. He was a wise leader. His life was wholly devoted to God. Before he died, he assembled the Hebrew host, and, following the example of Moses, he recapitulated their travels in the wilderness, and also the merciful dealings of God with them. He then eloquently addressed them. He related to them that the king of Moab warred against them, and called Balaam to curse them; but God "would not hearken unto Balaam, therefore he blessed you still." He then said to them, "And if it seem evil unto you to serve the Lord, choose you this day whom you will serve; whether the gods which your fathers served that were on the other side of the flood, or the gods of the Amorites, in whose land ye dwell. But as for me and my house, we will serve the Lord. And the people answered, and said, God forbid that we should forsake the Lord, to serve other gods; for the Lord our God, he it is that brought us up, and our fathers, out of the land of Egypt, from the house of bondage, and which did those great signs in our sight, and preserved us in all the way wherein we went, and among all the people through whom we passed." (1SP 351.3)

The people renewed their covenant with Joshua. They said unto him, "The Lord our God will we serve, and his voice will we obey." Joshua wrote the words of their covenant in the book containing the laws and statutes given to Moses. Joshua was loved and respected by all Israel, and his death was much lamented by them. (1SP 352.1)

*****

Chapter 33
Samuel and Saul

The children of Israel were a highly-favored people. God had brought them from Egyptian bondage, and acknowledged them as his own peculiar treasure. Moses said, "What nation is there so great, who hath God so nigh them, as the Lord our God is in all things that we call upon him for?" (1SP 352.2)

Samuel had judged Israel from his youth. He had been a righteous and impartial judge, faithful in all his work. He was becoming old; and the people saw that his sons did not follow his footsteps. Although they were not vile, like the children of Eli, yet they were dishonest and double-minded. While they aided their father in his laborious work, their love of reward led them to favor the cause of the unrighteous. (1SP 353.1)

The Hebrews demanded a king of Samuel, like the nations around them. By preferring a despotic monarchy to the wise and mild government of God himself, by the jurisdiction of his prophets, they showed a great want of faith in God, and confidence in his providence to raise them up rulers to lead and govern them. The children of Israel being peculiarly the people of God, their form of government was essentially different from all the nations around them. God had given them statutes and laws, and had chosen their rulers for them; and these leaders the people were to obey in the Lord. In all cases of difficulty and great perplexity, God was to be inquired of. Their demand for a king was a rebellious departure from God, their special leader. He knew that a king would not be best for his chosen people. They would render to an earthly monarch that honor which was due to God alone. And if they had a king whose heart was lifted up and not right with God, he would lead them away from him, and cause them to rebel against him. The Lord knew that no one could occupy the position of king, and receive the honors usually given to a king, without becoming exalted, and his ways seeming right in his own eyes, while at the same time he was sinning against God. At the word of a king, innocent persons would be made to suffer, while the most unworthy would be exalted, unless he continually trusted in God, and received wisdom from him. (1SP 353.2)

If the Hebrews had continued to obey God after they left Egypt, and had kept his righteous law, he would have gone before them and prospered them, and made them always a terror to the heathen nations around them. But they so often followed their own rebellious hearts, and departed from God, and went into idolatry, that he suffered them to be overcome by other nations, to humble and punish them. When in their affliction they cried unto God, he always heard them, and raised them up a ruler to deliver them from their enemies. They were so blinded that they did not acknowledge that it was their sins which had caused God to depart from them, and to leave them weak and a prey to their enemies; but they reasoned that it was because they had no one invested with kingly authority to command the armies of Israel. They had not kept in grateful remembrance the many instances God had given them of his care and great love, but often distrusted his goodness and mercy. (1SP 354.1)

God had raised up Samuel to judge Israel. He was honored by all the people. God was to be acknowledged as their great head; yet he designated their rulers, and imbued them with his Spirit, and communicated his will to them through his angels, that they might instruct the people. God also gave special evidences to the people, by his mighty works performed through the agency of his chosen rulers, that they might have confidence that he had invested them with authority which could not be lightly set aside. (1SP 354.2)

God was angry with his people because they demanded a king. He gave them a king in his wrath. Yet he bade Samuel to tell the people faithfully the manner of the kings of the nations around them: that they would not be as a judge of difficulties of church and state, to instruct them in the ways of the Lord, like their rulers; that their king would be exalted, and would require kingly honors, and would exact a heavy tax or tribute; that they would be oppressed; and that God would not manifest to them his mighty power to deliver them, as he had in Egypt, but when they should cry unto him in their distress, he would not hear them. (1SP 355.1)

But the people would not receive the advice of Samuel, and continued to demand a king. "And the Lord said unto Samuel, Hearken unto the voice of the people in all that they say unto thee; for they have not rejected thee, but they have rejected me, that I should not reign over them." Here, God granted to rebellious Israel that which would prove a heavy curse to them, because they would not submit to have the Lord rule over them. They thought that it would be more honorable in the sight of other nations to have it said, The Hebrews have a king. The Lord directed Samuel to anoint Saul as king of Israel. His appearance was noble, such as would suit the pride of the children of Israel. But God gave them an exhibition of his displeasure. It was not a season of the year when they were visited with heavy rains accompanied with thunder. "So Samuel called unto the Lord, and the Lord sent thunder and rain that day. And all the people greatly feared the Lord and Samuel. And all the people said unto Samuel, Pray for thy servants unto the Lord thy God, that we die not; for we have added unto all our sins this evil, to ask us a king." Samuel sought to encourage the people, that although they had sinned, yet if they from that time followed the Lord, he would not forsake them, for his great name's sake. "Moreover, as for me, God forbid that I should sin against the Lord in ceasing to pray for you; but I will teach you the good and the right way; only fear the Lord, and serve him in truth with all your heart; for consider how great things he hath done for you. But if ye shall still do wickedly, ye shall be consumed, both ye and your king." (1SP 355.2)

When the Philistines, with their large army, prepared to make war with Israel, then the people were afraid. They had not that confidence that God would appear for them, as before they had wickedly demanded a king. They knew that they were but a handful, compared with the armies of the Philistines, and to go out to battle with them seemed to be certain death. They did not feel as secure as they thought they should in possession of their king. In their perplexity, they dared not call upon God whom they had slighted. The Lord said to Samuel, They have not rejected you, but me, by desiring a king. (1SP 356.1)

Now these men, who had been valiant and a terror to their numerous enemies, were afraid to go out against the Philistines to battle. They had their king, but did not dare to trust in him; and they felt that they had chosen him before the Strength of Israel. When they were brought into this perplexing condition, their hearts fainted. In their distress, the people scattered, and hid themselves in caves, and in thickets, and in high places, and in pits, as though escaping from captivity. Those who ventured to go with Saul, followed him trembling. He was in great perplexity as he saw that the people were scattered from him. He anxiously awaited the promised coming of Samuel; but the time expired, and he came not. God had designedly detained Samuel, that his people might be proved, and might realize their sin, and how small was their strength, and how weak their judgment and wisdom, without God. (1SP 356.2)

In their calamity, they repented that they had chosen a king. They had possessed greater courage and confidence while they had God-fearing rulers to instruct and lead them; for they obtained counsel direct from God, and it was like being led by God himself. Now, they realized that they were commanded by an erring king, who could not save them in their distress. Saul had not a high and exalted sense of the excellence and terrible majesty of God. He had not a sacred regard for his appointed ordinances. With an impetuous spirit because Samuel did not appear at the appointed time, he rushed before God presumptuously, and undertook the sacred work of sacrifice. While equipped for war, he built the altar and officiated for himself and the people. This work was sacredly given to those appointed for the purpose. This act was a crime in Saul, and such an example would lead the people to have a low estimate of the religious ceremonies and ordinances sanctified and appointed of God, prefiguring the sinless offering of his dear Son. God would have his people have a holy regard and sacred reverence for the sacrificial work of the priests, which pointed to the sacrifice of his Son. (1SP 357.1)

Chapter 33 - Samuel and Saul (1SP 358.1)

As soon as Saul had finished his presumptuous work, Samuel appears, and, beholding the evidences of Saul's sin, cries out in grief to him, "What hast thou done?" Saul explains the matter to Samuel, justifying himself, setting before Samuel his perplexity and distress, and his delay, as an excuse. Samuel reproves Saul, and tells him that he has done foolishly in not keeping the commandments of the Lord, which if he had obeyed, the Lord would have established his kingdom forever. "But now thy kingdom shall not continue. The Lord hath sought him a man after his own heart, and the Lord hath commanded him to be captain over his people, because thou hast not kept that which the Lord commanded thee." (1SP 358.1)

Because of the sin of Saul in his presumptuous offering, the Lord would not give to him the honor of commanding the armies of Israel in battle with the Philistines. The Lord would have his name alone magnified, lest the armies of Israel should exalt themselves as though it were on account of their righteousness, valor, or wisdom, that their enemies were overcome. He moved upon the heart of Jonathan, a righteous man, and his armor-bearer, to go over to the garrison of the Philistines. Jonathan believed that God was able to work for them, and to save by many or by few. He did not rush up presumptuously. He asked counsel of God, and then, with a fearless heart, trusting in him alone, moved forward. Through these two men, the Lord accomplished his work of subduing the Philistines. He sent angels to protect Jonathan and his armor-bearer, and to shield them from the instruments of death in the hands of their enemies. (1SP 358.2)

Angels of God fought by the side of Jonathan, and the Philistines fell all around him. Great fear seized the host of the Philistines in the field and in the garrison; and the spoilers that had been divided into separate companies, and sent in different directions, ready for their work of slaughter, were terribly afraid. The earth trembled beneath them, as though a great multitude with horsemen and chariots were upon the ground, prepared for battle. Jonathan and his armor-bearer, and even the Philistine host, knew that the Lord was working for the deliverance of the Hebrews. The Philistines became perplexed. It seemed to them that there were men of Israel among them, fighting against them; and they fought against one another, and slaughtered their own armies. (1SP 359.1)

The battle had progressed quite a length of time before Saul and his men were aware that deliverance was being wrought for Israel. The watchmen of Saul perceived great confusion among the Philistines, and saw their numbers decreasing, and yet no one was missed from the armies of Israel. After numbering the men of war, Jonathan and his armor-bearer were reported missing. Saul and the people were perplexed. He had the ark of God brought; and while the priest was inquiring of God, the noise among the Philistines increased. It sounded like two great armies in close battle. When Saul and the people of Israel perceived that God was fighting for them, those who had fled and hid in their terror, and those who had joined the Philistines through fear, united with Saul and Jonathan, and pursued the Philistines. The Lord wrought for Israel, and delivered them for his own name's glory, lest the heathen army should triumph over his people, and exalt themselves proudly against God. (1SP 359.2)

Again, Saul erred in his rash vow that no man should eat until the evening. There was a great lack of wisdom in Saul's zeal in making such a vow. It was a great day's labor for the people, and they suffered much through faintness; and when the time of the vow expired, the people were so faint that they transgressed the commandment of the Lord, and ate meat with the blood, which had been forbidden of God. Saul was determined to slay his son Jonathan, because in his faintness he had tasted of a little honey, being ignorant of his father's vow. (1SP 360.1)

Here was seen Saul's blind zeal, and failure to judge righteously and wisely in difficult matters. He should have reasoned thus: God has been pleased to work in a special manner through Jonathan, thus choosing him among the children of Israel to deliver them; and it would be a crime to destroy his life, which God has miraculously preserved. He knew that if he spared his life, he must acknowledge that he had committed an error in making such a vow. This would humble his pride before the people. Saul should have respected the ones whom God had honored by choosing them to deliver Israel. In putting Jonathan to death, he would slay one whom God loved, while those whose hearts were not right with God, he would preserve alive. God would not suffer Jonathan to die, but led the people to oppose Saul's judgment, although he were a ruling monarch, that he might be convinced that he sinned in making so rash a vow. "And the people said unto Saul, Shall Jonathan die, who hath wrought this great salvation in Israel? God forbid; as the Lord liveth, there shall not one hair of his head fall to the ground; for he hath wrought with God this day. So the people rescued Jonathan, that he died not." (1SP 360.2)

Saul was an impulsive man, and the people of Israel were soon made to feel their sin in demanding a king. The Lord directed Samuel to go unto Saul with a special command from him. Before he related to him the words of the Lord, he said to him, "The Lord sent me to anoint thee to be king over his people, over Israel; now, therefore, hearken thou unto the voice of the words of the Lord." (1SP 361.1)

Samuel had lost confidence in Saul's religious character, because he had been so regardless of following the word of the Lord. He had sinned in his presumptuous offering, and greatly erred in his rash vow. Therefore, Samuel gave him a special charge to heed the words of the Lord. "Thus saith the Lord of hosts, I remember that which Amalek did to Israel, how he laid wait for him in the way, when he came up from Egypt. Now go and smite Amalek, and utterly destroy all that they have, and spare them not." (1SP 361.2)

Many years before, God had appointed Amalek to utter destruction. They had lifted up their hands against God and his throne, and had taken oath by their gods that Israel should be utterly consumed, and the God of Israel brought down so that he would not be able to deliver them out of their hands. (1SP 361.3)

Amalek had made derision of the fears of his people, and made sport of God's wonderful works for the deliverance of Israel performed by the hand of Moses before the Egyptians. They had boasted that their wise men and magicians could perform all those wonders; and that if the children of Israel had been their captives, in their power as they were in Pharaoh's, the God of Israel himself would not have been able to deliver them out of their hands. They despised Israel, and vowed to plague them until there should not be one left. (1SP 361.4)

God marked their boastful words against him, and appointed them to be utterly destroyed by the very people they had despised, that all nations might mark the end of that most proud and powerful people. (1SP 362.1)

God proved Saul by intrusting him with the important commission to execute his threatened wrath upon Amalek. But he disobeyed God, and spared the wicked, blasphemous king Agag, whom God had appointed unto death, and spared the best of the cattle. He destroyed utterly all the refuse that would not profit them. Saul thought it would add to his greatness to spare Agag, a noble monarch splendidly attired; and that to return from battle with him captive, with great spoil of oxen, sheep, and much cattle, would get to himself much renown, and cause the nations to fear him, and tremble before him. And the people united with him in this. They excused their sin among themselves in not destroying the cattle, because they could reserve them to sacrifice to God, and spare their own cattle to themselves. (1SP 362.2)

Samuel visits Saul with a curse from the Lord for his disobedience, for thus exalting himself before the Lord, to choose his own course, and follow his own reasoning, instead of strictly following the Lord. Saul goes forth to meet Samuel, like an innocent man, greeting him with these words: "Blessed be thou of the Lord. I have performed the commandment of the Lord. And Samuel said, What meaneth, then, this bleating of the sheep in mine ears, and the lowing of the oxen which I hear? And Saul said, They have brought them from the Amalekites; for the people spared the best of the sheep and of the oxen, to sacrifice unto the Lord thy God; and the rest we have utterly destroyed." (1SP 362.3)

Samuel relates to Saul what God had said unto him the night before, which night Samuel spent in sorrowful prayer because of Saul's sin. "When thou wast little in thine own sight, wast thou not made the head of the tribes of Israel, and the Lord anointed thee king over Israel?" He reminds Saul of the commands of God which he had wickedly transgressed, and inquires, "Wherefore, then, didst thou not obey the voice of the Lord, but didst fly upon the spoil, and didst evil in the sight of the Lord?" (1SP 363.1)

"And Saul said unto Samuel, Yea, I have obeyed the voice of the Lord, and have gone the way which the Lord sent me, and have brought Agag, the king of Amalek, and have utterly destroyed the Amalekites. But the people took of the spoil, sheep and oxen, the chief of the things, which should have been utterly destroyed, to sacrifice unto the Lord thy God in Gilgal." (1SP 363.2)

Saul here uttered a falsehood. The people had obeyed his directions; but in order to shield himself, he was willing the people should bear the sin of his disobedience. (1SP 363.3)

"And Samuel said, Hath the Lord as great delight in burnt offerings and sacrifices, as in obeying the voice of the Lord? Behold, to obey is better than sacrifice, and to hearken, than the fat of rams. For rebellion is as the sin of witchcraft, and stubbornness is as iniquity and idolatry. Because thou hast rejected the word of the Lord, he hath also rejected thee from being king. And Saul said unto Samuel, I have sinned; for I have transgressed the commandments of the Lord, and thy words; because I feared the people, and obeyed their voice." (1SP 363.4)

God did not wish his people to possess anything which belonged to the Amalekites, for his curse rested upon them and their possessions. He designed that they should have an end, and that his people should not preserve anything for themselves which he had cursed. He also wished the nations to see the end of that people who had defied him, and to mark that they were destroyed by the very people they had despised. They were not to destroy them to add to their own possessions, or to get glory to themselves, but to fulfill the word of the Lord spoken in regard to Amalek. (1SP 364.1)

The Lord had said unto Moses, "Write this for a memorial in a book, and rehearse it in the ears of Joshua; for I will utterly put out the remembrance of Amalek from under heaven." "Remember what Amalek did unto thee by the way, when ye were come forth out of Egypt; how he met thee by the way, and smote the hindermost of thee, even all that were feeble behind thee, when thou wast faint and weary, and he feared not God. Therefore it shall be, when the Lord thy God hath given thee rest from all thine enemies round about, in the land which the Lord thy God giveth thee for an inheritance to possess it, that thou shalt blot out the remembrance of Amalek from under heaven; thou shalt not forget it." (1SP 364.2)

And yet Saul had ventured to disobey God, and reserve that which he had cursed and appointed unto death, to offer before God as a sacrifice for sin. (1SP 365.1)

Samuel presented before Saul his wicked course, and then inquired, "Hath the Lord as great delight in burnt-offerings and sacrifices, as in obeying the voice of the Lord?" It would have been better had he obeyed God, than to make such provisions for sacrifices and offerings for their sins of disobedience. (1SP 365.2)

God did not have as great delight in their shedding the blood of beasts, as in obedience to his commandments. The offerings were divinely appointed to remind sinful man that sin brought death, and that the blood of the innocent beast could atone for the guilt of the transgressor, by virtue of the great sacrifice yet to be offered. God required of his people obedience rather than sacrifice. All the riches of the earth were his. The cattle upon a thousand hills belonged to him. He did not require the spoil of a corrupt people, upon whom his curse rested, even to their utter extinction, to be presented to him to prefigure the holy Saviour, as a lamb without blemish. (1SP 365.3)

Samuel informed Saul that his rebellion was as the sin of witchcraft. That is, when one commences to travel in the path of rebellion, he yields himself to be controlled by an influence that is in opposition to the will of God. Satan controls the rebellious mind. Those who are thus controlled lose a calm trust in God, and have less and less disposition to yield loving obedience to his will. Satan becomes more and more familiar with them, until they seem to have no power to cease to rebel. In this respect, rebellion is as the sin of witchcraft. (1SP 365.4)

Saul's stubbornness in persisting before Samuel that he had obeyed God, was an iniquity and idolatry. His love to carry out his own will was more desirable to him than to obtain the favor of God, or the approbation of a clear conscience. And when his sin was opened clearly before him, and his wrong definitely pointed out, his pride of opinion, his excessive self-love, led him to justify himself in his wrong course, in defiance of the reproof of Samuel, and the word of the Lord by the mouth of his prophet. Such obstinacy in a known transgression, separated him forever from God. (1SP 366.1)

He knew that he had gone contrary to God's express command; yet when reproved by God through Samuel, he would not humbly acknowledge his sin, but in a determined manner uttered a falsehood in self-justification. If he had humbly repented, and received the reproof, the Lord would have had mercy and forgiven Saul of his great sin. But the Lord left Saul for his stubbornly refusing to be corrected, and for uttering falsehoods to Samuel, his messenger. Samuel told Saul that, as he had rejected the word of the Lord, God had rejected him from being king. (1SP 366.2)

This last startling denunciation from Samuel gave Saul a sense of his true condition, and, through fear, he acknowledged that he had sinned, and had transgressed the commandment of the Lord, which he had before firmly denied. He entreated Samuel to pardon his sin, and to worship with him before the Lord. Samuel refused, and told Saul that God had rent the kingdom from him; and lest he should be deceived, he told him that the Strength of Israel would not lie, nor be as changeable as he was. (1SP 366.3)

Again Saul earnestly entreated that Samuel would honor him with his presence once more before the elders of Israel and all the people. Samuel yielded to his request, and called for the cruel king Agag; and he came to him very politely. "And Samuel said, As thy sword hath made women childless, so shall thy mother be childless among women. And Samuel hewed Agag in pieces before the Lord in Gilgal." (1SP 367.1)

And the Lord no more communicated with Saul, or instructed him through Samuel. He had chosen to follow his own will, and had rejected the word of the Lord. God left him to be guided by his own judgment, which he had chosen to follow rather than to obey God. Saul had no true repentance. He had become exalted because he was made king. He manifested greater anxiety to be honored by Samuel before the people, than to obtain forgiveness and the favor of God. (1SP 367.2)

Samuel came no more to Saul with directions from God. The Lord could not employ him to carry out his purposes. But he sent Samuel to the house of Jesse, to anoint David, whom he had selected to be ruler in the place of Saul, whom he had rejected. (1SP 367.3)

As the sons of Jesse passed before Samuel, he would have selected Eliab, who was of high stature and dignified appearance, but the angel of God stood by him to guide him in the important decision, and instructed him that he should not judge from appearances. Eliab did not fear the Lord. His heart was not right with God. He would make a proud, exacting ruler. None was found among the sons of Jesse, but David, the youngest, whose humble occupation was that of tending sheep. He had filled the humble office of shepherd with such faithfulness and courage that God selected him to be captain of his people. In course of time, he was to change his shepherd's crook for the scepter. (1SP 367.4)

David was not of lofty stature; but his countenance was beautiful, expressive of humility, honesty, and true courage. The angel of God signified to Samuel that David was the one for him to anoint, for he was God's chosen. From that time the Lord gave David a prudent and understanding heart. (1SP 368.1)

When Saul saw that Samuel came no more to instruct him, he knew that the Lord had rejected him for his wicked course, and his character seemed ever after to be marked with extremes. His servants, whom he directed in regard to things connected with the kingdom, at times dared not approach him, for he seemed like an insane man, violent and abusive. He often seemed filled with remorse. He was melancholy, and often afraid when there was no danger. This disqualified him for being ruler. He was always full of anxiety; and when in his gloomy moods, he wished not to be disturbed, and at times would suffer none to approach him. He would speak prophetically of his being dethroned, and another's occupying his position as ruler, and that his posterity would never be exalted to the throne, and receive kingly honors, but that they would all perish because of his sins. He would repeat, prophetically, sayings against himself with distracted energy, even in the presence of his lords, and of the people. (1SP 368.2)

Those who witnessed these strange exhibitions in Saul recommended to him music, as calculated to have a soothing influence upon his mind when thus distracted. In the providence of God, David was brought to his notice as a skillful musician. He was also recommended for being a valiant man of war, prudent and faithful in all matters, because he was especially guided by the Lord. Saul felt humbled at times, and was even anxious that one should take charge of the government of the kingdom, who should know from the Lord how to move in accordance with his will. While in a favorable state of mind, he sent messengers for David. He soon loved him, and gave him the position of armor-bearer, making him his attendant. He thought that if David was favored of God, he would be a safeguard to him, and perhaps save his life, when he should be exposed to his enemies. David's skillful playing upon the harp soothed the troubled spirit of Saul. As he listened to the enchanting strains of music, it had an influence to dispel the gloom which had settled upon him, and to bring his excited mind into a more rational, happy state. (1SP 368.3)

Especially was the heart of Jonathan knit with David's; and there was a most sacred bond of union established between them, which remained unbroken till the death of Saul and Jonathan. This was the Lord's doings, that Jonathan might be the means of preserving the life of David when Saul would try to kill him. God's providence connected David with Saul, that by his wise behaviour he might obtain the confidence of the people, and by a long course of hardships and vicissitudes, be led to put his entire trust in God, while he was preparing him to become ruler of his people. (1SP 369.1)

When the Philistines renewed war with Israel, David was permitted to go to his father's house to resume the occupation of shepherd, which he loved. The Philistines dare not venture their large armies against Israel, as they had heretofore done, fearing they would be overcome, and fall before Israel. They are ignorant of the weakness of Israel. They know not that Saul and his people have great anxiety, and they dare not commence the battle with them, fearing that Israel will be overcome. But the Philistines propose their own manner of warfare, in selecting a man of great size and strength, whose height is about twelve feet; and they send this champion forth to provoke a combat with Israel, requesting them to send out a man to fight with him. He was terrible in appearance, and spoke proudly, and defied the armies of Israel and their God. (1SP 370.1)

For forty days this proud boaster filled Israel with terror, and made Saul greatly afraid; for no one dared to combat with the mighty giant. Israel, on account of their transgressions, had not that sacred trust in God which would lead them to battle in his name. But God would not suffer an idolatrous nation to lift their heads proudly against the Ruler of the universe. He saved Israel, not by the hand of Saul, but by the hand of David, whom he had raised up to rule his people. (1SP 370.2)

Saul knows not what to do. He imagines Israel as Philistine slaves. He can see no way of escape. In his trouble, he offers great reward to any one who will slay the proud boaster. But all feel their weakness. They have a king whom God does not instruct, who dares not engage in any perilous enterprise, for he expects no special interposition from God to save his life. As Israel had been partakers with him in transgression, he had no hope that God would work specially for them, and deliver them out of the hands of the Philistines. The armies of Israel seemed paralyzed with terror. They could not trust in their king, whom they had demanded of God. Saul's mind was changeable. He would for a short time direct the armies, and then fear and discouragement would seize him, and he would countermand his orders. (1SP 370.3)

As David is performing a humble errand from his father to his brethren, he hears the proud boaster defying Israel, and his spirit is stirred within him. He is jealous for the armies of the living God, whom the blasphemous boaster has defied. He expresses his indignation that a heathen, who has no fear of God, and no power from him, should be left to thus hold all Israel in fear, and triumph over them. (1SP 371.1)

David's eldest brother, Eliab, whom God would not choose to be king, was jealous of David, because he was honored before him. He despised David, and looked upon him as inferior to himself. He accused him before others of stealing away unknown to his father to see the battle. He taunts him with the small business in which he is engaged, in tending a few sheep in the wilderness. David repels the unjust charge, and says, "What have I now done? Is there not a cause?" David is not careful to explain to his brother that he had come to the help of Israel; that God had sent him to slay Goliath. God had chosen him to be a ruler of Israel; and as the armies of the living God were in such peril, he had been directed by an angel to save Israel. (1SP 371.2)

David is brought before Saul, and tells him that Israel need not fear: "Thy servant will go and fight with this Philistine." Saul objects, because of his youth. David refers to the perils he had experienced in the wilderness, to save the sheep under his care. He humbly ascribes his

Chapter 33 - Samuel and Saul (1SP 374.1)

deliverance to God. "The Lord that delivered me out of the paw of the lion, and out of the paw of the bear, he will deliver me out of the hand of this Philistine." Saul gives David permission to go. He places upon David his own kingly armor; but David laid it off, and merely chose him five smooth stones from the brook, a sling, and a staff. As the proud defier of Israel saw the young man of beautiful countenance approaching him with this equipment, he inquired," Am I a dog, that thou comest to me with staves?" He cursed David by his gods, and boastingly invited him to come to him, that he might give his flesh to the fowls of the air, and to the beasts of the field. "Then said David to the Philistine, Thou comest to me with a sword, and with a spear, and with a shield;" but I come to thee, not in display of armor, nor with powerful weapons, but "in the name of the Lord of hosts, the God of the armies of Israel, whom thou hast defied." David makes no boast of superior skill. His boast is in the Lord. "This day will the Lord deliver thee into mine hand, ... that all the earth may know that there is a God in Israel. And all this assembly shall know that the Lord saveth not with sword and spear; for the battle is the Lord's, and he will give you into our hands. And it came to pass, when the Philistine arose, and came and drew nigh to meet David, that David hasted, and ran toward the army to meet the Philistine. And David put his hand in his bag, and took thence a stone, and slang it, and smote the Philistine in his forehead, that the stone sunk into his forehead; and he fell upon his face to the earth." (1SP 371.3)

David cut off the head of the proud boaster with his own powerful sword, of which he had boasted. And when the Philistines saw that their champion was dead, they were confused, and fled in every direction, Israel pursuing them. (1SP 373.1)

When Saul and David were returning from the slaughter of the Philistines, the women of the cities came out to meet them with demonstrations of joy, and with singing. One company sang, "Saul hath slain his thousands." Another company responded to the first, "And David his ten thousands." This made Saul very angry. Instead of manifesting humble gratitude to God that Israel had been saved out of the hand of their enemies by the hand of David, a cruel spirit of jealousy comes upon him, and, as in times past, he yields himself to its control. "And Saul was very wroth, and the saying displeased him; and he said, They have ascribed unto David ten thousands, and to me they have ascribed but thousands; and what can he have more but the kingdom?" His fears were aroused that this was indeed the man who would take his place as ruler. Yet because the people all esteemed and loved David, Saul was afraid to harm him openly. (1SP 373.2)

Through the influence of the people, David was promoted to take charge of the business connected with warfare. He was leader in all their important enterprises. As Saul saw that David had won the love and confidence of the people, he hated him; for he thought that he was preferred before him. He watched an opportunity to slay him; and when the evil spirit was upon him, and David played before him as usual to soothe his troubled mind, he tried to kill him, by throwing with force a sharp-pointed instrument at his heart. Angels of God preserved the life of David. They made him understand what was the purpose of Saul; and as the instrument was hurled at him, he sprang to one side, and received no harm, while the instrument was driven deep into the wall where David had been sitting. (1SP 373.3)

The people of Israel were now made to feel their peculiar position. They had daily evidence that God had left Saul to his own guilty course, and that they were commanded by a ruler who dared to commit murder, and slay a righteous person whom the Lord had chosen to save them. And by the cruel acts of Saul they were having living evidences to what extremes of guilt and crime a king might go who rebelled against God, and was governed by his own passions. (1SP 374.1)

David had obeyed Saul as a servant, and his conduct was humble. His life was irreproachable. His faithfulness in doing the will of God was a constant rebuke to Saul's extravagant, rebellious course. Saul determined to leave no means untried, that David might be slain. As long as Saul lived, this was the great object of his life, notwithstanding he was compelled to ascribe to the providence of God the escape of David from his hands. Yet his heart was destitute of the love of God, and he was a self-idolater. True honor, justice, and humanity, were sacrificed to his pride and ambition. He hunted David as a wild beast. David often had Saul in his power, and was urged by the men whom he commanded to slay him.

Chapter 33 - Samuel and Saul (1SP 374.2)

Although David knew that he was chosen of God as ruler in Israel, yet he would not lift his hand against Saul, whom God had anointed. He chose to find an asylum among the Philistines. He made even his enemies to be at peace with him, by his prudent, humble course, with whom he remained until the death of Saul. (1SP 374.2)

When the Philistines again make war with Israel, Saul is afraid. He has no rest in any season of peril, and the people are divided. Some go with Saul in all his wickedness. Others cannot trust to his judgment, and wish a righteous ruler. Saul's last acts have been so cruel, presumptuous and daring, that his conscience is as a scourge, continually upbraiding him. Yet he does not repent of his wickedness, but pursues his relentless course with despairing desperation, and at the prospect of a battle, he is distracted and melancholy. He presumes, with his load of guilt upon him, to inquire of God; but God answers him not. He has barbarously massacred the priests of the Lord, because they suffered David to escape. He destroyed the city where the priests lived, and put a multitude of righteous persons to death, to satisfy his envious rage. Yet in his peril he dares to approach God, to inquire whether he shall make war with the Philistines. But as God has left him, he seeks a woman with a familiar spirit, who is in communion with Satan. He has forsaken God, and at length seeks one who has made a covenant with death, and an agreement with hell, for knowledge. The witch of Endor had made agreement with Satan to follow his directions in all things; and he would perform wonders and miracles for her, and would reveal to her the most secret things, if she would yield herself unreservedly to be controlled by his satanic majesty. This she had done. (1SP 375.1)

When Saul inquired for Samuel, the Lord did not cause Samuel to appear to Saul. He saw nothing. Satan was not allowed to disturb the rest of Samuel in the grave, and bring him up in reality to the witch of Endor. God does not give Satan power to resurrect the dead. But Satan's angels assume the form of dead friends, and speak and act like them, that through professed dead friends he can the better carry on his work of deception. Satan knew Samuel well, and he knew how to represent him before the witch of Endor, and to utter correctly the fate of Saul and his sons. (1SP 376.1)

Satan will come in a very plausible manner to such as he can deceive, and will insinuate himself into their favor, and lead them almost imperceptibly from God. He wins them under his control, cautiously at first, until their perceptibilities become blunted. Then he will make bolder suggestions, until he can lead them to commit almost any degree of crime. When he has led them fully into his snare, he is then willing that they should see where they are, and he exults in their confusion, as in the case of Saul. He had suffered Satan to lead him a willing captive, and now Satan spreads before Saul a correct description of his fate. By giving Saul a correct statement of his end, through the woman of Endor, Satan opens a way for Israel to be instructed by his satanic cunning, that they may, in their rebellion against God, learn of him, and by thus doing, sever the last link which would hold them to God. (1SP 376.2)

Saul knew that in this last act, of consulting the witch of Endor, he cut the last shred which held him to God. He knew that if he had not before willfully separated himself from God, this act sealed that separation, and made it final. He had made an agreement with death, and a covenant with hell. The cup of his iniquity was full. (1SP 376.3)

*****

Chapter 34
David

God selected David, a humble shepherd, to rule his people. He was strict in all the ceremonies connected with the Jewish religion, and he distinguished himself by his boldness and unwavering trust in God. He was remarkable for his fidelity and reverence. His firmness, humility, love of justice, and decision of character, qualified him to carry out the high purposes of God, to instruct Israel in their devotions, and to rule them as a generous and wise monarch. (1SP 377.1)

His religious character was sincere and fervent. It was while David was thus true to God, and possessing these exalted traits of character, that God calls him a man after his own heart. When exalted to the throne, his general course was in striking contrast with the kings of other nations. He abhorred idolatry, and zealously kept the people of Israel from being seduced into it by the surrounding nations. He was greatly beloved and honored by his people. (1SP 377.2)

He often conquered, and triumphed. He increased in wealth and greatness. But his prosperity had an influence to lead him from God. His temptations were many and strong. He finally fell into the common practice of other kings around him, of having a plurality of wives, and his life was imbittered by the evil results of polygamy. His first wrong was in taking more than one wife, thus departing from God's wise arrangement. This departure from right, prepared the way for greater errors. The kingly idolatrous nations considered it an addition to their honor and dignity to have many wives, and David regarded it an honor to his throne to possess several wives. But he was made to see the wretched evil of such a course, by the unhappy discord, rivalry and jealousy among his numerous wives and children. (1SP 377.3)

His crime in the case of Uriah and Bath-sheba, was heinous in the sight of God. A just and impartial God did not sanction or excuse these sins in David, but sent a reproof and heavy denunciation by Nathan, his prophet, which portrayed in living colors his grievous offense. David had been blinded to his wonderful departure from God. He had excused his own sinful course to himself, until his ways seemed passable in his own eyes. One wrong step had prepared the way for another, until his sins called for the rebuke from Jehovah through Nathan. David awakens as from a dream. He feels the sense of his sin. He does not seek to excuse his course, or palliate his sin, as did Saul; but with remorse and sincere grief, he bows his head before the prophet of God, and acknowledges his guilt. Nathan tells David that, because of his repentance and humble confession, God will forgive his sin, and avert a part of the threatened calamity, and spare his life; yet he should be punished, because he had given great occasion to the enemies of the Lord to blaspheme. This occasion has been improved by the enemies of God, from David's day until the present time. Skeptics have assailed Christianity, and ridiculed the Bible, because David gave them occasion. They bring up to Christians the case of David, his sin in the case of Uriah and Bath-sheba, his polygamy, and then assert that David is called a man after God's own heart, and that if the Bible record is correct, God justified David in his crimes. (1SP 378.1)

I was shown that it was when David was pure, and walking in the counsel of God, that God called him a man after his own heart. When David departed from God, and stained his virtuous character by his crimes, he was no longer a man after God's own heart. God did not in the least degree justify him in his sins, but sent Nathan, his prophet, with dreadful denunciations to David because he had transgressed the commandment of the Lord. God shows his displeasure at David's having a plurality of wives, by visiting him with judgments, and permitting evils to rise up against him from his own house. The terrible calamity that God permitted to come upon David, who, for his integrity, was once

Chapter 34 - David (1SP 379.1)

called a man after God's own heart, is evidence to after generations that God would not justify any one in transgressing his commandments; but that he would surely punish the guilty, however righteous and favored of God they might once have been while they followed the Lord in purity of heart. When the righteous turn from their righteousness and do evil, their past righteousness will not save them from the wrath of a just and holy God. (1SP 379.1)

Leading men of Bible history have sinned grievously. Their sins are not concealed, but faithfully recorded in the history of God's church, with the punishment from God, which followed the offenses. These instances are left on record for the benefit of after generations, and should inspire faith in the word of God, as a faithful history. Men who wish to doubt God, doubt Christianity, and the word of God, will not judge candidly and impartially, but with prejudiced minds will scan the life and character, to detect all the defects in the lives of those who have been the most eminent leaders of Israel. God has caused a faithful delineation of character to be given in inspired history, of the best and greatest men in their day. These men were mortal, subject to a tempting devil. Their weaknesses and sins are not covered, but are faithfully recorded, with the reproofs and punishments which followed. These things "were written for our admonition upon whom the ends of the world are come." (1SP 379.2)

God has not allowed much to be said in his word to extol the virtues of the best men that have lived upon the earth. All their victories, and great and good works, were ascribed to God. He alone was to receive the glory, he alone to be exalted. He was all and in all. Man was only an agent, a feeble instrument in his hands. The power and excellence were all of God. God saw in man a continual disposition to depart from, and forget, him, and to worship the creature instead of the Creator. Therefore, God would not suffer much in the praise of man to be left upon the pages of sacred history. (1SP 380.1)

David repented of his sin in dust and ashes. He entreated the forgiveness of God, and concealed not his repentance from the great men, and even servants, of his kingdom. He composed a penitential psalm, recounting his sin and repentance, which psalm he knew would be sung by after generations. He wished others to be instructed by the sad history of his life. (1SP 380.2)

The songs which David composed were sung by all Israel, especially in the presence of the assembled court, and before priests, elders and lords. He knew that the confession of his guilt would bring his sins to the notice of other generations. He presents his case, showing in whom was his trust and hope for pardon: "Have mercy upon me, O God, according to thy loving-kindness; according unto the multitude of thy tender mercies, blot out my transgressions. Wash me thoroughly from mine iniquity, and cleanse me from my sin." "Deliver me from blood guiltiness, O God, thou God of my salvation." (1SP 381.1)

David does not manifest the spirit of an unconverted man. If he had possessed the spirit of the rulers of the nations around him, he would not have borne, from Nathan, the picture of his crime before him in its truly abominable colors, but would have taken the life of the faithful reprover. But notwithstanding the loftiness of his throne, and his unlimited power, his humble acknowledgment of all with which he was charged, is evidence that he still feared and trembled at the word of the Lord. (1SP 381.2)

David was made to feel bitterly the fruits of wrong-doing. His sons acted over the sins of which he had been guilty. Amnon committed a great crime; Absalom revenged it by slaying him. Thus was David's sin brought continually to his mind, and he made to feel the full weight of the injustice done to Uriah and Bath-sheba. (1SP 381.3)

Absalom, his own son, whom he loved above all his children, rebelled against him. By his remarkable beauty, winning manners, and pretended kindness, he cunningly stole the hearts of the people. He did not possess benevolence at heart, but was ambitious, and, as his course shows, would resort to intrigue and crime to obtain the kingdom. He would have requited his father's love and kindness by taking his life. He was proclaimed king by his followers in Hebron, and led them out to pursue his father. He was defeated and slain. (1SP 382.1)

David was brought into great distress by this rebellion. It was unlike any war that he had been connected with. His wisdom from God, with his energy and warlike skill, had enabled him to successfully resist the assaults of his enemies. But this unnatural warfare, arising in his own house, and the rebel being his own son, seemed to confuse and weaken his calm judgment. And the knowledge that this evil had been predicted by the prophet, and that he had brought it upon himself by transgressing the commandments of God, destroyed his skill and former unequaled courage. (1SP 382.2)

David was humbled and greatly distressed. He fled from Jerusalem to save his life. He did not go forth with confidence and kingly honor, trusting in God, as he had in previous battles; but as he went up by the ascent of the Mount of Olivet, surrounded by his people, and his mighty men, he covered his head in his humility, and walked barefoot, weeping; and his people imitated the example of deep humility manifested by their king, while fleeing before Absalom. (1SP 382.3)

Shimei, a kinsman of Saul, who had ever been envious of David because he received the throne and kingly honors which had once been given to Saul, improved this opportunity of venting his rebellious rage upon David in his misfortune. He cursed the king, and cast stones and dirt at him and his servants, and accused David of being a bloody and mischievous man. The followers of David beg permission to go and take his life; but David rebukes them, and tells them to "let him curse, because the Lord hath said unto him, Curse David. Who shall then say, Wherefore hast thou done so?" Behold my son "seeketh my life; how much more now may this Benjamite do it? Let him alone, and let him curse; for the Lord hath bidden him." (1SP 382.4)

He thus acknowledges, before his people and chief men, that this is the punishment God has brought upon him because of his sin, which has given the enemies of the Lord occasion to blaspheme; that the enraged Benjamite might be accomplishing his part of the punishment predicted, and that if he bore these things with humility, the Lord would lessen his affliction, and turn the curse of Shimei into a blessing. David does not manifest the spirit of an unconverted man. He shows that he has had an experience in the things of God. He manifests a disposition to receive correction from God, and, in confidence turns to him as his only trust. God rewards David's humble trust in him, by defeating the counsel of Ahithophel, and preserving his life. (1SP 383.1)

David was not the character Shimei represented him to be. When Saul was repeatedly placed in his power, and his followers would have killed him, David would not permit them to do so, although he was in continual fear of his own life, and was pursued, like a wild beast, by Saul. At one time when Saul was in his power, he cut off a piece of the skirt of his robe, that he might evidence to Saul that he would not harm him, although he might have taken his life if he had been so disposed. David repented even of this, because Saul was the Lord's anointed. (1SP 383.2)

When David was thirsty, and greatly desired water of the well of Bethlehem, three men, without his knowledge, broke through the host of the Philistines, and drew water out of the well of Bethlehem, and brought it to David. He considered it too sacred to drink to quench his thirst, because three men, through their love for him, had periled their lives to obtain it. He did not lightly regard life. It seemed to him that if he drank the water these brave men had put their lives in jeopardy to obtain, it would be like drinking their blood. He solemnly poured out the water as a sacred offering to God. (1SP 384.1)

After the death of Absalom, God turned the hearts of Israel, as the heart of one man, to David. Shimei, who had cursed David in his humility, through fear of his life, was among the first of the rebellious to meet David on his return to Jerusalem. He made confession of his rebellious conduct toward David. Those who witnessed his abusive course urged David not to spare his life, because he cursed the Lord's anointed. But David rebuked them. He not only spared the life of Shimei, but mercifully forgave him. Had David possessed a revengeful spirit, he could readily have gratified it, by putting the offender to death. (1SP 384.2)

Israel prospered and increased in numbers under David's rule; and, as they became strong, and had increased in wealth and greatness, they became exalted and proud. They forgot the Giver of all their mercies, and were fast losing their peculiar and holy character, which separated them from the nations around them. (1SP 384.3)

David, in his prosperity, did not preserve that humility of character and trust in God which characterized the earlier part of his life. He looked upon the accession to the kingdom with pride, and contrasted their then prosperous condition with their few numbers and little

Chapter 34 - David (1SP 385.1)

strength when he ascended the throne, taking glory to himself. He gratified his ambitious feelings in yielding to the temptation of the devil to number Israel, that he might compare their former weakness with their then prosperous state under his rule. This was displeasing to God, and contrary to his express command. It would lead Israel to rely upon their strength of numbers, instead of the living God. (1SP 385.1)

The work of numbering Israel is not fully completed before David feels convicted that he has committed a great sin against God. He sees his error, and humbles himself before God, confessing his great sin in foolishly numbering the people. But his repentance came too late. The word had already gone forth from the Lord to his faithful prophet, to carry a message to David, and offer him his choice of punishments for his transgression. David still shows that he has confidence in God. He chooses to fall into the hands of a merciful God, rather than to be left to the cruel mercies of wicked men. (1SP 385.2)

Swift destruction followed. Seventy thousand were destroyed by pestilence. David and the elders of Israel were in the deepest humiliation, mourning before the Lord. As the angel of the Lord was on his way to destroy Jerusalem, God bade him stay his work of death. A pitiful God loves his people still, notwithstanding their rebellion. The angel, clad in warlike garments, with a drawn sword in his hand, stretched out over Jerusalem, is revealed to David, and to those who are with him. David is terribly afraid, yet he cries out in his distress, and his compassion for Israel. He begs of God to save the sheep. In anguish he confesses, "I have sinned, and I have done wickedly; but these sheep, what have they done? Let thine hand, I pray thee, be against me, and against my father's house." God speaks to David, by his prophet, and bids him make atonement for his sin. David's heart was in the work, and his repentance was accepted. The threshing-floor of Araunah is offered him freely, where to build an altar unto the Lord; also cattle, and everything needful for the sacrifice. But David tells him who would make this generous offering, that the Lord will accept the sacrifice which he is willing to make, but that he would not come before the Lord with an offering which cost him nothing. He would buy it of him for full price. He offered there burnt-offerings and peace-offerings. God accepted the offerings by answering David in sending fire from Heaven to consume the sacrifice. The angel of the Lord was commanded to put his sword into his sheath, and cease his work of destruction. (1SP 385.3)

David composed many of the psalms in the wilderness, to which he was compelled to flee for safety. Saul even pursued him there; and David was several times preserved from falling into the hands of Saul, by the special interposition of Providence. While David was thus passing through severe trials and hardships, he manifested an unwavering trust in God, and was especially imbued with his Spirit as he composed his songs which recount his dangers and deliverances, ascribing praise and glory to God, his merciful preserver. In these psalms is seen a spirit of fervor, devotion, and holiness. He sung these songs, which express his thoughts and meditations of divine things, accompanied with skillful music upon the harp and other instruments. The psalm contained in 2 Samuel 22, was composed while Saul was hunting him to take his life. Nearly all the sacred songs of David were arranged in the earlier period of his life, while he was serving the Lord with integrity and purity of heart. (1SP 386.1)

David proposed to build a house for God, in which he could place the sacred ark, and to which all Israel should come to worship. The Lord informed David, through his prophet, that he should not build the house, but that he should have a son who should build a house for God. "I will be his father, and he shall be my son. If he commit iniquity, I will chasten him with the rod of men, and with the stripes of the children of men. But my mercy shall not depart away from him, as I took it from Saul, whom I put away before thee." God manifests pity and compassion for the weakness of erring man, and promises, if he transgress, to punish him; and if he repent, to forgive him. (1SP 387.1)

The closing years of David's life were marked with faithful devotion to God. He mourned over his sins and departure from God's just precepts, which had darkened his character, and given occasion for the enemies of the Lord to blaspheme. The Lord, through his angel, instructed David, and gave him a pattern of the house which Solomon should build for him. An angel was commissioned to stand by David while he was writing out, for the benefit of Solomon, the important directions in regard to the arrangement of the house. David's heart was in the work. He manifested an earnestness and devotion in making extensive preparations for the building, and spared neither labor nor expense, but made large donations from his own treasury, thereby setting a noble example before his people, which they did not hesitate to follow with willing hearts. **(1SP 387.2)**

David feels the greatest solicitude for Solomon. He fears that he may follow his example in wrong-doing. He can see with the deepest sorrow the spots and blemishes he has brought upon his character by falling into grievous sins; and he would save his son from the evil if he could. He has learned by experience that the Lord will in no case sanction wrong-doing, whether it be found in the loftiest prince or the humblest subject, but would visit the leader of his people with as much severer punishment as his position is more responsible than that of the humblest subject. The sins committed by the leaders of Israel would have an influence to lessen the heinousness of crime in the minds and consciences of the people, and would be brought to the notice of other nations, who fear not God, but who trample upon his authority; and they would be led to blaspheme the God of Israel. **(1SP 388.1)**

David solemnly charges his son to adhere strictly to the law of God, and to keep all his statutes. He relates to Solomon the word of the Lord, spoken unto him through his prophets: "Moreover, I will establish his kingdom forever, if he be constant to do my commandments and my judgments, as at this day. Now, therefore, in the sight of all Israel, the congregation of the Lord, and in the audience of our God, keep and seek for all the commandments of the Lord your God, that ye may possess this good land, and leave it for an inheritance for your children after you forever. And thou, Solomon, my son, know thou the God of thy father, and serve him with a perfect heart, and with a willing mind; for the Lord searcheth all hearts, and understandeth all the imaginations of the thoughts. If thou seek him, he will be found of thee; but if thou forsake him, he will cast thee off forever. Take heed now; for the Lord hath chosen thee to build an house for the sanctuary. Be strong, and do it." **(1SP 388.2)**

After giving this charge to his son in the audience of the people, and in the presence of God, he offers grateful thanks to God for disposing his own heart, and the hearts of the people, to give willingly for the great work of building. He also entreats the Lord to incline the heart of Solomon to his commandments. He says, "I know also, my God, that thou triest the heart, and hast pleasure in uprightness. As for me, in the uprightness of mine heart I have willingly offered all these things. And now have I seen with joy thy people, which are present here to offer willingly unto thee. O Lord God of Abraham, Isaac, and of Israel, our fathers, keep this forever in the imagination of the thoughts of the heart of thy people, and prepare their heart unto thee. And give unto Solomon, my son, a perfect heart, to keep thy commandments, thy testimonies, and thy statutes, and to do all these things, and to build the palace, for the which I have made provision." **(1SP 389.1)**

David's public labor was about to close. He knew that he should soon die, and he does not leave his business matters in confusion, to vex the soul of his son; but while he has sufficient physical and mental strength, he arranges the affairs of his kingdom, even to the minutest matters, not forgetting to warn Solomon in regard to the case of Shimei. He knew that the latter would cause trouble in the kingdom. He was a dangerous man, of violent temper, and was kept in control only through fear. Whenever he dared, he would cause rebellion, or, if he had a favorable opportunity, would not hesitate to take the life of Solomon. **(1SP 389.2)**

David, in arranging his business, sets a good example to all who are advanced in years, to settle their matters while they are capable of doing so, that when they shall be drawing near to death, and their mental faculties are dimmed, they shall have nothing of a worldly nature to divert their minds from God. **(1SP 390.1)**

*****

Chapter 35
Solomon

The hearts of the people are turned toward Solomon, as they were to David, and they obey him in all things. The Lord sends his angel to instruct Solomon by a dream in the night season. He dreams that God converses with him. "And God said, Ask what I shall give thee. And Solomon said, Thou hast showed unto thy servant David, my father, great mercy, according as he walked before thee in truth, and in righteousness, and in uprightness of heart with thee; and thou hast kept for him this great kindness, that thou hast given him a son to sit on his throne, as it is this day. And now, O Lord my God, thou hast made thy servant king instead of David my father; and I am but a little child; I know not how to go out or come in. And thy servant is in the midst of thy people which thou hast chosen, a great people, that cannot be numbered nor counted for multitude. Give, therefore, thy servant an understanding heart to judge thy people, that I may discern between good and bad; for who is able to judge this thy so great a people? (1SP 390.2)

"And the speech pleased the Lord, that Solomon had asked this thing. And God said unto him, Because thou hast asked this thing, and hast not asked for thyself long life; neither hast asked riches for thyself, nor hast asked the life of thine enemies; but hast asked for thyself understanding to discern judgment; behold, I have done according to thy word. Lo, I have given thee a wise and an understanding heart; so that there was none like thee before thee, neither after thee shall any arise like unto thee. And I have also given thee that which thou hast not asked, both riches and honor, so that there shall not be any among the kings like unto thee all thy days. And if thou wilt walk in my ways, to keep my statutes and my commandments, as thy father David did walk, then I will lengthen thy days." (1SP 391.1)

God promises that, as he has been with David, he will be with Solomon. If he will walk before the Lord in integrity of heart, and in uprightness, to do according to all that God commanded him, and if he will keep his statutes and judgments, he promises to establish his throne upon Israel forever. Solomon feels the magnitude of the work of building a house for God. He thus gives expression to his ideas: "Who is able to build him an house, seeing the heaven and Heaven of heavens cannot contain him?" (1SP 391.2)

The Lord imparted unto Solomon that wisdom which he desired above earthly riches, honor, or long life. He was the wisest king that ever sat upon the throne. God gave him an understanding heart. He wrote many proverbs, and composed many songs. For many years his life was marked with devotion to God, and with uprightness, firm principle, and strict obedience to God's commands. He directed in every important enterprise, and managed the business matters connected with the kingdom, with the greatest wisdom. His faithfully carrying out the directions, in constructing the most magnificent building the world ever saw, caused his fame to spread among the nations everywhere. He was greatly blessed and honored of God. All nations acknowledged, and marveled at, his superior knowledge and wisdom, the excellence of his character, and the greatness of his power. Many came to him from all parts of the world to behold his unlimited power, and to be instructed how to conduct difficult matters. The temple built for God could not be excelled for richness, beauty, and costly design. (1SP 392.1)

After the temple was finished, Solomon assembled all Israel, and many nations also came to witness the dedication of the house of God. It was dedicated with great splendor. Solomon addresses the people, and seeks to tear away from the minds of all present the superstitions which have clouded the minds of heathen nations in regard to Jehovah. He tells them that God is not like the heathen gods, who are confined to temples built for them; but that the God of Israel would meet them by his Spirit when the people should assemble in that house dedicated to his worship. (**1SP 392.2**)

Solomon kneels before God, in the presence of that immense congregation, and makes supplication to God. He inquires in his prayer, "But will God indeed dwell on the earth? Behold, heaven and the Heaven of heavens cannot contain thee; how much less this house that I have builded!" He continues: "That thine eyes may be open toward this house night and day, even toward the place of which thou hast said, My name shall be there; that thou mayest hearken unto the prayer which thy servant shall make toward this place." (**1SP 393.1**)

"Now, when Solomon had made an end of praying, the fire came down from Heaven, and consumed the burnt-offering and the sacrifices; and the glory of the Lord filled the house. And the priests could not enter into the house of the Lord, because the glory of the Lord had filled the Lord's house. And when all the children of Israel saw how the fire came down, and the glory of the Lord upon the house, they bowed themselves with their faces toward the ground upon the pavement, and worshiped, and praised the Lord, saying, For he is good; for his mercy endureth forever." (**1SP 393.2**)

Seven days was Solomon engaged in the dedication of the house of God. And after the ceremonies of dedicating the house were ended, "the Lord said unto him, I have heard thy prayer and thy supplication that thou hast made before me. I have hallowed this house which thou hast built, to put my name there forever; and mine eyes and mine heart shall be there perpetually. And if thou wilt walk before me as David, thy father, walked, in integrity of heart, and in uprightness, to do according to all that I have commanded thee, and wilt keep my statutes and my judgments, then I will establish the throne of thy kingdom upon Israel forever, as I promised to David, thy father, saying, There shall not fail thee a man upon the throne of Israel. But if ye shall at all turn from following me, ye or your children, and will not keep my commandments and my statutes which I have set before you, but go and serve other gods, and worship them; then will I cut off Israel out of the land which I have given them; and this house which I have hallowed for my name, will I cast out of my sight; and Israel shall be a proverb and a by-word among all people." (**1SP 393.3**)

If Israel remained faithful and true to God, this glorious building was to stand forever, as a perpetual sign of God's especial favor to his chosen people. They were called peculiar, because they alone, among all the nations of earth, preserved the true worship of God, by keeping his commandments. (**1SP 394.1**)

While Solomon remained pure, God was with him. In the dedication of the temple, he exalts God's law before the people. While blessing the people he repeats these words: "The Lord our God be with us, as he was with our fathers. Let him not leave us, nor forsake us; that he may incline our hearts unto him, to walk in all his ways, and to keep his commandments, and his statutes, and his judgments, which he commanded our fathers." (**1SP 394.2**)

In the uprightness of his heart, he exhorts the congregation of Israel: "Let your heart, therefore, be perfect with the Lord our God, to walk in his statutes, and to keep his commandments, as at this day." As long as Solomon steadfastly obeyed the commandments, God was with him, as he had entreated that he might be, as he was with David. "Thou hast shown unto my father David great mercy, according as he walked before thee in truth, and in righteousness, and in uprightness of heart." (**1SP 395.1**)

There is enough contained in these words to silence every skeptic in regard to God's sanctioning the sins of David and Solomon. God was merciful to them according as they walked before him in truth, righteousness, and uprightness of heart. Just according to their faithfulness, God dealt with them. (**1SP 395.2**)

Solomon walked for many years uprightly before God. Wisdom was given him of God to judge the people with impartiality and mercy. But even this exalted, learned, and once good, man, fell through yielding to temptations connected with his prosperity and honored position. He forgot God, and the solemn conditions of his success. He fell into the sinful practice of other kings, of having many wives, which was contrary to God's arrangement. God commanded Moses to warn the people against their having a plurality of wives. "Neither shall he multiply wives to himself, that his heart turn not away. Neither shall he greatly multiply to himself silver and gold." (**1SP 395.3**)

Chapter 35 - Solomon (1SP 395.4)

True goodness is accounted of Heaven as true greatness. The condition of the moral affections determines the worth of the man. A man may have property and intellect, and yet be valueless, because the glowing fire of goodness has never burned upon the altar of his heart, because his conscience has been seared, blackened and crisped, with selfishness and sin. When the lust of the flesh is controlling the man, and the evil passions of the carnal nature are permitted to rule, skepticism in regard to the realities of the Christian religion is encouraged, and doubts are expressed, as though it was a special virtue to doubt. (1SP 395.4)

The life of Solomon might have been remarkable until its close, if virtue had been preserved. But he surrendered this special grace to lustful passion. In his youth he looked to God for guidance. He trusted in him, and God chose for him, and wisdom was given to him–wisdom that astonished the world. His power and wisdom were extolled throughout the land. His love of women was his sin. This passion he did not control in his manhood. It proved a snare to him. His wives led him into idolatry, and the wisdom God had given him was removed when he began to descend the declivity of life; he lost his firmness of character, and became more like the giddy youth, wavering between right and wrong. He yielded his principles, and placed himself in the current of evil, and thus separated himself from God, the source of his strength. He was a man who had moved from principle. Wisdom had been more precious to him than the gold of Ophir. But alas! lustful passions obtained the victory. He was deceived and ruined through women. What a lesson for watchfulness! What a testimony as to the need of strength from God to the very last! (1SP 396.1)

In the battle with inward corruptions and outward temptations, even the wise and powerful Solomon was vanquished. It is not safe to permit the least departure from the strictest integrity. "Abstain from all appearance of evil." Remember Solomon. Among many nations there was no king like him, beloved of his God. He fell. He was led from God and became corrupt through the indulgence of lustful passions. This is the prevailing sin of this age, and its progress is fearful. None but the pure and lowly can dwell in his presence. "Who shall ascend into the hill of the Lord? and who shall stand in his holy place? He that hath clean hands, and a pure heart; who hath not lifted up his soul unto vanity, nor sworn deceitfully." (1SP 396.2)

Solomon's heart was turned from God when he multiplied to himself wives of idolatrous nations. God had expressly forbidden his people to intermarry with idolatrous nations, for he had chosen them as his peculiar treasure. "For it came to pass, when Solomon was old, that his wives turned away his heart after other gods; and his heart was not perfect with the Lord his God, as was the heart of David, his father." "And the Lord was angry with Solomon, because his heart was turned from the Lord God of Israel, which had appeared unto him twice, and had commanded him concerning this thing, that he should not go after other gods; but he kept not that which the Lord commanded. Wherefore the Lord said unto Solomon, Forasmuch as this is done of thee, and thou hast not kept my covenant and my statutes which I have commanded thee, I will surely rend the kingdom from thee, and will give it to thy servant." The Lord informed Solomon, by his prophet, of his purpose concerning him: that he would cause his prosperity to cease, and would raise up adversaries against him, and he should no longer reign as universal monarch upon the throne of Israel. Had Solomon died prior to his departing from God, his life would have been one of the most remarkable upon record. But he tarnished his luster, and exhibited a striking example of the weakness of the wisest of mortals. The greatest men, and the wisest, will surely fail unless their lives are marked with trust in God, and obedience to his commandments. (1SP 397.1)

*****

Chapter 36
The Ark of God

The ark of God was a sacred chest, made to be the depository of the ten commandments, which law was the representative of God himself. This ark was considered the glory and strength of Israel. The token of the Divine Presence abode upon it day and night. The priests who ministered before it were sacredly consecrated to the holy office. They wore a breast-plate bordered with precious stones of different materials, the same as compose the twelve foundations of the city of God. Within the border were the names of the twelve tribes of Israel, graven on precious stones set in gold. This was a very rich and beautiful work, suspended from the shoulders of the priests, covering the breast. (1SP 398.1)

At the right and left of the breast-plate were set two larger stones, which shone with great brilliancy. When difficult matters were brought to the judges, which they could not decide, they were referred to the priests, and they inquired of God, who answered them. If he favored, and if he would grant them success, a halo of light and glory especially rested upon the precious stone at the right. If he disapproved, a vapor or cloud seemed to settle upon the precious stone at the left hand. When they inquired of God in regard to going to battle, the precious stone at the right, when circled with light, said, Go, and prosper. The stone at the left, when shadowed with a cloud, said, Thou shalt not go; thou shalt not prosper. (1SP 398.2)

When the high priest entered within the most holy, once a year, and ministered before the ark in the awful presence of God, he inquired, and God often answered him with an audible voice. When the Lord did not answer by a voice, he let the sacred beams of light and glory rest upon the cherubim upon the right of the ark, in approbation, or favor. If their requests were refused, a cloud rested upon the cherubim at the left. (1SP 399.1)

Four heavenly angels always accompanied the ark of God in all its journeyings, to guard it from all danger, and to fulfill any mission required of them in connection with the ark. Jesus the Son of God, followed by heavenly angels, went before the ark as it came to Jordan; and the waters were cut off before his presence. Christ and angels stood by the ark and the priests in the bed of the river, until all Israel had passed over Jordan. Christ and angels attended the circuit of the ark around Jericho, and finally cast down the massive walls of the city, and delivered Jericho into the hands of Israel. (1SP 399.2)

When Eli was high priest, he exalted his sons to the priesthood. Eli alone was permitted to enter the most holy once a year. His sons ministered at the door of the tabernacle, and officiated in the slaying of the beasts, and at the altar of sacrifice. They continually abused this sacred office. They were selfish, covetous, gluttonous, and profligate. God reproved Eli for his criminal neglect of family discipline. Eli reproved his sons, but did not restrain them. And after they were placed in the sacred office of priesthood, Eli heard of their conduct in defrauding the children of Israel in their offerings, also their bold transgressions of the law of God, and their violent conduct, which caused Israel to sin. (1SP 400.1)

Their crimes were known to all Israel. Eli reproved them. He presented before them the enormity of their sin. It was not like a sin against each other, which officiating priests could atone for. But if the priests themselves sin against God, and show open contempt for his authority, who should atone for them? They regarded not the counsel of their father. Eli was judge, and also high priest, in Israel, and he was responsible for the conduct of his sons. He should have removed them at once from the priesthood, and judged them as their case deserved. He knew that if he should do this, they must suffer death for their abominable example to Israel. Permitting them, loaded with guilt, to occupy the relation of priests to Israel, would lead the people to lightly

Chapter 36 - The Ark of God (1SP 400.2)

regard crime, and to despise the sacrificial offerings. (1SP 400.2)

The Lord, by his prophet, sent a reproof to Eli: "Wherefore kick ye at my sacrifice and at mine offering, which I have commanded in my habitation; and honorest thy sons above me, to make yourselves fat with the chiefest of all the offerings of Israel, my people? Wherefore the Lord God of Israel saith, I said indeed that thy house, and the house of thy father, should walk before me forever; but now the Lord saith, Be it far from me; for them that honor me I will honor, and they that despise me shall be lightly esteemed." (1SP 400.3)

Eli's undue affection for his sons made him a partial judge. He excused sins in them which he would have condemned in others. The Lord informed Eli, by his prophet, that because he had thus suffered his sons to remain in sacred office, while they were compelling Israel to sin, and because of their transgressions of his law, he would cut off both his sons in one day. As Eli had neglected his sacred duty, God would punish them, and they should both perish. (1SP 401.1)

Here is a standing rebuke to parents, who are professed followers of Christ, who neglect to restrain their children, but merely entreat them, like Eli; and who say, "Why do ye so wickedly?" but do not decidedly restrain them. Such suffer God's cause to be dishonored, because they do not exercise that authority which belongs to them in order to restrain wickedness. (1SP 401.2)

The Lord made known to the child Samuel the judgments he would bring upon Eli's house because of his negligence. "And the Lord said to Samuel, Behold, I will do a thing in Israel, at which both the ears of every one that heareth it shall tingle. In that day I will perform against Eli all things which I have spoken concerning his house. When I begin, I will also make an end. For I have told him that I will judge his house forever, for the iniquity which he knoweth; because his sons made themselves vile, and he restrained them not. And therefore I have sworn unto the house of Eli, that the iniquity of Eli's house shall not be purged with sacrifice nor offering forever." (1SP 401.3)

The transgressions of Eli's sons were so daring, so insulting to a holy God, that no sacrifice could atone for such willful transgression. These sinful priests profaned the sacrifices which typified the Son of God. And by their blasphemous conduct they were trampling upon the blood of the atonement, from which was derived the virtue of all sacrifices. (1SP 402.1)

Samuel told Eli the words of the Lord; "and he said, It is the Lord; let him do what seemeth him good." Eli knew that God had been dishonored, and he felt that he had sinned. He submitted that God was just in thus punishing his sinful neglect. The word of the Lord to Samuel was made known by Eli to all Israel. In doing this, he thought to correct in a measure his past sinful negligence. The evil pronounced upon Eli was not long delayed. (1SP 402.2)

The Israelites made war with the Philistines, and were overcome, and four thousand of them were slain. The Hebrews were afraid. They knew that if other nations should hear of their defeat, they would be encouraged to also make war with them. The elders of Israel decided that their defeat was because the ark of God was not with them. They sent to Shiloh for the ark of the covenant. They thought of their passage over Jordan, and the easy conquest of Jericho, when they bore the ark; and they decided that all that was necessary was to bring the ark to them, and they would triumph over their enemies. They did not realize that their strength was in their obedience to that law contained in the ark, which was a representative of God himself. The polluted priests, Hophni and Phinehas, were with the sacred ark, transgressing the law of God. These sinners conducted the ark to the camp of Israel. The confidence of the men of war was restored, and they felt confident of success. (1SP 402.3)

"And when the ark of the covenant of the Lord came into the camp, all Israel shouted with a great shout, so that the earth rang again. And when the Philistines heard the noise of the shout, they said, What meaneth the noise of this great shout in the camp of the Hebrews? And they understood that the ark of the Lord was come into the camp. And the Philistines were afraid; for they said, God is come into the camp. And they said, Woe unto us! for there hath not been such a thing heretofore. Woe unto us! Who shall deliver us out of the hand of these mighty gods? These are the gods that smote the Egyptians with all the plagues in the wilderness. Be strong, and quit yourselves like men, O ye Philistines, that ye be not servants unto the Hebrews, as they have been to you. Quit yourselves like men, and fight. And the Philistines fought, and Israel was smitten, and they fled every man into his tent. And there was a very great slaughter; for there fell of Israel thirty thousand footmen. And the ark of God was taken; and the two sons of Eli, Hophni and Phinehas, were slain." (1SP 403.1)

The Philistines thought that this ark was the Israelites' god. They knew not that the living God, who created the heavens and the earth, and gave his law upon Sinai, sent prosperity and adversity according to the obedience or transgression of his law contained in the sacred chest. (1SP 403.2)

There was a very great slaughter in Israel. Eli was sitting by the wayside, watching with a trembling heart to receive news from the army. He was afraid that the ark of God might be taken, and polluted by the Philistine host. A messenger from the army ran to Shiloh and informed Eli that his two sons had been slain. He could bear this with a degree of calmness, for he had reason to expect it. But when the messenger added, "And the ark of God is taken," Eli wavered in anguish upon his seat, and fell backward and died. He shared the wrath of God which came upon his sons. He was guilty in a great measure of their transgressions, because he had criminally neglected to restrain them. The capture of the ark of God by the Philistines was considered the greatest calamity which could befall Israel. The wife of Phinehas, as she was about to die, named her child Ichabod, saying, "The glory is departed from Israel, for the ark of God is taken." (1SP 404.1)

God permitted his ark to be taken by their enemies, to show Israel how vain it was to trust in the ark, the symbol of his presence, while they were profaning the commandments contained in the ark. God would humble them by removing from them that sacred ark, their boasted strength and confidence. (1SP 404.2)

The Philistines were triumphant, because they had, as they thought, the famous God of the Israelites, which had performed such wonders for them, and had made them a terror to their enemies. They took the ark of God to Ashdod, and set it in a splendid temple, made in honor of their most popular God, Dagon, and placed it by the side of their god. In the morning, the priests of these gods entered the temple, and they were terrified to find Dagon fallen upon his face to the ground before the ark of the Lord. They raised Dagon and placed him in his former position.

They thought he might have accidentally fallen. But the next morning they found him fallen as before upon his face to the ground, and the head of Dagon and both his hands were cut off. The angels of God, who ever accompanied the ark, prostrated the senseless idol God, and afterward mutilated it, to show that God, the living God, was above all gods, and that before him every heathen God was as nothing. The heathen possessed great reverence for their God, Dagon; and when they found it ruinously mutilated, and lying upon its face before the ark of God, they were sad, and considered it a very bad omen to the Philistines. It was interpreted by them that the Philistines and all their gods would yet be subdued and destroyed by the Hebrews, and the Hebrews' God would be greater and more powerful than all gods. They removed the ark of God from their idol temple, and placed it by itself. (1SP 404.3)

The men of Ashdod began to be greatly afflicted. The Lord destroyed them; and they remembered the plagues brought upon Egypt, and their mutilated God, and were convinced that it was because they kept the ark of God, that these distressing afflictions came upon them. God would evidence to the idolatrous Philistines, and also to his people, that the ark was strength and power to those who were obedient to his law; and that to the disobedient and wicked it was punishment and death. (1SP 405.1)

When the men of Ashdod became convinced that it was the God of the Hebrews who caused their afflictions, because of his ark, they decided that the ark of the God of Israel should not abide with them. "For," said they, "his hand is sore upon us, and upon Dagon, our god." The great men and rulers consulted together, relative to what they should do with the ark of the God of Israel. They had taken it in triumph, but knew not what to do with the sacred chest; for instead of its being a power and strength to them, it was a great burden and a heavy curse. They decided to send it to Gath. But the destroying angels carried on their work of destruction in that place also. Very many of the people of Gath died; and they dared not retain the ark longer there, lest the God of Israel should consume them all by his curse. (1SP 406.1)

They of Gath decided to send the ark to Ekron. And as the idolatrous priests bore the ark of God to Ekron, the people of that place were greatly alarmed, and cried out, "They have

Chapter 36 - The Ark of God (1SP 406.2)

brought about the ark of the God of Israel to us, to slay us and our people." The Ekronites were also afflicted, and great numbers of them died. They went to their gods for help, as the cities of Ashdod and Gath had done, but they obtained no relief. They then humbled themselves to cry to the God of Israel, to whom the ark belonged, for relief from their affliction. "So they sent and gathered together all the lords of the Philistines, and said, Send away the ark of the God of Israel, and let it go again to his own place, that it slay us not, and our people; for there was a deadly destruction throughout all the city; the hand of God was very heavy there. And the men that died not, were smitten with the emerods; and the cry of the city went up to Heaven." (1SP 406.2)

The ark of God was kept seven months by the Philistines. They had overcome the Israelites, and had taken the ark of God, wherein they supposed their power consisted, and thought that they should ever be in safety, and have no more fear of the armies of Israel. But in the midst of their joy at their success, a wailing was heard all over the land, and the cause was at length credited to the ark of God. It was borne from place to place in terror, and destruction from God followed its course, until the Philistines were greatly perplexed to know what to do with it. Angels, who accompanied it, guarded it from all harm. And the Philistines did not dare to open the chest; for their God Dagon had met with such a fate that they feared to touch it, or to have it near them. They called for the priests and the diviners, and inquired of them what they should do with the ark of God. They advised them to send it back to the people to whom it belonged, and to send with it a costly trespass-offering, which if God would be pleased to accept, they would be healed. They should also understand that God's hand was upon them because they had taken his ark, which belonged alone to Israel. (1SP 407.1)

Some were not in favor of this. It was too humiliating to carry back the ark; and they urged that no one of the Philistines would dare venture his life, to carry the ark of the God of Israel, which had brought such death upon them. Their counselors entreated the people not to harden their hearts, as the Egyptians and Pharaoh had done, and cause still greater afflictions and plagues to come upon them. And as they were all afraid to take the ark of God, they advised them, saying, "Now, therefore, make a new cart, and take two milch kine, on which there hath come no yoke, and tie the kine to the cart, and bring their calves home from them. And take the ark of the Lord, and lay it upon the cart; and put the jewels of gold, which ye return him for a trespass-offering, in a coffer by the side thereof; and send it away, that it may go. And see, if it goeth up by the way of his own coast to Beth-shemesh, then he hath done us this great evil; but if not, then we shall know that it is not his hand that smote us; it was a chance that happened to us. And the men did so; and took two milch kine, and tied them to the cart, and shut up their calves at home." "And the kine took the straight way to the way of Beth-shemesh, and went along the highway, lowing as they went, and turned not aside to the right hand or to the left." (1SP 407.2)

The Philistines knew that the cows would not be induced to leave their young calves at home, unless they should be urged by some unseen power. The cows went direct to Beth-shemesh, lowing for their calves, yet going directly from them. The lords of the Philistines followed after the ark unto the border of Beth-shemesh. They dared not trust that sacred chest wholly to the cows. They feared that if any evil happened to it, greater calamities would come upon them. They knew not that angels of God accompanied the ark, and guided the cows in their course to the place where it belonged. The people of Beth-shemesh were reaping in the field; and when they saw the ark of God upon the cart, drawn by the cows, they were greatly rejoiced. They knew that it was the work of God. The cows drew the cart containing the ark, to a large stone, and stood still of themselves. The Levites took down the ark of the Lord and the offering of the Philistines, and they offered the cart and the cows which had borne the sacred ark, and the offering of the Philistines, unto God as a burnt-sacrifice. The lords of the Philistines returned to Ekron, and the plague was stayed. (1SP 408.1)

The men of Beth-shemesh were curious to know what great power could be in that ark, which caused it to accomplish such marvelous things. They looked upon the ark alone as being so powerful, and were not accrediting the power to God. None but men sacredly appointed for the purpose could look upon the ark, divested of its coverings, without being slain; for it was as though looking upon God himself. And as the

Chapter 36 - The Ark of God (1SP 411.1)

people gratified their curiosity, and opened the ark to gaze into its sacred recesses, which the heathen idolaters had not dared to do, the angels attending the ark slew above fifty thousand of the people. (1SP 409.1)

And the people of Beth-shemesh were afraid of the ark; and they said, "Who is able to stand before this holy Lord God? And to whom shall he go up from us? And they sent messengers to the inhabitants of Kirjath-jearim, saying, The Philistines have brought again the ark of the Lord. Come ye down, and fetch it up to you." The people of Kirjath-jearim brought the ark of the Lord to the house of Abinadab, and sanctified his son to keep it. For twenty years the Hebrews were in the power of the Philistines, and they were greatly humbled, and repented of their sins; and Samuel interceded for them, and God was again merciful to them. And the Philistines made war with them; and the Lord again wrought in a miraculous manner for Israel, and they overcame their enemies. (1SP 409.2)

The ark remained in the house of Abinadab until David was made king. He gathered together all the chosen men of Israel, thirty thousand, and went to bring up the ark of God. They set the ark upon a new cart, and brought it out of the house of Abinadab. Uzzah and Ahio, sons of Abinadab, drove the cart. David and all the house of Israel played before the Lord on all manner of musical instruments. "And when they came to Nachon's threshing-floor, Uzzah put forth his hand to the ark of God, and took hold of it; for the oxen shook it. And the anger of the Lord was kindled against Uzzah, and God smote him there for his error; and there he died by the ark of God." Uzzah was angry with the oxen, because they stumbled. He showed a manifest distrust of God, as though he who had brought the ark from the land of the Philistines, could not take care of it. Angels who attended the ark struck down Uzzah for presuming impatiently to put his hand upon the ark of God. (1SP 410.1)

"And David was afraid of the Lord that day, and said, How shall the ark of the Lord come to me? So David would not remove the ark of the Lord unto him into the city of David; but David carried it aside into the house of Obed-edom, the Gittite." David knew that he was a sinful man; and he was afraid that, like Uzzah, he should in some way be presumptuous, and call forth the wrath of God upon himself. "And the ark of the Lord continued in the house of Obed-edom, the Gittite, three months; and the Lord blessed Obed-edom, and all his household." (1SP 410.2)

God would teach his people that, while his ark was a terror and death to those who transgressed his commandments contained in it, it was also a blessing and strength to those who were obedient to his commandments. When David heard that the house of Obed-edom was greatly blessed, and that all that he had prospered, because of the ark of God, he was very anxious to bring it to his own city. But before David ventured to move the sacred ark, he sanctified himself to God, and also commanded that all the men highest in authority in the kingdom should keep themselves from all worldly business, and everything which would distract their minds from sacred devotion. Thus should they sanctify themselves for the purpose of conducting the sacred ark to the city of David. "So David went and brought up the ark of God from the house of Obed-edom into the city of David with gladness. And it was so, that when they that bare the ark of the Lord had gone six paces, he sacrificed oxen and fatlings." (1SP 410.3)

David laid off his kingly attire, and clothed himself with garments similar to the priests', which had never been worn before, that not the least impurity might be upon his clothing. Every six paces, they erected an altar and solemnly sacrificed to God. The special blessing of the Lord rested upon king David, who thus manifested before his people his exalted reverence for the ark of God. "And David danced before the Lord with all his might; and David was girded with a linen ephod. So David and all the house of Israel brought up the ark of the Lord with shouting, and with the sound of the trumpet. And as the ark of the Lord came into the city of David, Michal, Saul's daughter, looked through a window, and saw king David leaping and dancing before the Lord; and she despised him in her heart." (1SP 411.1)

The dignity and pride of king Saul's daughter were shocked that king David should lay aside his garments of royalty, and his royal scepter, and be clothed with the simple linen garments worn by the priests. She thought that he was greatly dishonoring himself before the people of Israel. But God honored David in the sight of all Israel by letting his Spirit abide upon him. David humbled himself, but God exalted him. He sung in an inspired manner, playing

Chapter 36 - The Ark of God (1SP 412.1)

upon the harp, producing the most enchanting music. He felt, in a small degree, that holy joy that all the saints will experience at the voice of God when their captivity is turned, and God makes a covenant of peace with all who have kept his commandments. (1SP 412.1)

"And they brought in the ark of the Lord, and set it in his place, in the midst of the tabernacle that David had pitched for it. And David offered burnt-offerings and peace-offerings before the Lord." (1SP 412.2)

After Solomon had finished building the temple, he assembled the elders of Israel, and the most influential men among the people, to bring up the ark of the covenant of the Lord out of the city of David. These men consecrated themselves to God, and, with great solemnity and reverence, accompanied the priests who bore the ark. "And they brought up the ark of the Lord, and the tabernacle of the congregation, and all the holy vessels that were in the tabernacle, even those did the priests and the Levites bring up. And king Solomon, and all the congregation of Israel, that were assembled unto him, were with him before the ark, sacrificing sheep and oxen, that could not be told nor numbered for multitude." (1SP 412.3)

Solomon followed the example of his father David. Every six paces, he sacrificed. With singing, and with music, and great ceremony, "the priests brought in the ark of the covenant of the Lord unto his place, into the oracle of the house, to the most holy place, even under the wings of the cherubim. For the cherubim spread forth their two wings over the place of the ark, and the cherubim covered the ark and the staves thereof above." (1SP 413.1)

A most splendid sanctuary had been made, according to the pattern showed to Moses in the mount, and afterward presented by the Lord to David. The earthly sanctuary was made like the heavenly. In addition to the cherubim on the top of the ark, Solomon made two other angels of larger size, standing at each end of the ark, representing the heavenly angels always guarding the law of God. It is impossible to describe the beauty and splendor of this tabernacle. There, as in the tabernacle, the sacred ark was borne in solemn, reverential order, and set in its place beneath the wings of the two stately cherubim that stood upon the floor. (1SP 413.2)

The sacred choir united their voices with all kinds of musical instruments, in praise to God. And while the voices, in harmony with instruments of music, resounded through the temple, and were borne upon the air through Jerusalem, the cloud of God's glory took possession of the house, as it had formerly filled the tabernacle. "And it came to pass, when the priests were come out of the holy place, that the cloud filled the house of the Lord, so that the priests could not stand to minister because of the cloud; for the glory of the Lord had filled the house of the Lord." (1SP 413.3)

King Solomon stood upon a brazen scaffold before the altar, and blessed the people. He then knelt down, and, with his hands raised upward, poured forth earnest and solemn prayer to God, while the congregation were bowed with their faces to the ground. After Solomon had ended his prayer, a miraculous fire came from Heaven and consumed the sacrifice. (1SP 414.1)

Because of the sins of Israel, the calamity which God said should come upon the temple if his people departed from him, was fulfilled some hundreds of years after the temple was built. God promised Solomon, if he would remain faithful, and his people would obey all his commandments, that that glorious temple should stand forever in all its splendor, as an evidence of the prosperity and exalted blessings resting upon Israel for their obedience. (1SP 414.2)

Because of Israel's transgression of the commandments of God, and their wicked acts, God suffered them to go into captivity, to humble and punish them. Before the temple was destroyed, God made known to a few of his faithful servants the fate of the temple, which was the pride of Israel, and which they regarded with idolatry, while they were sinning against God. He also revealed to them the captivity of Israel. These righteous men, just before the destruction of the temple, removed the sacred ark containing the tables of stone, and, with mourning and sadness, secreted it in a cave where it was to be hid from the people of Israel, because of their sins, and was to be no more restored to them. That sacred ark is yet hid. It has never been disturbed since it was secreted. (1SP 414.3)

Made in United States
Troutdale, OR
10/06/2023